MathFlare

Name: ___________________

Class: __________

Teacher: ___________________

Introduction

As parents and educators, we recognize the pivotal role mathematics plays in shaping a child's academic journey and future success. Yet, the path to mathematical proficiency can often seem daunting, fraught with challenges and complexities. That's where the transformative power of MathFlare Workbooks shine through, illuminating the way forward with clarity, precision, and purpose.

Introducing MathFlare Workbooks – a beacon of guidance, a testament to excellence, and a catalyst for achievement. Crafted with meticulous care and expertise, MathFlare Workbooks stand as paragons of educational excellence, designed to nurture young minds, ignite a passion for learning, and develop a deep-rooted understanding of mathematical concepts.

Picture this: your child eagerly delves into the pages of Mathflare Workbook, greeted by a step-by-step guide illuminated with vivid examples that demystify complex mathematical concepts. With each turn of the page, they embark on a journey of discovery, encountering thoughtfully curated practice questions that reinforce learning and hone problem-solving skills. And when they unveil the answers to those very questions, a sense of accomplishment blossoms within them – a tangible reward for their hard work and dedication.

But MathFlare Workbooks are more than just tools for learning; they are pathways to comprehension, fostering a deep-seated understanding of mathematical concepts through a sequential, logical flow. From fundamental principles to advanced problem-solving strategies, every chapter builds upon the last, ensuring a robust foundation upon which future knowledge can be constructed.

As parents, we yearn for nothing more than to see our children thrive, to witness the spark of inspiration ignited within them as they conquer academic challenges with confidence and poise. MathFlare Workbooks serve as partners in this noble endeavor, offering not just practice questions, but the keys to unlocking a world of opportunity.

And for teachers, MathFlare Workbooks stand as invaluable allies in the quest to cultivate mathematical proficiency in the classroom. With answers readily available, instructors can focus on guiding and nurturing their students, confident in the knowledge that MathFlare Workbooks provide a solid framework upon which to build.

In the pages of MathFlare Workbooks, we find not just the promise of academic excellence, but the seeds of a brighter tomorrow. So let us embrace the power of mathematics, let us champion the journey of learning, and let us pave the way for a generation of young minds poised to shape the world. With MathFlare Workbooks as our guide, the possibilities are infinite, and the future, bright.

Table of Contents

Chapter. 07
Exponents and Scientific Notations

Answers

MathFlare
Grade 1-2
MATH WORKBOOK
Step by Step Guide and Essential Practice with Answers
Counting and Numbers
Addition and Subtraction
Place Value and Expanded Notations
Understanding Time
MathFlare Publishing

MathFlare
Grade 2
MATH WORKBOOK
Step by Step Guide and Essential Practice with Answers
Addition Subtraction
Multiplication
Place Value and Expanded Notations
Geometry
MathFlare Publishing

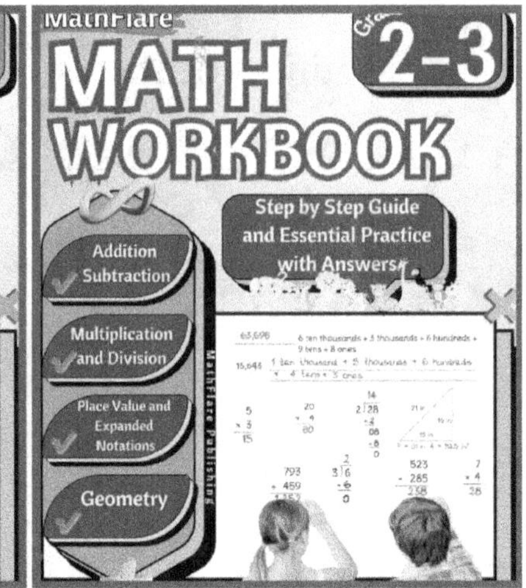
MathFlare
Grade 2-3
MATH WORKBOOK
Step by Step Guide and Essential Practice with Answers
Addition Subtraction
Multiplication and Division
Place Value and Expanded Notations
Geometry
MathFlare Publishing

MathFlare
Grade 3
MATH WORKBOOK
Step by Step Guide and Essential Practice with Answers
Multiplication and Division
Decimals
Place Value and Expanded Notations
Fractions and Geometry
MathFlare Publishing

MathFlare
Grade 3-4
MATH WORKBOOK
Step by Step Guide and Essential Practice with Answers
Addition Subtraction
Multiplication Division
Place Value and Expanded Notations
Fractions and Geometry
MathFlare Publishing

MathFlare
Grade 4
MATH WORKBOOK
Step by Step Guide and Essential Practice with Answers
Addition Subtraction
Multiplication Division
Place Value and Expanded Notations
Fractions and Geometry
MathFlare Publishing

MathFlare
Grade 4-5
MATH WORKBOOK
Step by Step Guide and Essential Practice with Answers
Multiplication Division
Place Value and Expanded Notations
Fractions and Geometry
Unit Conversion
MathFlare Publishing

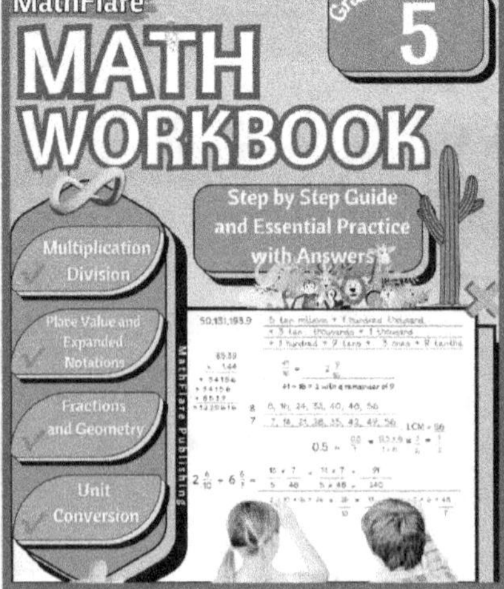
MathFlare
Grade 5
MATH WORKBOOK
Step by Step Guide and Essential Practice with Answers
Multiplication Division
Place Value and Expanded Notations
Fractions and Geometry
Unit Conversion
MathFlare Publishing

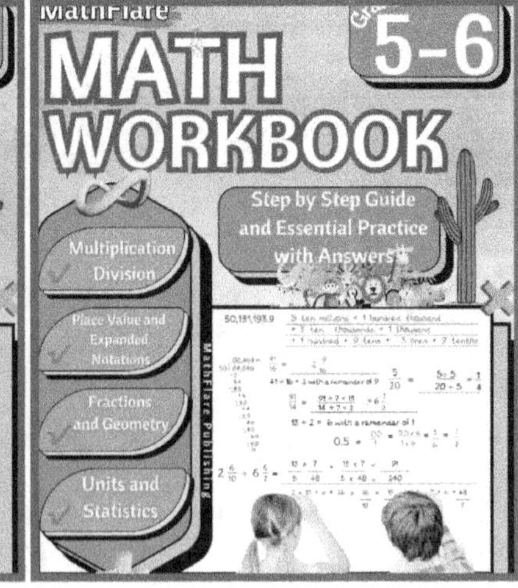
MathFlare
Grade 5-6
MATH WORKBOOK
Step by Step Guide and Essential Practice with Answers
Multiplication Division
Place Value and Expanded Notations
Fractions and Geometry
Units and Statistics
MathFlare Publishing

MathFlare
MATH WORKBOOK
Grade 6
Step by Step Guide and Essential Practice with Answers
Integers and Statistics
Arithmetic and Pre-Algebra
Fractions and Geometry
Ratio and Percentage
MathFlare Publishing

MathFlare
MATH WORKBOOK
Grade 6-7
Step by Step Guide and Essential Practice with Answers
Arithmetic and Pre-Algebra
Ratio, Percent Proportion
Geometry
Statistics
MathFlare Publishing

MathFlare
MATH WORKBOOK
Grade 7
Step by Step Guide and Essential Practice with Answers
Pre-Algebra
Ratio, Percent Proportion
Geometry
Statistics
MathFlare Publishing

MathFlare
MATH WORKBOOK
Grade 7-8
Step by Step Guide and Essential Practice with Answers
Pre-Algebra
Ratio, Percent Proportion
Geometry and Cartesian Plane
Statistics
MathFlare Publishing

MathFlare
MATH WORKBOOK
Grade 8
Step by Step Guide and Essential Practice with Answers
Pre-Algebra
Percentage
Linear Equations
Geometry
MathFlare Publishing

MathFlare
MATH WORKBOOK
Grade 8-9
Step by Step Guide and Essential Practice with Answers
Pre-Algebra
Ratio, Proportion and Percentage
Linear Equations
Geometry and Cartesian Plane
MathFlare Publishing

MathFlare
MATH WORKBOOK
Grade 9
Step by Step Guide and Essential Practice with Answers
Equations and Expressions
Linear Equations and Systems
Quadratic Equations
Geometry
MathFlare Publishing

MathFlare
MATH WORKBOOK
Grade 9-10
Step by Step Guide and Essential Practice with Answers
Equations and Expressions
Linear Equations and Systems
Quadratic Equations
Polynomials Geometry
MathFlare Publishing

MathFlare
MATH WORKBOOK
Grade 10
Step by Step Guide and Essential Practice with Answers
Equations and Expressions
Linear Equations and Systems
Quadratic Equations
Polynomials Scientific Notations
MathFlare Publishing

Chapter. 01

Equations and Expressions

Solving One-Step Equations

Solving one-step equations involves finding the value of the variable that makes the equation true. In a one-step equation, there is only one operation (addition, subtraction, multiplication, or division) performed on the variable.

The goal is to isolate the variable on one side of the equation by performing inverse operations.

For example:

Given the equation $6 = -3z$, where we want to solve for z.

The given equation is already in the form of a one-step equation, with z being multiplied by -3.

To isolate z, we need to perform the inverse operation of multiplication, which is division.

Divide both sides by -3:

$$\frac{6}{-3} = \frac{-3z}{-3}$$

Simplify:

$$-2 = z$$

So, the solution to the equation is $z = -2$.

When we substitute the value of z = −2 back into the original equation, 6 = −3(−2), it simplifies to 6 = 6. This confirms that our solution is correct because it satisfies the original equation.

Solving Two-Step Equations

Solving two-step equations involves finding the value of the variable that makes the equation true. In a two-step equation, two operations (addition, subtraction, multiplication, or division) are performed on the variable.

The goal is to isolate the variable on one side of the equation by performing inverse operations in the reverse order of operations.

For example:

Given the equation 18 = (10 + b) − 2, where we want to solve for b.

To solve for b, we need to undo the operations that have been performed on b.

1. Undo the subtraction by adding 2 to both sides:

$$18 + 2 = (10 + b) -2 + 2$$

$$20 = 10 + b$$

2. Undo the addition by subtracting 10 from both sides:

$$20 - 10 = 10 + b - 10$$

$$10 = b$$

So, the solution to the equation is b = 10

Let's substitute b = 10 back into the original equation to verify if it satisfies the equation:

Original equation:

$$18 = (10 + b) - 2:$$

Substitute b = 10:

$$18 = (10 + 10) - 2$$

simplify:

$$18 = 20 - 2$$

$$18 = 18$$

Since the equation simplifies to 18 =1 8, it confirms that our solution b = 10 is correct.

Solving Multi-Step Equations

Solving multi-step equations involves finding the value of the variable that makes the equation true. In a multi-step equation, multiple operations (addition, subtraction, multiplication, or division) are performed on the variable.

The goal is to isolate the variable on one side of the equation by performing inverse operations in the reverse order of operations.

Example:

Given the equation $-3m - m = -8$, where we want to solve for m.

To solve for m, we need to undo the operations that have been performed on m.

1. Combine like terms on the left side:

$$-3m - m = -4m$$

2. Substitute the combined term back into the equation:

$$-4m = -8$$

3. Undo the multiplication by dividing both sides by $-4-4$:

$$\frac{-4m}{-4} = \frac{-8}{-4}$$

$$m = 2$$

Let's substitute m = 2 back into the original equation to verify if it satisfies the equation:

Original equation:

$$-3m - m = -8$$

Substitute m = 2:

$$-3(2) - 2 = -8$$

simplify:

$$-6 - 2 = -8$$

$$-8 = -8$$

Since the equation simplifies to 8 = 8, it confirms that our solution m = 2 is correct.

<u>Solving Equations (One Side)</u>

Solving one-step equations involves performing a single operation to isolate the variable and find its value.

Let's solve an equation step by step: **16 + x = 31**

1. **Identify the Goal:**

    The goal is to isolate the variable x on one side of the equation.

2. **Simplify the Equation:** Combine like terms on both sides of the equation, if necessary.

    The equation is already simplified.

3. **Undo Addition or Subtraction:** If there's addition or subtraction involving the variable, undo it by performing the opposite operation on both sides of the equation.

Since x is being added to 16, we'll undo this operation by subtracting 16 from both sides of the equation:

$$16 + x - 16 = 31 - 16$$

4. **Isolate the Variable**: Ensure that the variable is alone on one side of the equation.

$$x = 15$$

5. **Check Your Solution**: Substitute the value of x back into the original equation to verify that it satisfies the equation.

$$16 + 15 = 31$$

$$31 = 31$$

The equation is balanced.

Equations (Two Sides)

A two-sided equation is an equation where both sides have expressions with variables and constants. The goal when solving a two-sided equation is to find the value of the variable that makes both sides equal.

For example: Let's solve an equation:

$$9 + 8x + 8 = 64 + x + 2$$

- **Combine Like Terms**: Simplify each side of the equation by combining like terms (terms with the same variable or constants).

$$9 + 8x + 8 = 64 + x + 2$$
$$17 + 8x = 66 + x$$

- **Isolate the Variable**: Use inverse operations to isolate the variable on one side of the equation.

subtract x from both sides:

$$17 + 8x - x = 66 + x - x$$

$$17 + 7x = 66$$

subtracting 17 from both sides:

$$17 - 17 + 7x = 66 - 17$$

$$7x = 49$$

divide both sides by 7:

$$\frac{7x}{7} = \frac{49}{7} = x = 7$$

- **Check Solution:** Once you find the solution, substitute it back into the original equation to ensure it makes the equation true.

Substitute $x = 7$ back into the original equation:

$$9 + 8(7) + 8 = 64 + 7 + 2$$

$$9 + 56 + 8 = 64 + 7 + 2$$

$$73 = 73$$

Simplifying expressions

It involves combining like terms and performing operations to make the expression easier to understand and work with.

Let's simplify the expression:

$$2x - 2x + 8 + 4$$

- **Combine like terms:** First, we look for terms with the same variable and exponent. In this expression, $2x$ and $-2x$ are like terms, so they can be combined:

$$2x - 2x = 0$$

- **Substitute the simplified terms:** After combining the like terms, the expression becomes:

$$0 + 8 + 4$$

- **Combine the remaining terms:** Now, we add the constants together:

$$8 + 4 = 12$$

Let's solve another problem:

$$-7m - 3 - 3 - 6m$$

combine like terms

$$-7m - 6m - 3 - 3$$

$$13m - 6$$

1. Example: $10 - 4 \div 2 = 10 - 2 = 8$

Evaluating Equations

Evaluating expressions involves substituting given values for variables in an expression and then performing the indicated operations to find the result.

For example: Let's evaluate $4x - 10$, when $x = 3$:

Step 1: Substitute the given value for the variable:

Replace every occurrence of x in the expression $4x - 10$ with the given value, which is 3:

$$= 4(3) - 10$$

Step 2: Perform the operations:

Perform the indicated operations according to the order of operations (PEMDAS - Parentheses, Exponents, Multiplication and Division, Addition and Subtraction):

$$= 4 \times 3 - 10$$

Step 3: Simplify:

Calculate the result:

$$12 - 10 = 2$$

<u>Verbal Algebra Expressions</u>

Verbal algebra involves translating word problems or verbal statements into algebraic expressions or equations.

For example: The product of the two numbers is 91. One number is six less than the other. What are the numbers?

We're given a verbal description of a problem, and we need to represent it using algebraic symbols and equations.

Let's break down the given problem into algebraic expressions:

- Given that the product of the two numbers is 91, we can write the equation: $xy = 91$
- Also, given that one number is six less than the other, we can write another equation: $x = y - 6$

Now, we can use algebraic techniques to solve the system of equations to find the values of x and y, which represent the two numbers.

$$x(x - 6) = 91$$

1. Solve the equation:

- Expand the equation:

$$x^2 - 6x = 91$$

- Rearrange the equation into standard quadratic form:

$$x^2 - 6x - 91 = 0$$

- Factor the quadratic equation:

$$(x - 13)(x + 7) = 0$$

2. Find the solutions for x:

- From the factored form, we have two possible values for x:

$$x = 13 \text{ or } x = -7$$

3. Check the validity of the solutions:

- Since one number is six less than the other, we discard the negative solution.

- Therefore, the solution is $x = 13$.

4. Find the other number:

- Substitute $x = 13$ into the expression for the other number:

Other number $= x - 6 = 13 - 6 = 7$

So, the two numbers are 13 and 7.

Solving One-Step Equations

Solve for the variable.

1. $9 = 9y$

2. $4 = \dfrac{b}{1}$

3. $-k = -2$

4. $-6 = -3z$

5. $y - 8 = 0$

6. $z - 7 = 1$

7. $\dfrac{k}{2} = 2$

8. $-45 = -9z$

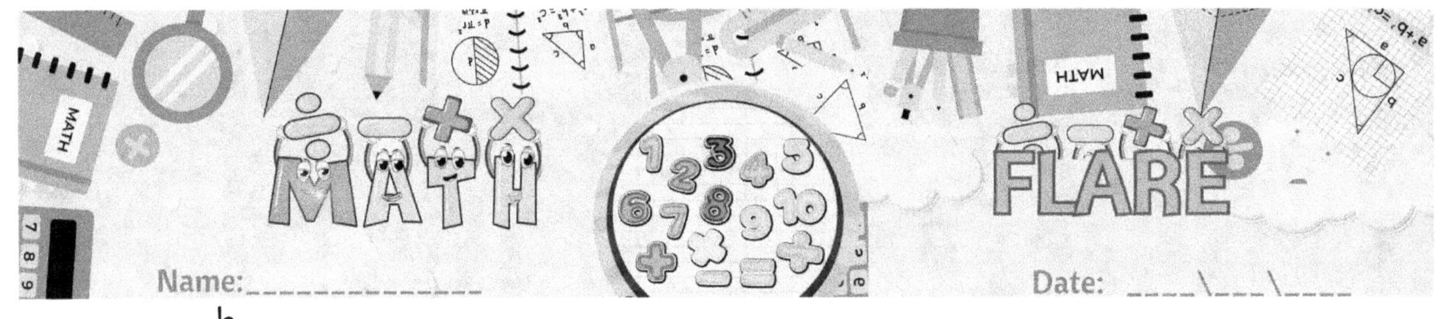

9. $6 = \dfrac{k}{1}$

10. $1 = x - 9$

11. $-9 + z = -4$

12. $11 = x + 9$

13. $-12 = -3b$

14. $12 = y + 9$

15. $14 = 7z$

16. $x - 4 = 5$

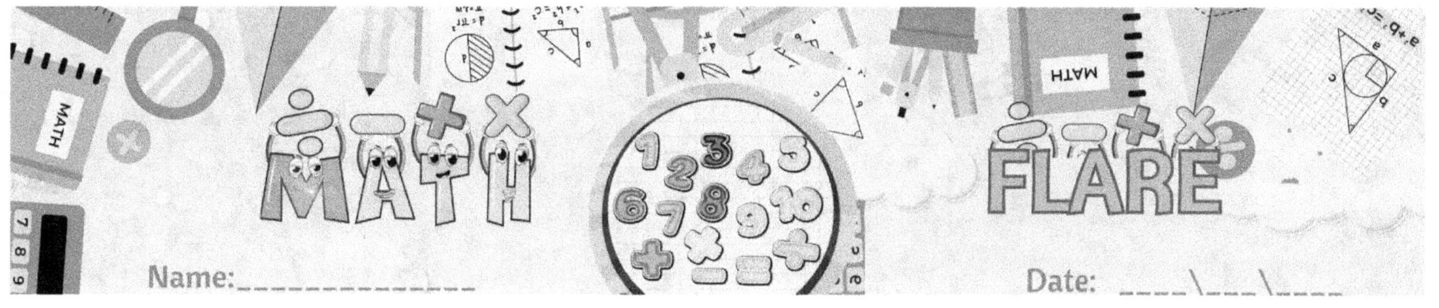

17. $-3 + s = 6$

18. $7 = b + 4$

19. $\dfrac{k}{4} = 1$

20. $7k = 35$

21. $42 = 7y$

22. $y + 1 = 11$

23. $9x = 18$

24. $-10z = -100$

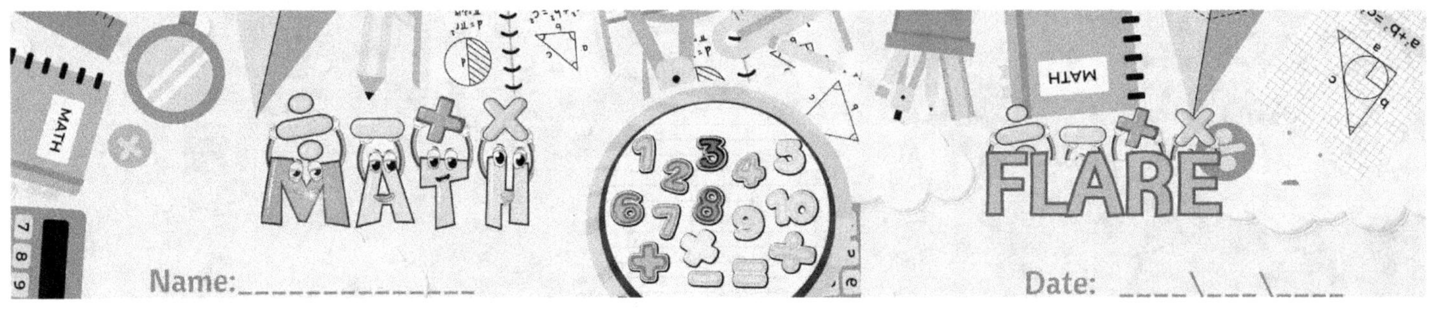

25. $-8s = -72$

26. $-10 + m = -1$

27. $-8 + m = 2$

28. $\dfrac{x}{10} = 1$

29. $8b = 40$

30. $13 = s + 3$

31. $k + 1 = 2$

32. $y - 3 = 5$

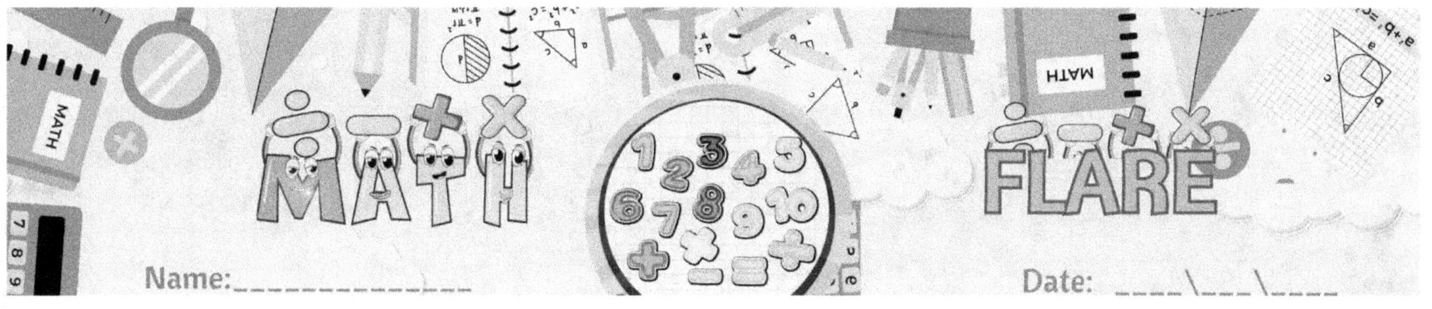

33. $-4 = x - 10$

34. $14 = z + 4$

35. $3 = \dfrac{a}{3}$

36. $7 = k + 5$

37. $\dfrac{x}{1} = 9$

38. $\dfrac{a}{4} = 2$

39. $-3 + x = 1$

40. $-6 = -6z$

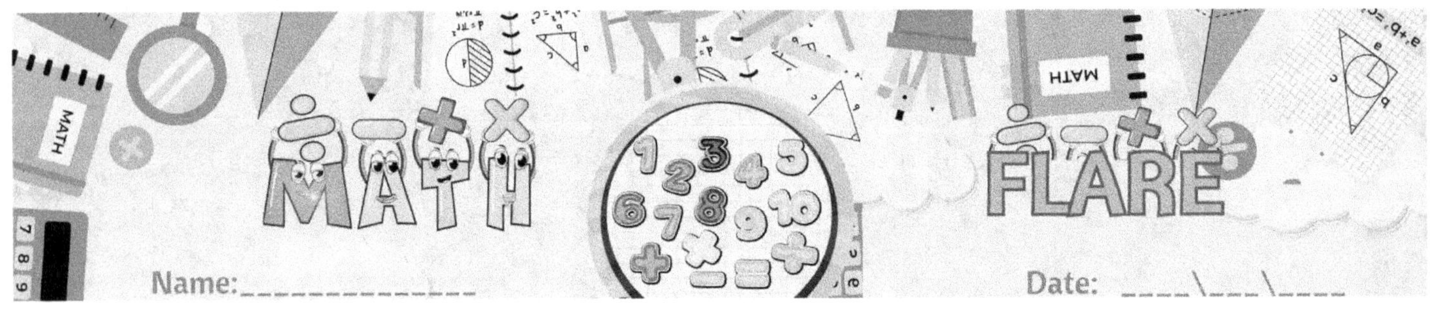

41. $8x = 32$

42. $-5 = -z$

43. $k - 2 = 2$

44. $s - 5 = 3$

45. $14 = 2x$

46. $5 = -4 + x$

47. $-10 = -z$

48. $9a = 54$

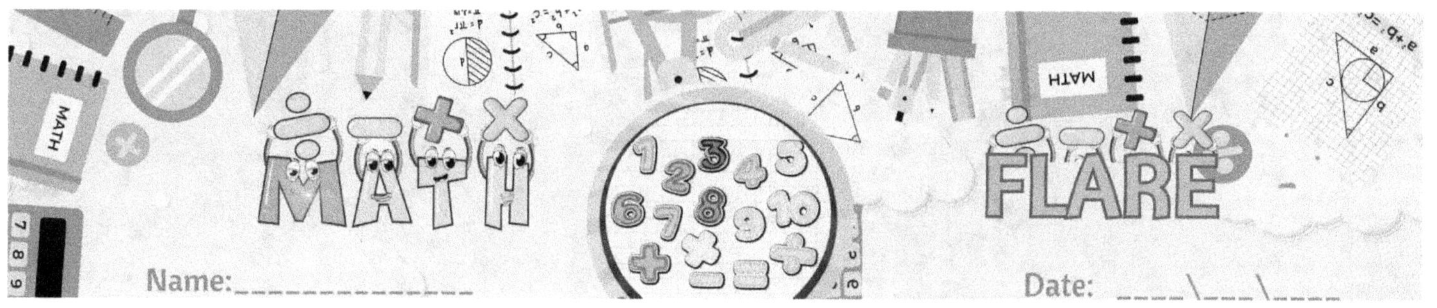

49. $8 = y + 7$

50. $36 = 4s$

51. $\dfrac{s}{2} = 5$

52. $5 = -2 + k$

53. $\dfrac{x}{2} = 3$

54. $-8 + s = -1$

55. $-2a = -6$

56. $63 = 9x$

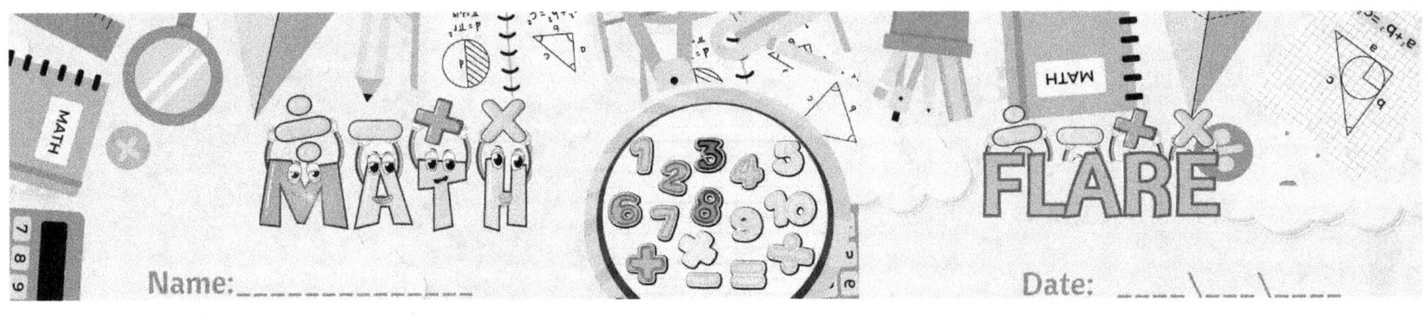

Solving Two-Step Equations

Solve for the variable.

1. $-8\dfrac{m}{-8} = 10$

2. $(-1 + x) - 7 = -4$

3. $18 = (10 + b) - 2$

4. $(3 - b)10 = 10$

5. $\dfrac{-4 + x}{1} = 2$

6. $(7 + a)6 = 60$

7. $-3 = (-5 + b) - 8$

8. $10z - 1 = 99$

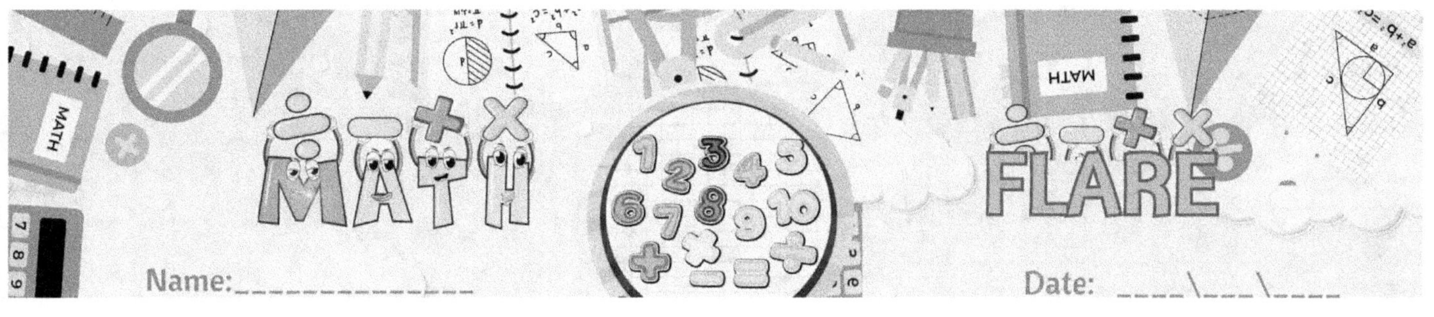

9. $10 = 4a - 10$

10. $10 - \dfrac{x}{1} = 1$

11. $\dfrac{x}{1} + 9 = 13$

12. $18 = k + 10$

13. $21 = 10b + 1$

14. $\dfrac{-9 + x}{1} = -8$

15. $-3 = -1(-6 + k)$

16. $\dfrac{y}{3} + 10 = 13$

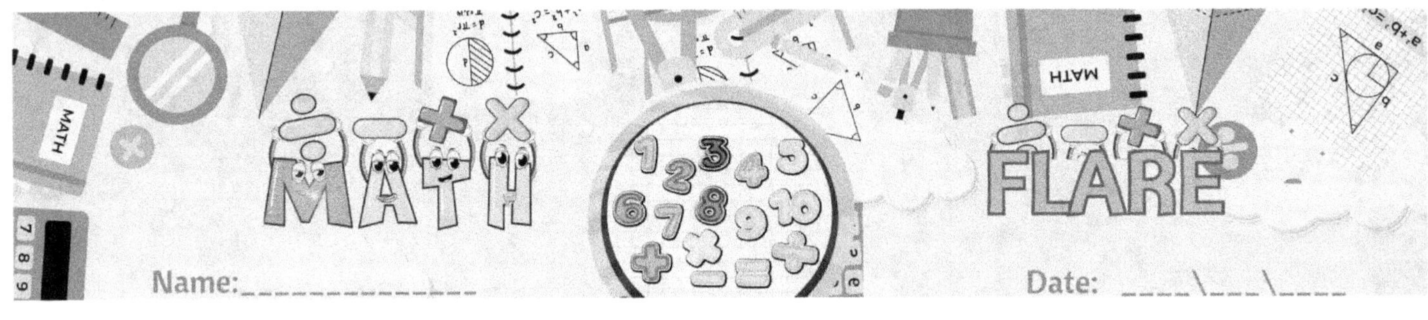

17. $8 + \dfrac{x}{2} = 11$

18. $10 = 10\dfrac{s}{8}$

19. $\dfrac{-9 + k}{2} = 0.5$

20. $-8(-7 + m) = 40$

21. $(3 - y) - 4 = -7$

22. $28 = 2(8 + a)$

23. $5(6 - s) = 0$

24. $-16 = \dfrac{8 + z}{-1}$

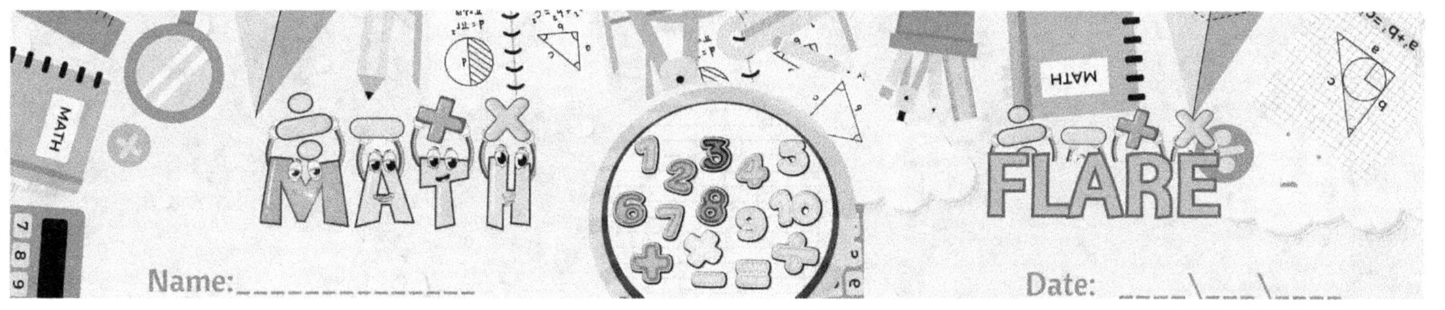

25. $11 = (9 + z) - 8$

26. $7(8 + k) = 63$

27. $-8s - 9 = -17$

28. $(-9 + z) - 8 = -10$

29. $(2 - a) - 4 = -10$

30. $-10 = 10\dfrac{-y}{8}$

31. $-0.1 = \dfrac{-10 + b}{9}$

32. $-13 = -y - 5$

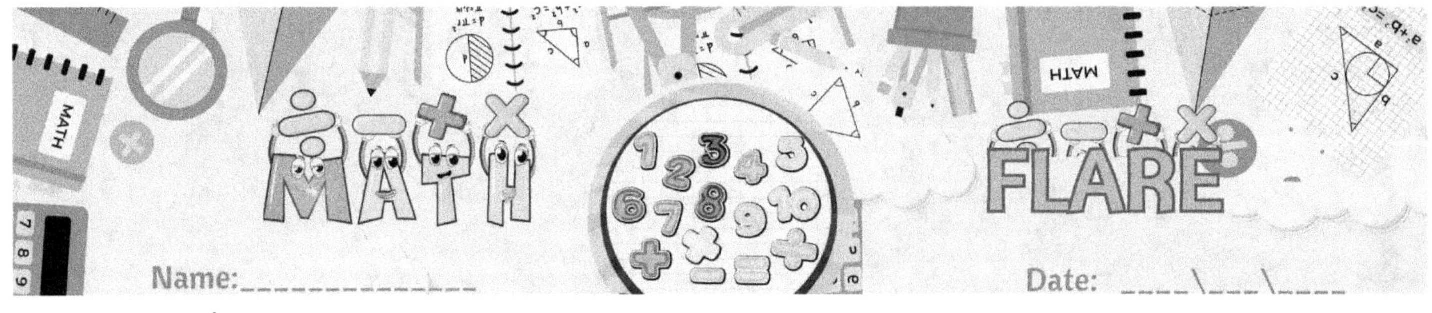

33. $9 = \dfrac{k}{1} + 8$

34. $5 = (10 + k) - 8$

35. $9(2 + m) = 108$

36. $72 = 9(1 + b)$

37. $-4\,\dfrac{m}{-10} = 4$

38. $50 = 10(2 + x)$

39. $2 = (5 + a) - 6$

40. $6 = (6 + a) - 9$

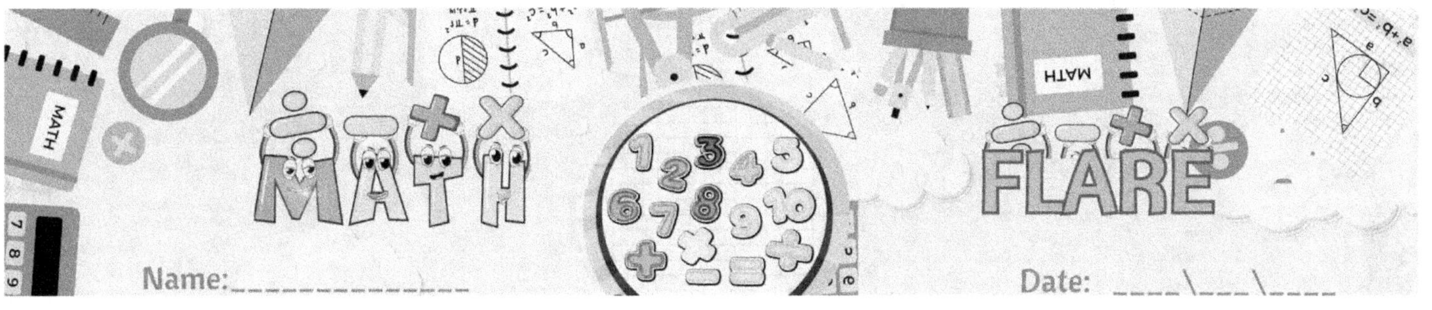

41. $(-2 + x) - 3 = 4$

42. $114 = 6(10 + k)$

43. $10\dfrac{-x}{10} = -10$

44. $\dfrac{x}{5} - 4 = -2$

45. $(4 - k)6 = 6$

46. $8(-4 + y) = -24$

47. $0 = 9(2 - b)$

48. $-6 = \dfrac{z}{4} - 8$

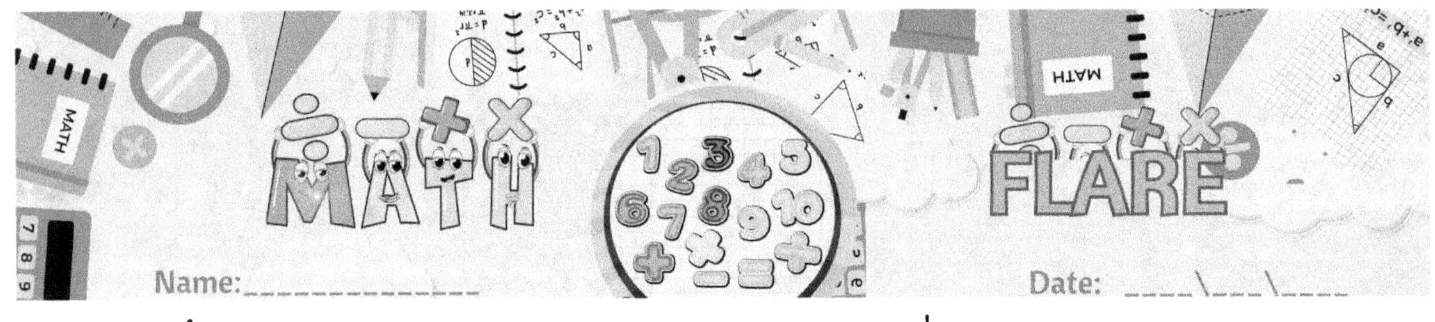

49. $\dfrac{-4+m}{3} = 0.7$

50. $3 = 1 + \dfrac{k}{5}$

51. $4\dfrac{-a}{2} = -20$

52. $4.5 = \dfrac{-1+b}{2}$

53. $4(-8+x) = 0$

54. $\dfrac{6+z}{2} = 6$

55. $(1+x) - 10 = -3$

56. $\dfrac{-8+b}{2} = 0$

Solving Multi-Step Equations

Solve for the variable.

1. $-3m - m = -8$

2. $-12 = 2y - 6y$

3. $-10 = 5 + k - 4k$

4. $-12 = 6k - 10k$

5. $8a - 4 - a = 38$

6. $70 = -a + 7 + 10a$

7. $-4x + 8 - 7 = -35$

8. $22 = 10x + 9 + 3$

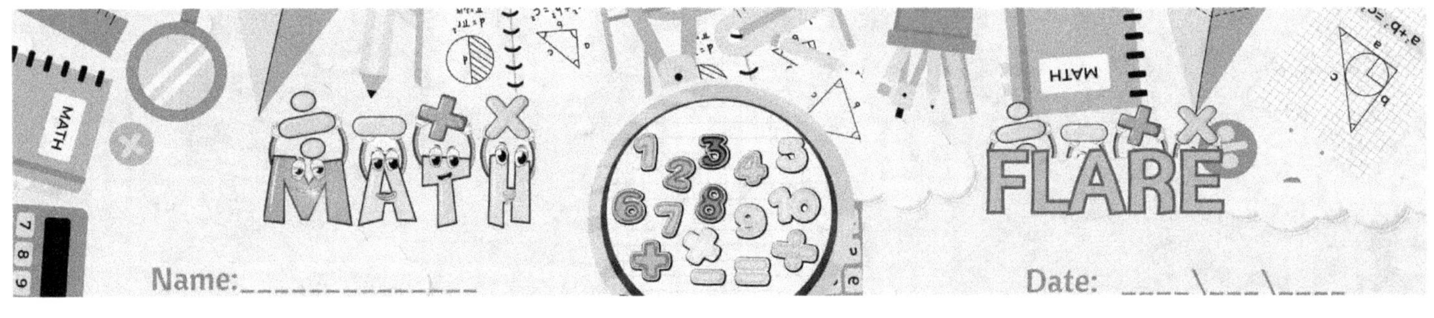

9. $1 = y + 10 - 2y$

10. $-39 = -8a + 5 + 4$

11. $6 + 10m - 9m = 16$

12. $s + 10 + 9s = 20$

13. $17 = -1 + 2y + 2$

14. $-8m + 9 - 1 = -48$

15. $16 = -2 - m + 3m$

16. $-9 = -4x + x$

17. $2x - x = 10$

18. $6 + z + 10z = 39$

19. $y - 1 - 8y = -29$

20. $-5k + 6 + k = -6$

21. $-35 = 10 - 8s + 3$

22. $-7 - 5x + 6 = -41$

23. $-1 - s - 8s = -46$

24. $41 = 6a - 9 - a$

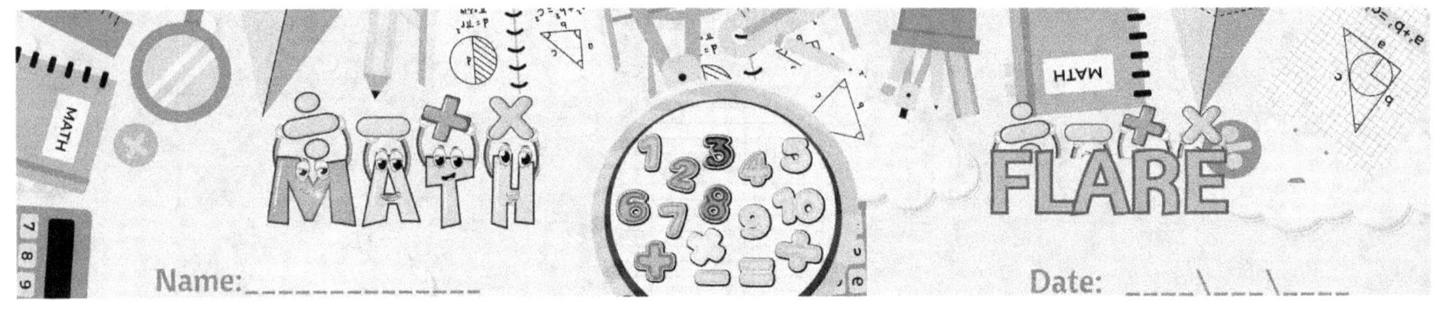

25. $-24 = -4s - 4s$

26. $24 = 8 + 9x - 5x$

27. $-3m - 3 - 6 = -18$

28. $4 - 8k + 8k = 4$

29. $-46 = 10 + m - 9m$

30. $-16 = -2z - 10 - z$

31. $-17 = -m - 5 - m$

32. $7s - 8 + 4 = 3$

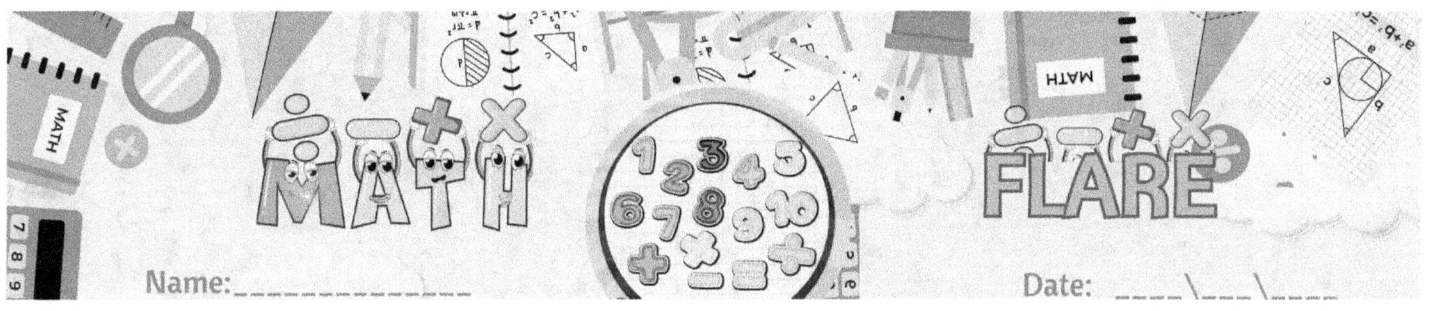

33. $-8s + 4 + 7 = -21$

34. $4 - 7k + 7k = 4$

35. $5 = k - 6 + 10k$

36. $15 = y + 8 + 6y$

37. $2 = m + 8 - 3m$

38. $65 = 8k - 9 + 2$

39. $-x + 2 + 8x = 37$

40. $x + 8 + 4x = 48$

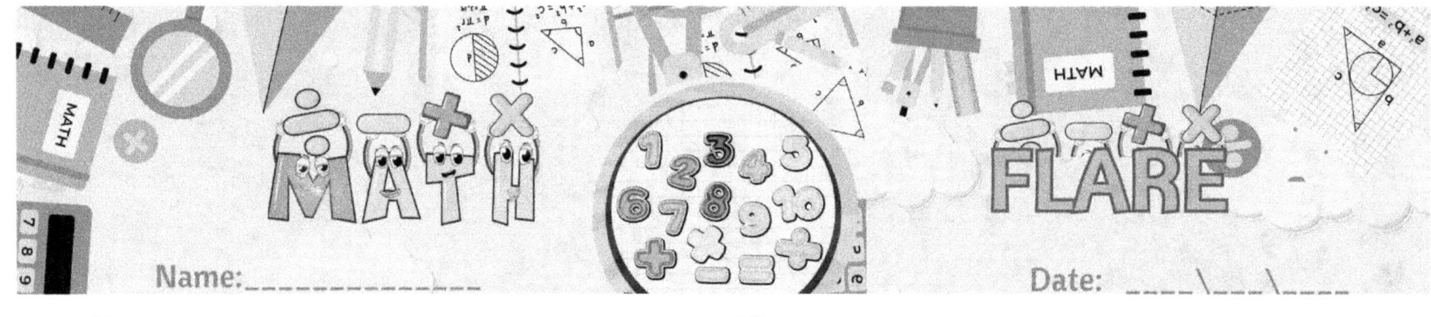

41. $-16 = 2 - 8m + 2m$

42. $-3y + y = -16$

43. $45 = 10z - 10 + z$

44. $-3b + 4b = 8$

45. $-31 = -4a + 4 - a$

46. $-s - 10 - 1 = -12$

47. $15 = 4b - b$

48. $-79 = -8z + 2 - z$

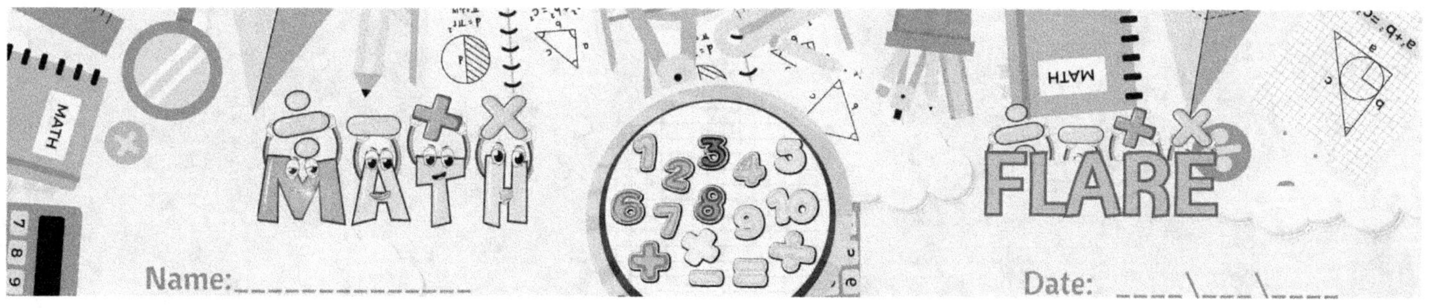

49. $10k - 9 + k = 24$

50. $-3x + x = -8$

51. $-2 = -2 - 7a + 7a$

52. $26 = 3s - 9 + 8$

53. $-5 + 7b - 9 = 7$

54. $0 = k - k$

55. $-54 = -5a - 4a$

56. $-6m - 8 - m = -22$

Equations: (One Side)

Solve the equations for the variable.

1. $5 - x = 6$

2. $x + -8 = 0$

3. $-76 \div k = 19$

4. $m + 4 = 8$

5. $11 - 4x = 23$

6. $4 + 10k = -6$

7. $m - -1 = 18$

8. $2m - 2 = 0$

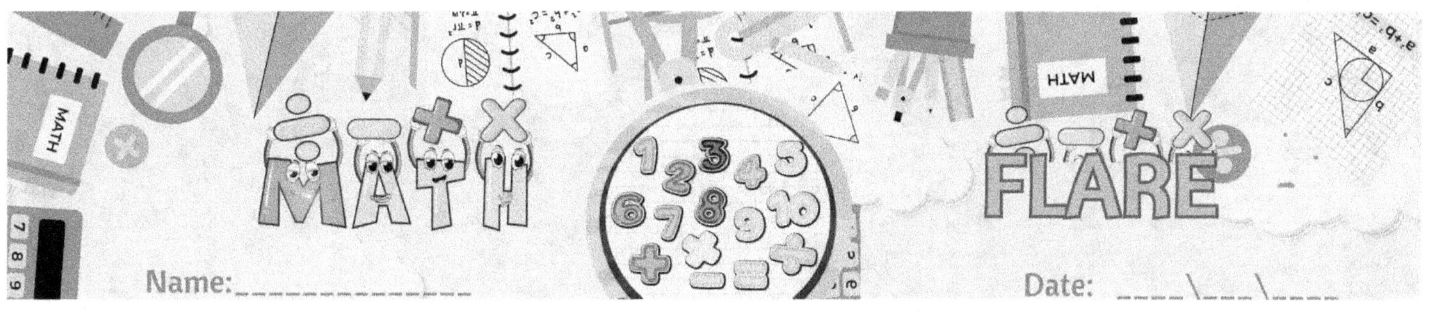

9. $8 \div x = 4$

10. $95 \div y = 19$

11. $-5x + -5 = -105$

12. $10m + -7 = 173$

13. $2m + 2 = -18$

14. $k \times 20 = 160$

15. $x \div 9 = 19$

16. $15z - 12 = 243$

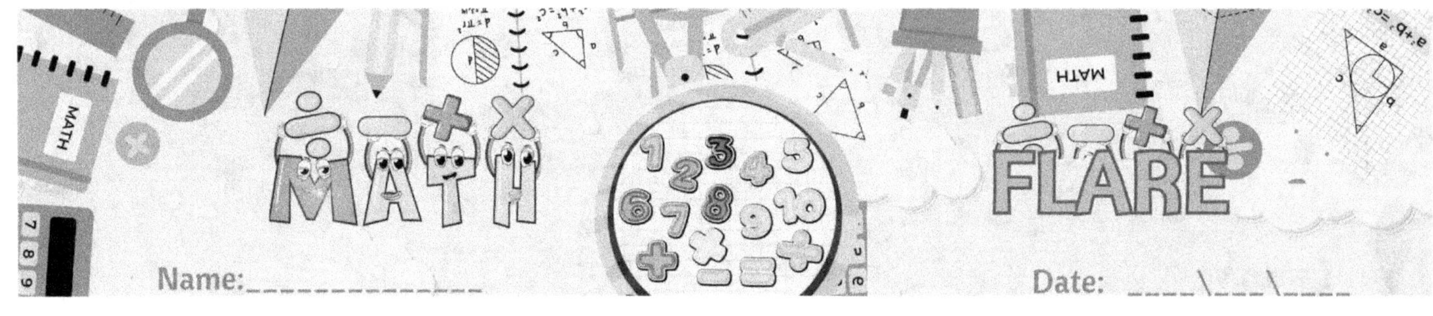

17. $15 - 7y = 57$

18. $12 + k = 21$

19. $323 \div k = 19$

20. $k \times -6 = 54$

21. $10 - m = 10$

22. $m \times 15 = 255$

23. $19 - m = 12$

24. $6 - z = 6$

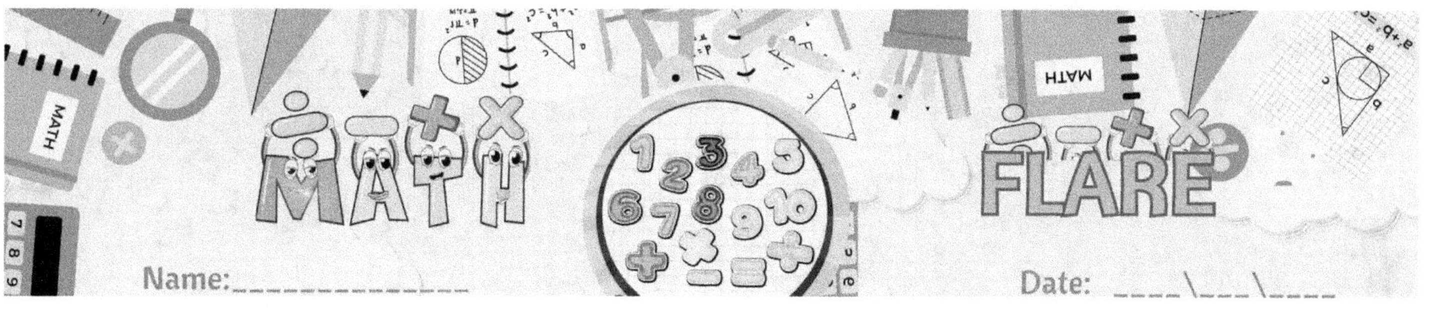

25. $k \div -5 = 3$

26. $8 - m = 8$

27. $-4 - 6x = 20$

28. $k + -5 = 14$

29. $-7 + -7y = 21$

30. $z \times 8 = 24$

31. $m - 11 = 4$

32. $-9 + k = 6$

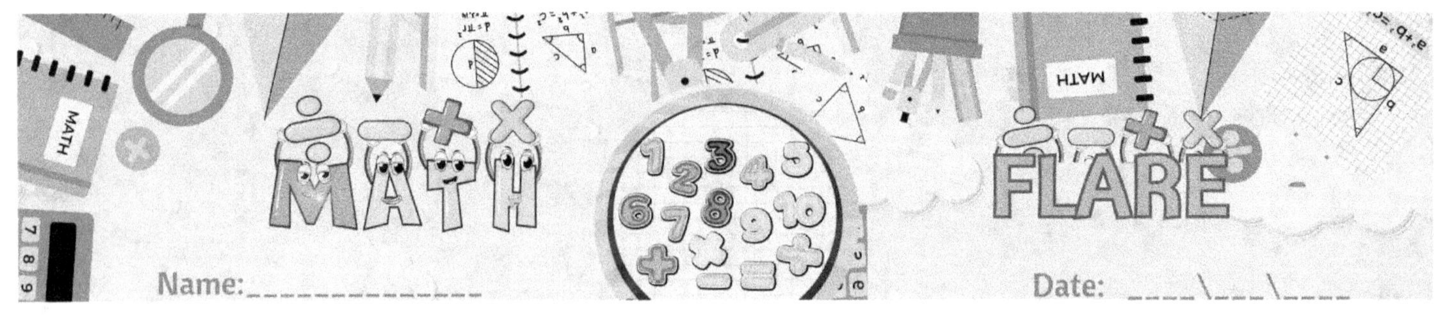

33. $y \times -9 = 72$

34. $9m - -3 = 165$

35. $6 + z = 11$

36. $11z + 0 = -33$

37. $y + 6 = -4$

38. $3 + m = 7$

39. $1z - 5 = 12$

40. $4 + 12k = 124$

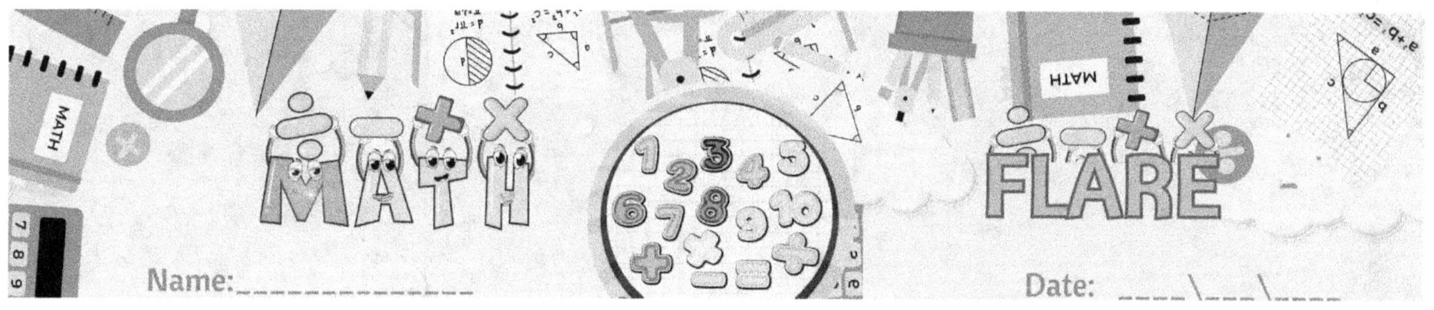

41. $1 \times z = -6$

42. $9 + k = 8$

43. $k \div 7 = -9$

44. $x + -2 = -2$

45. $-10 + 9y = -73$

46. $18 + m = 30$

47. $-4m + 1 = -31$

48. $14 \times x = 280$

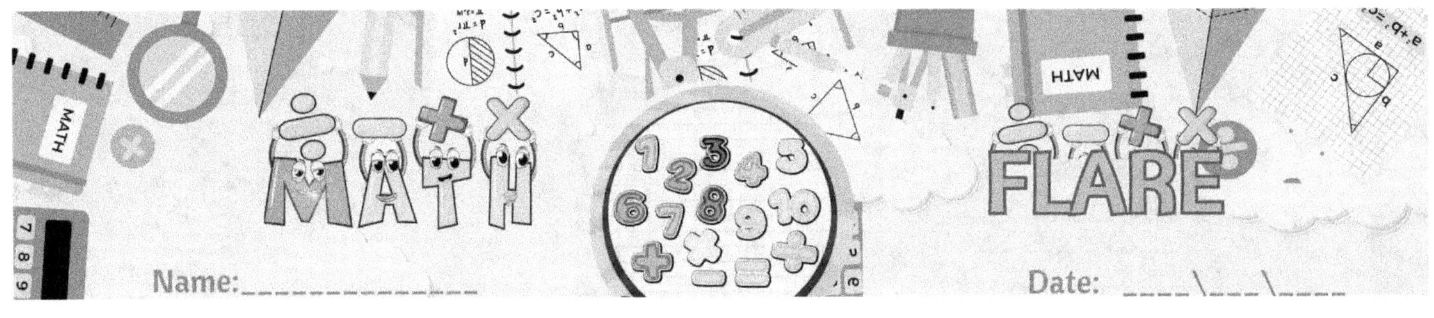

49. $x - 13 = 2$

50. $-40 \div x = -5$

51. $z \div 11 = 12$

52. $9 \times z = 81$

53. $0 \div k = 0$

54. $z \div -9 = 11$

55. $12k + -5 = 55$

56. $-7 + m = 12$

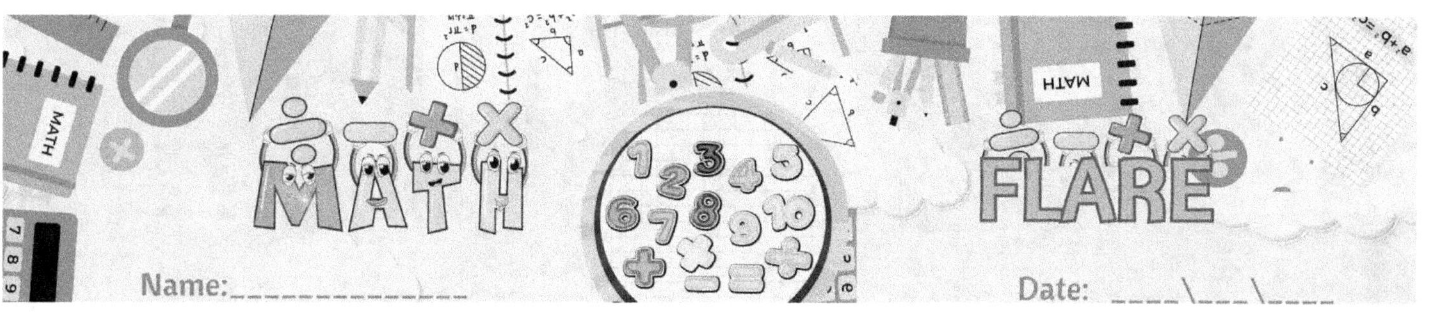

Equations (Two Sides)

Solve for the variable.

1. $2b = -9 + b$

2. $-2 + 2m + 1 = -7 - m + -6$

3. $16 + b = -7b$

4. $-7x = -24 - x$

5. $-56 + x = 8x$

6. $6m = 35 - m$

7. $-4 - x = -2x$

8. $-5m = 16 - m$

9. $-64 - a = 7a$

10. $9 - a = 8a$

11. $-5a + 119 = 8a + 2$

12. $1a + -1 = -4a + 44$

13. $-3 + -2m = -4 - m$

14. $8 + 9z = 6 + 7z$

15. $119 - 4x = 9 + 7x$

16. $81 - m = 1 + 7m$

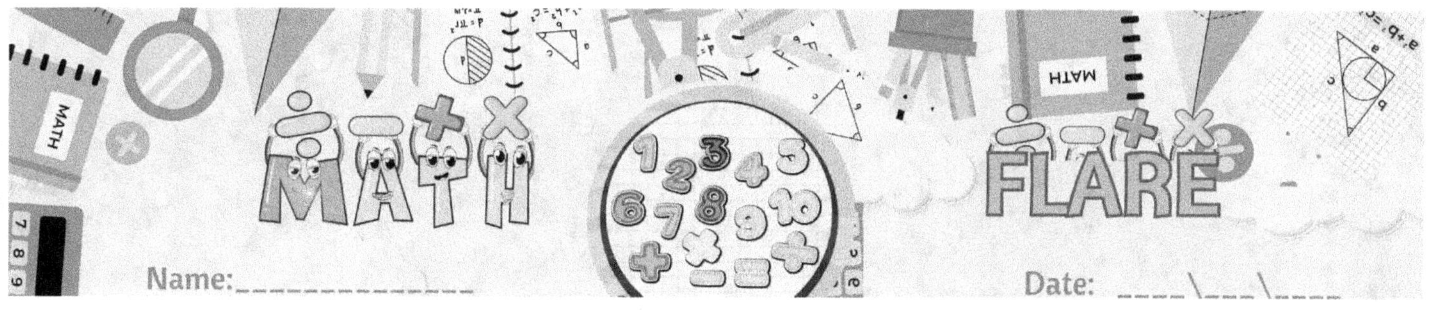

17. $9 + y = 2y$

18. $2m = -6 - m$

19. $6 + s = 10 + 2s + 1$

20. $9b + 6 = 2b + -8$

21. $13 - k = 2k + 1$

22. $-10 + -5y + -3 = -73 + y$

23. $-2m = 3 - m$

24. $-62 + k = -5k + -8$

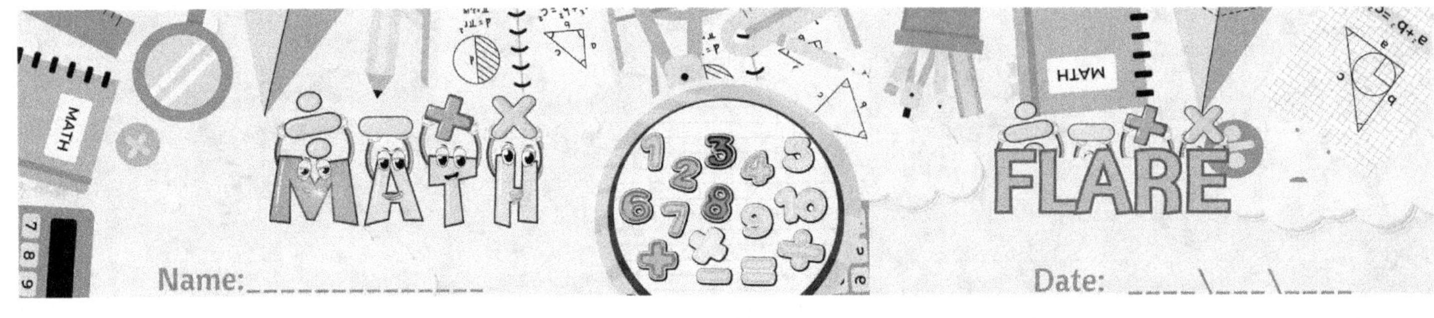

25. $40 + m = 9m$

26. $-10b = -9 - b$

27. $15 - s = 2s$

28. $47 - z + -15 = -8 + -6z + 5$

29. $10 - s = 9s$

30. $68 + 2m = -2 + 9m$

31. $8a = 27 - a$

32. $14 + b = -6b$

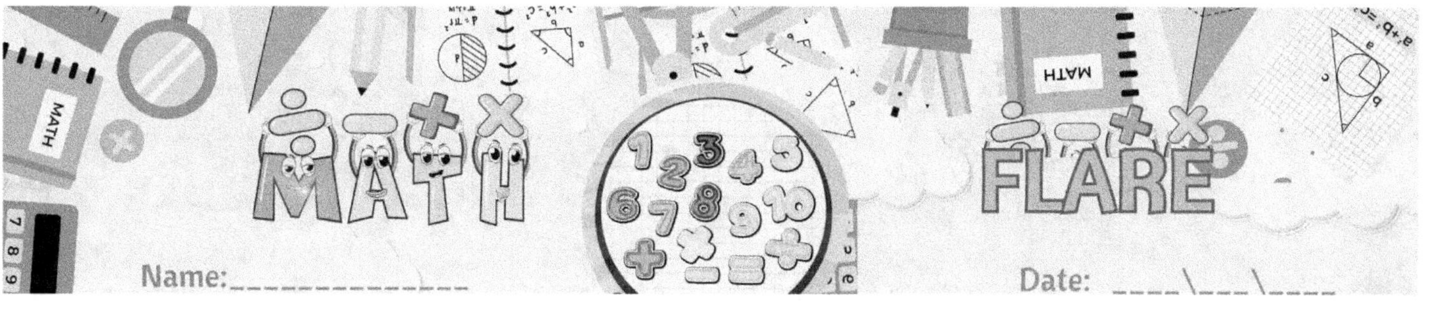

33. $3s + 10 = 14 - s$

34. $-8 - z = 2z + 1$

35. $-8 + 7m = 4m + -26$

36. $-2k + -9 = -12 - k$

37. $9 + -4m = -21 + m$

38. $2b + 14 = -1 + 7b$

39. $-13 + z = 1 + -6z$

40. $-33 + z = 9 + -7z + -2$

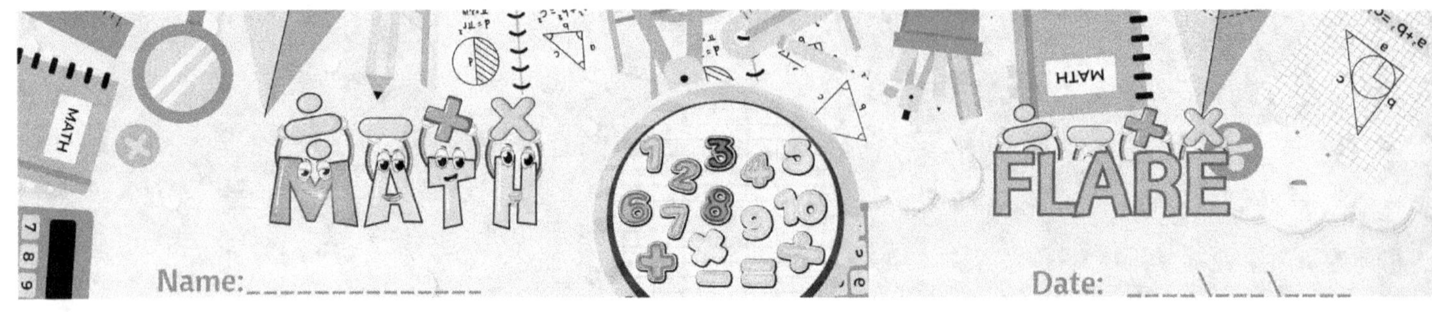

41. $8s = -56 + s$

42. $-3 - -7x = 6x + 5$

43. $3 - z = 2z$

44. $44 + a = 9a + -4$

45. $33 + z = -10z$

46. $5 + 2b + 1 = -2 + b$

47. $-68 - m = 4 + 7m$

48. $-3 - s = -2s$

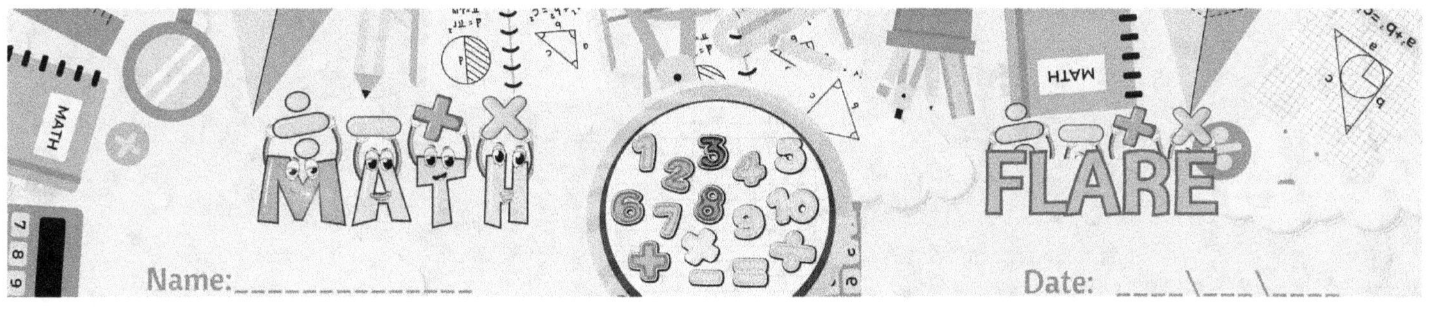

49. $-4m = -15 - m$

50. $-1 + 9z + -10 = 35 - z + -6$

51. $-9 + z = -2 + -6z$

52. $-10 + 7k = -17 - -8k$

53. $17 - z + 3 = -1 + 5z + -3$

54. $-118 + -8s = 9s + 1$

55. $2b = 21 - b$

56. $5m + 4 = 8 + m$

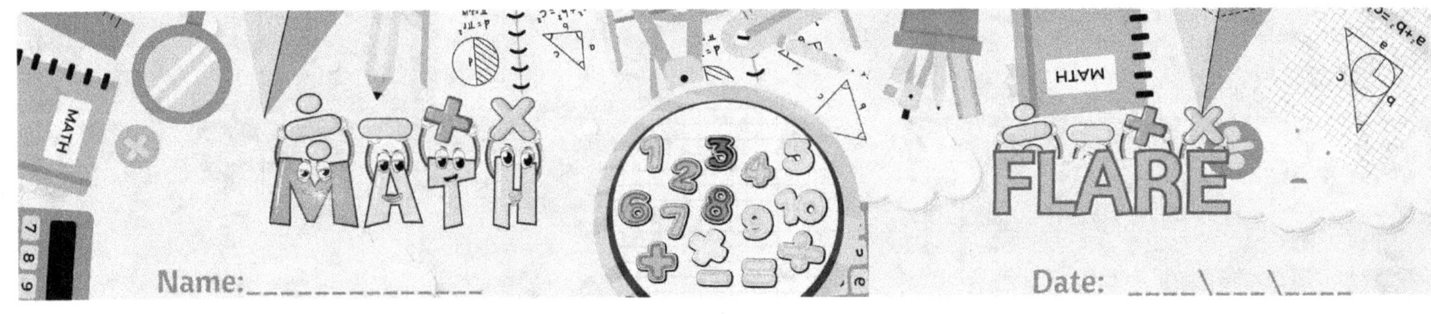

Simplify Expressions

1. $k + 15 + 11k$

2. $13 - 5(-7k + 3)$

3. $12 + 17x - 6x$

4. $1 + 16(3m + 9)$

5. $7 + 3x - 13x + 10 - x$

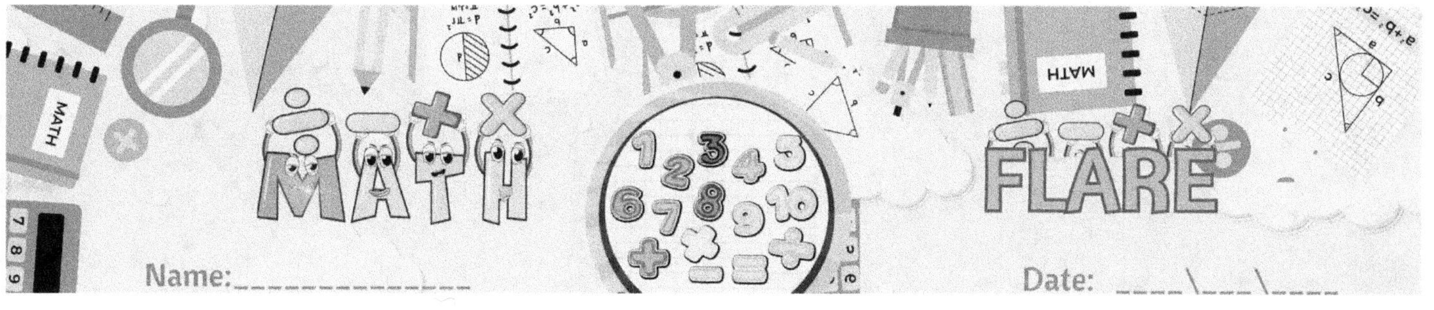

6. $k + k$

7. $-15x + 14 - 13 + 19x$

8. $-5m + 20m + 14 - 8m$

9. $10 + 14 + 13y - 3y + 11 - 6y$

10. $16 + 20m - 7m + 14 - m$

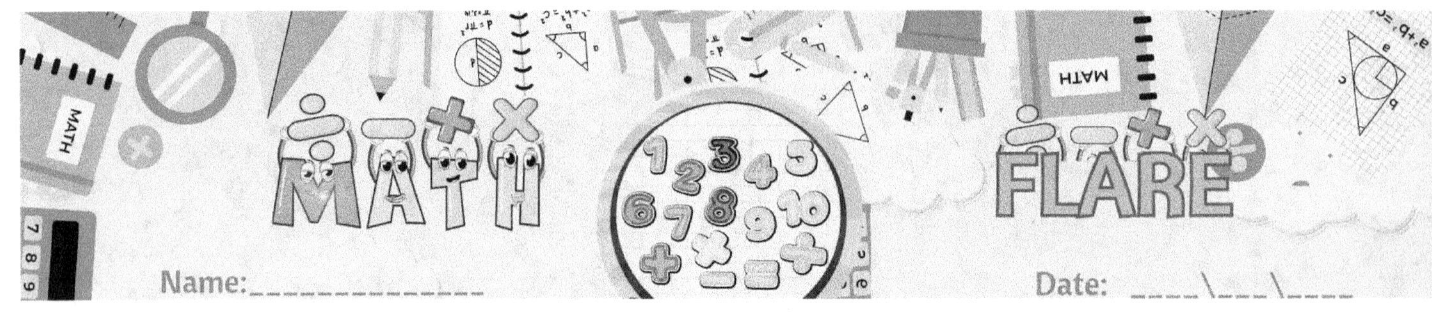

11. $-12 + 2k - 9k - 12 + 11k$

12. $-20x + 15 - 10x$

13. $-20m - 17 - 5m$

14. $z - 14z$

15. $-12k + 7 + 7k + 8 + 14k - 18$

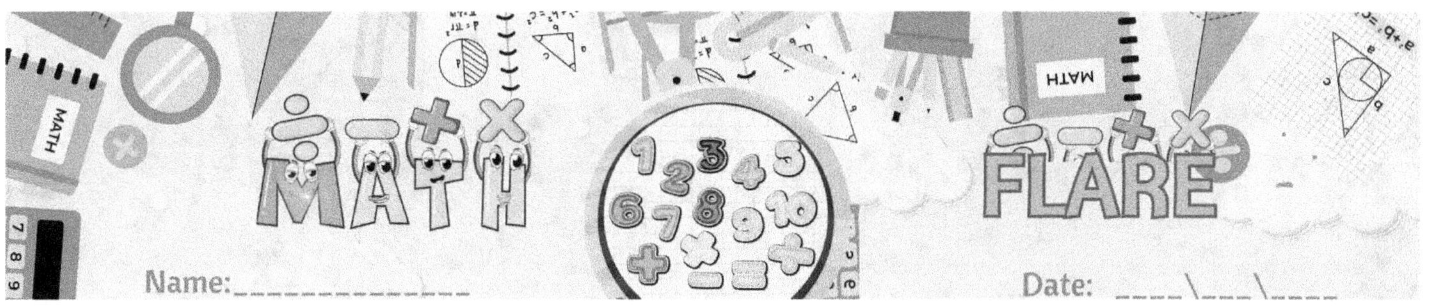

16. $17k - 20 - 20k + 8$

17. $14k + 3 + k$

18. $-7m + 10 - 3m$

19. $-12z - 17 - 2z$

20. $-10x - 13 - 15x$

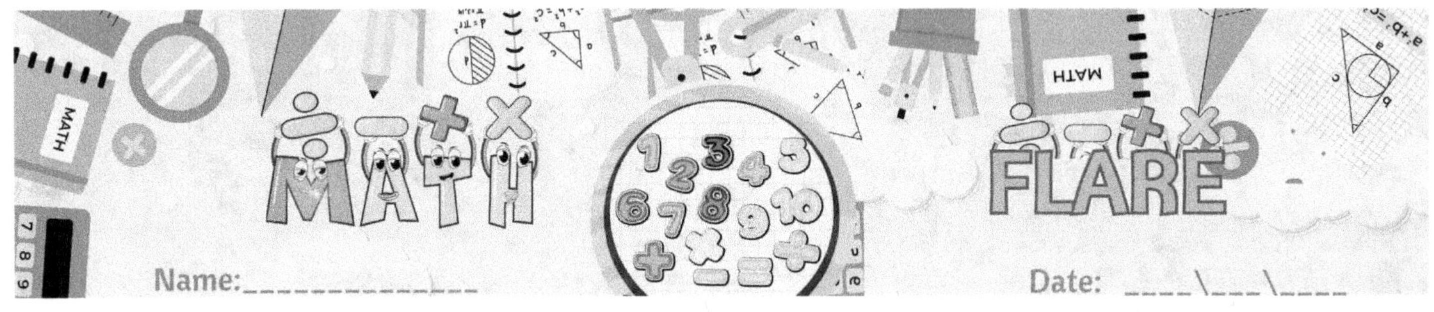

21. $4z - 4 - 7z + 6 - 15$

22. $-2 + 9x - x - 7 - 13x$

23. $y + 4 + 7y$

24. $-16z - 11 + 12 - 2z$

25. $15 + 7(14k + 7)$

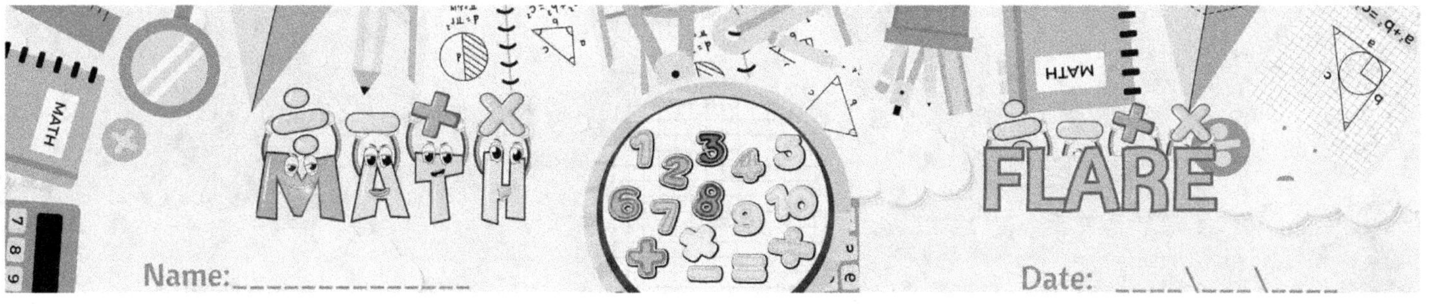

26. $2y + y$

27. $18z + 6 - 18z + 14 + 16z + 19$

28. $-14m + 10 + 13m + 14 + 14m - 13$

29. $13k + k$

30. $6k + 17 + 5k$

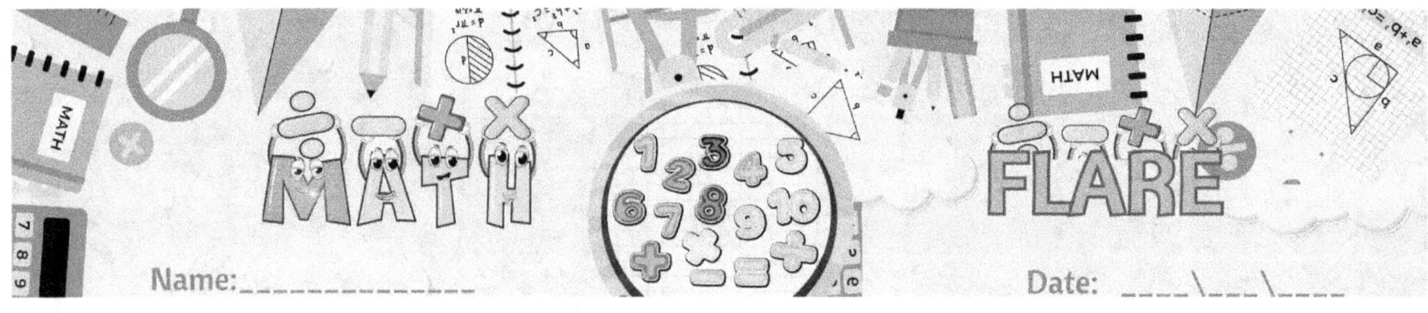

31. $8 + 10z - 10 + 19z$

32. $-2y + 1 + 18y$

33. $20 + 15m - 5 + 15m$

34. $-5x - 5x$

35. $4m - 18 - 20m + 10$

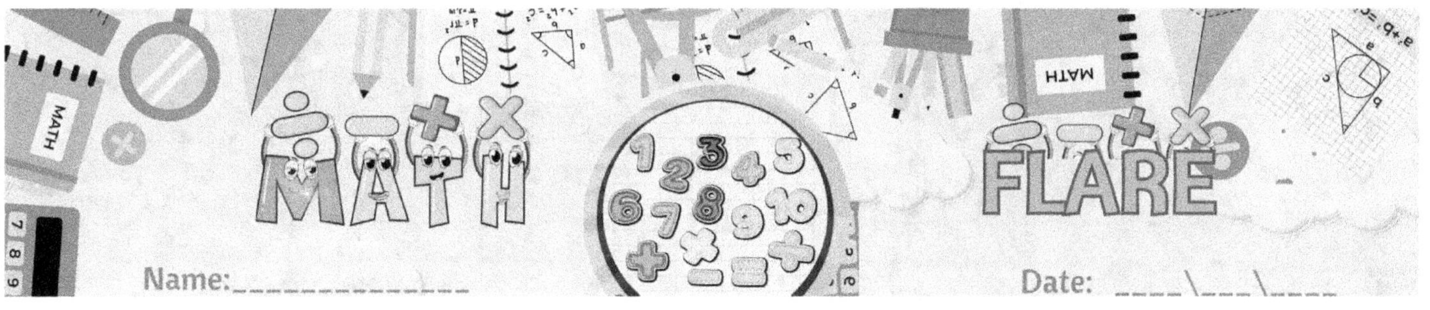

36. $3 - 7(20z - 19)$

37. $-10 + 2x + 8 - 15x$

38. $10 + 18(12k - 16)$

39. $17 + 19m - 6m$

40. $19k - 4k + 16 + 13$

41. $-10y - 8y$

42. $20k + 3k$

43. $y + 20 + 5y$

44. $19 + 7(14y + 2)$

45. $-4k - 19 - 5 - 13k$

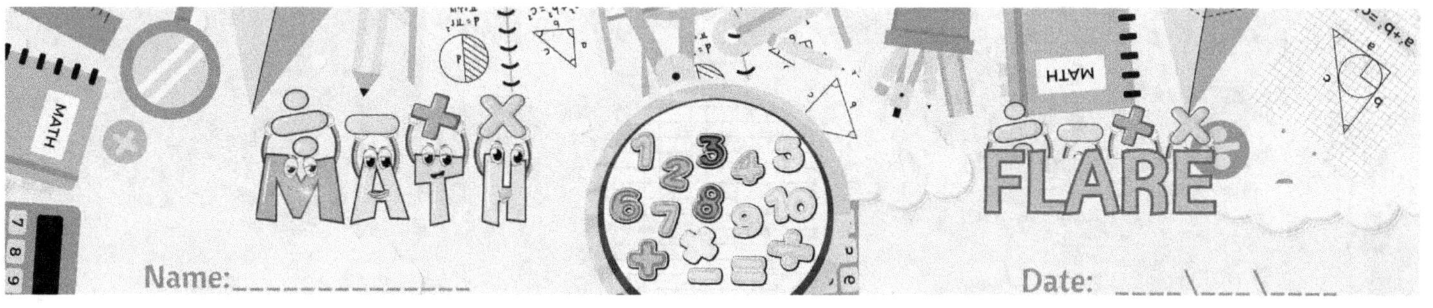

46. $20 + 11y + 4 + 17y$

47. $18 + 8m - 2 + 13m$

48. $-2k - 19 + 11k$

49. $-8m + 20 + 2m + 3 + 5m - 5$

50. $13 - 11(13m - 2)$

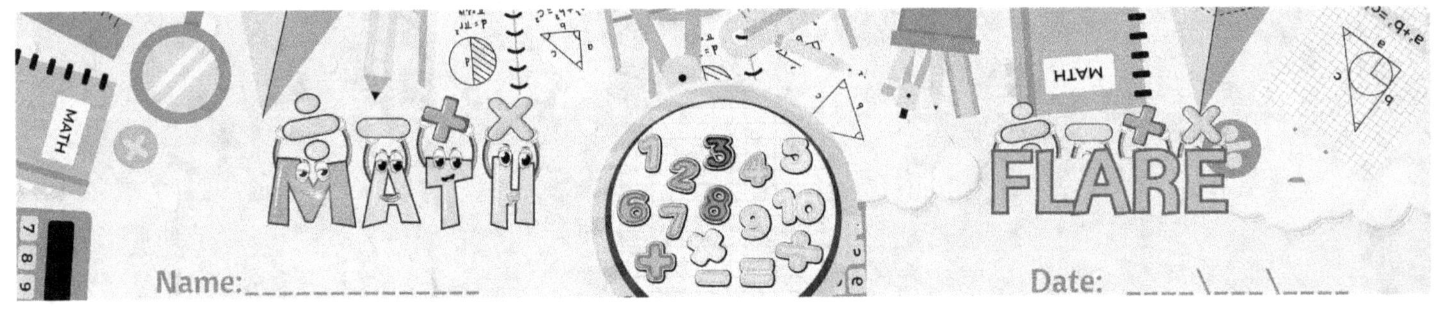

51. $-2 + 8y - 8y - 4 + 20y$

52. $12x - 16 - 2x + 4 - 16$

53. $-12x + 2 + 19x + 20 + 8x - 4$

54. $6y + 3 - 2 - 14y + 4y$

55. $20m - m + 8 + 7$

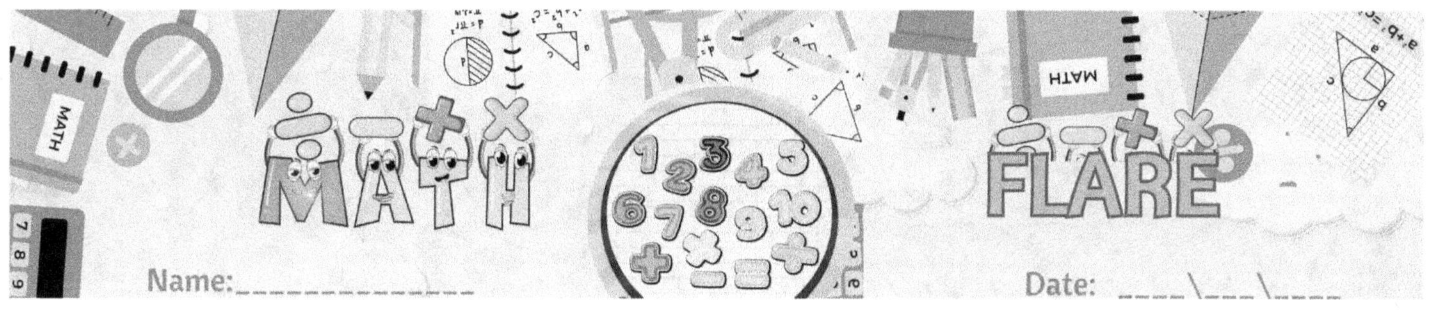

56. $-y - 11 + 16 - 17y$

57. $m + 14 + 9m + 2 + 2m + 7$

58. $16y + 5 - 5 - 11y + y$

59. $4 - 7(13k - 10)$

60. $-8 + 14y - 6y - 3 + 5y$

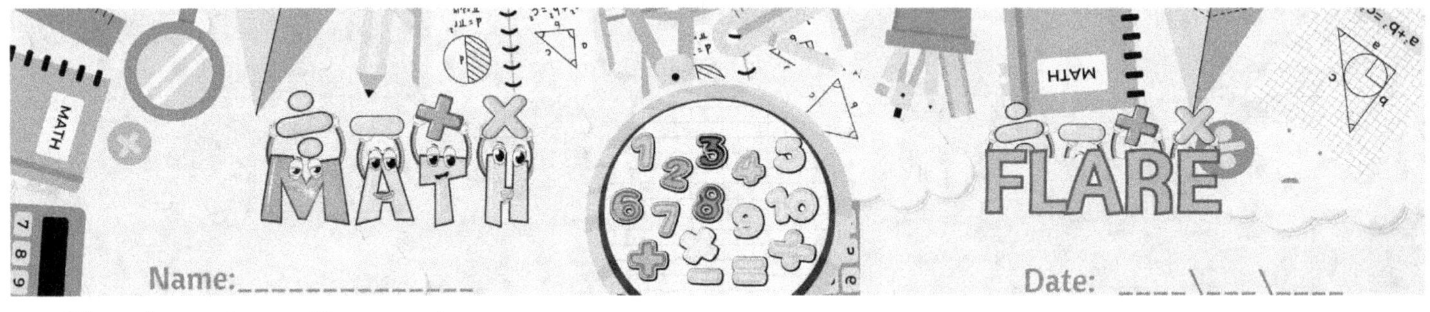

Evaluating Equations

Evaluate each expression when: $x = 2$

1. $7x + x - 2 =$

2. $1 - x =$

3. $9x + 3 - 3x =$

4. $10 - x =$

5. $9x - x =$

6. $(8x)(x) =$

7. $x + 8 =$

8. $8 + x =$

9. $x + 5 =$

10. $x^1 + x - 6 =$

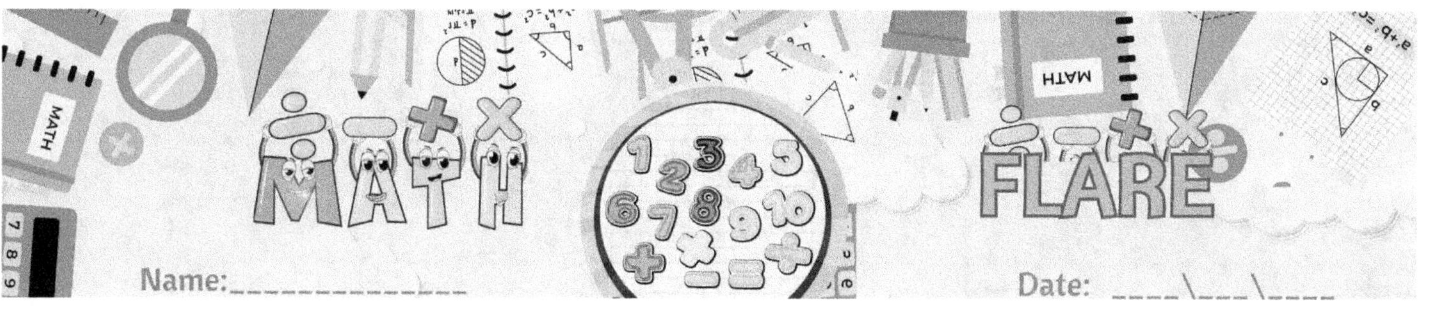

Evaluating Equations

Evaluate each expression when: x = 5

1. $8(2x) =$

2. $x - 9 =$

3. $x + 10 =$

4. $8x^1 + 10x^1 =$

5. $\dfrac{x}{1} + 4 =$

6. $7 + x =$

7. $10x^1 + 2x^1 =$

8. $8 - x =$

9. $6x - x =$

10. $7x + 1 =$

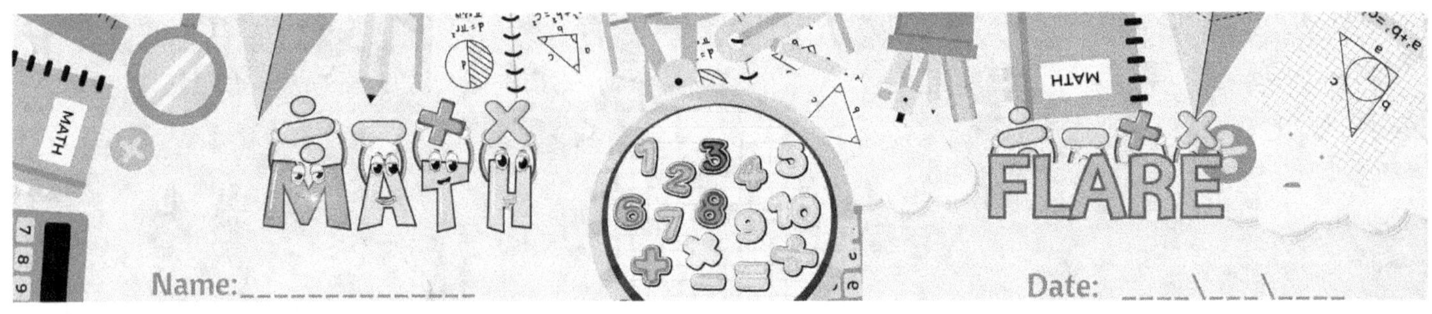

Evaluating Equations

Evaluate each expression when: x = 5

1. $x + 3 + 9x =$

2. $x \div 5 =$

3. $x - 3 =$

4. $5 \div x + 7 =$

5. $9(4x - 4) + 10(4 + x) =$

6. $5 \div x + 10 =$

7. $4 + x =$

8. $9 + (7x + 8) =$

9. $x^1 + 9x^1 =$

10. $8x + x =$

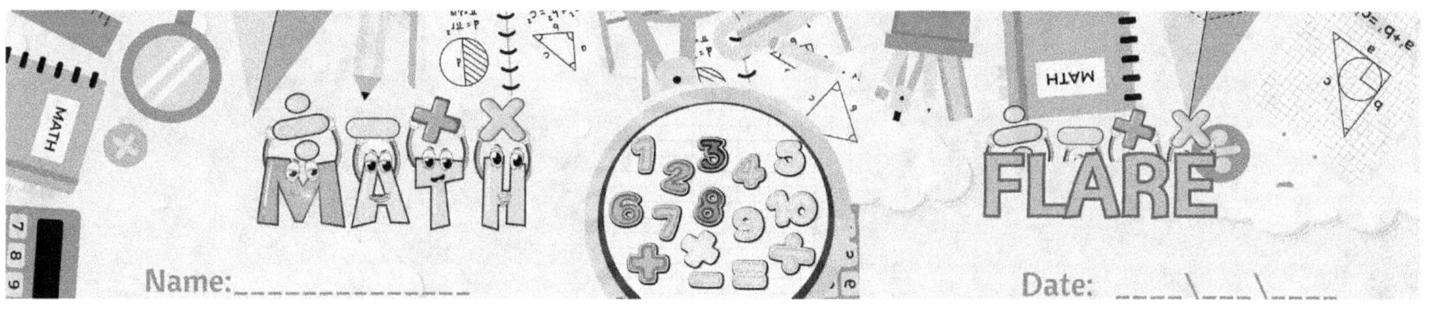

Evaluating Equations

Evaluate each expression when: $x = 4$

1. $\dfrac{2 + x}{x + 2} =$

2. $4x + 7x + 4x =$

3. $7x - x =$

4. $5(8 - x) =$

5. $6x + 1 + (2x - 4) =$

6. $8 \div x =$

7. $10x - x =$

8. $2x + 6x - 5 =$

9. $8 \div x + 8 =$

10. $6(10 - x) =$

Evaluating Equations

Evaluate each expression when: x = 4

1. $8x - x =$

2. $7 + 6x =$

3. $4x + 5x + 5x =$

4. $x + x - 2 =$

5. $x \div 2 =$

6. $\dfrac{x}{4} =$

7. $x - 1 =$

8. $2^1 + x^1 =$

9. $x + 2 + 7x =$

10. $(x^1 + 1) - 10(1 + x) =$

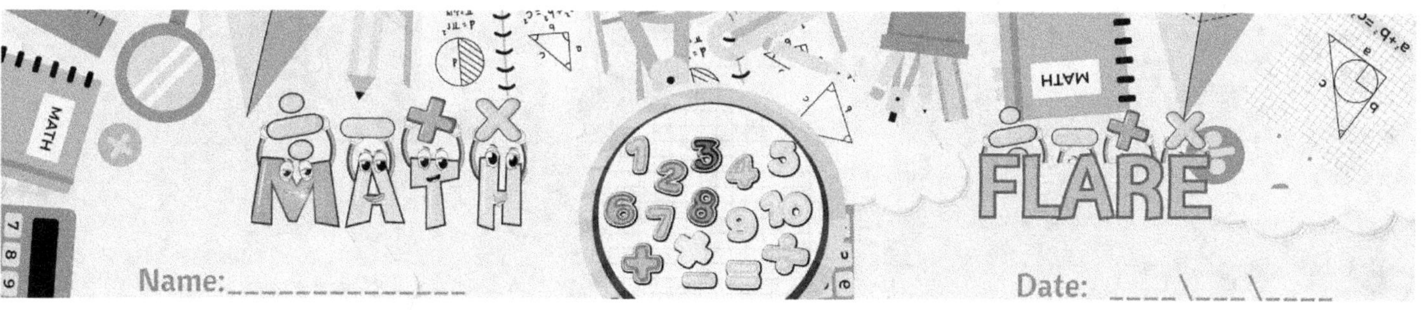

Evaluating Equations

Evaluate each expression when: x = 2

1. $9x + 7x + 3x =$

2. $9 - x =$

3. $8x + 8 =$

4. $8 + x =$

5. $x - 1 =$

6. $5x + 8 - 2x =$

7. $(x^1 + 10) - 7(7 + x) =$

8. $5x + 8x + 7x =$

9. $10x + 8x - 3 =$

10. $(x + 5) \div 7 =$

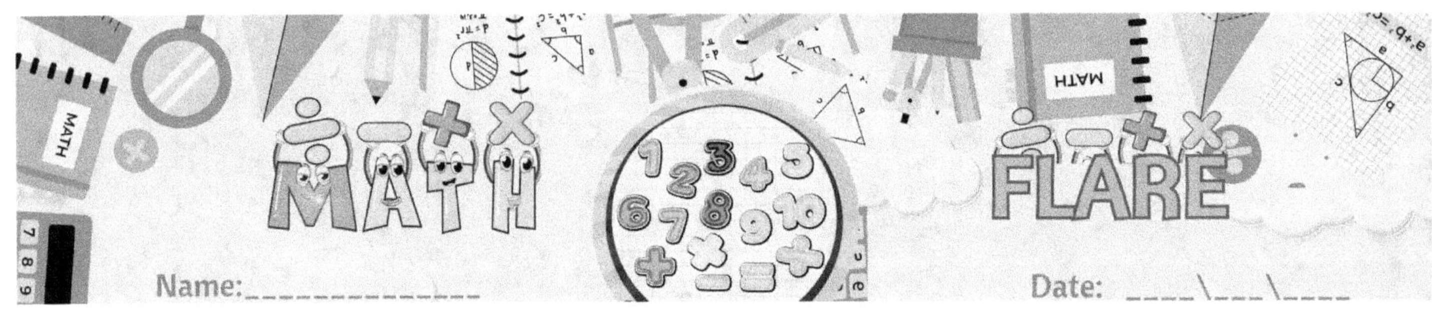

Evaluating Equations

Evaluate each expression when: $x = 7$

1. $7 \div x =$

2. $9 \div (x + 2) =$

3. $1(5 + x) =$

4. $10 \div x =$

5. $x^1 + x - 5 =$

6. $3 + x =$

7. $3 \div x =$

8. $x + 2 + 9x =$

9. $x + 4 + 7x =$

10. $\dfrac{x}{7} =$

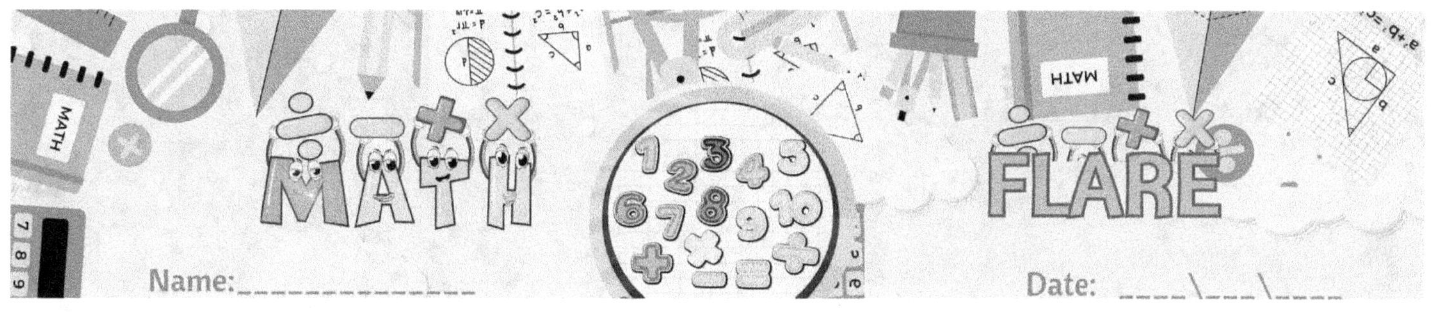

Evaluating Equations

Evaluate each expression when: $x = 2$

1. $2^1 + x^1 =$

2. $x(5 + x) =$

3. $\dfrac{x}{2} =$

4. $9x + 9x + x =$

5. $(7x + 8) + (10x - 8) =$

6. $\dfrac{4 + x}{x + 4} =$

7. $x^1 + x - 9 =$

8. $9x + 9 =$

9. $9 + \dfrac{6 + x}{x} - 9 =$

10. $\dfrac{20}{x} =$

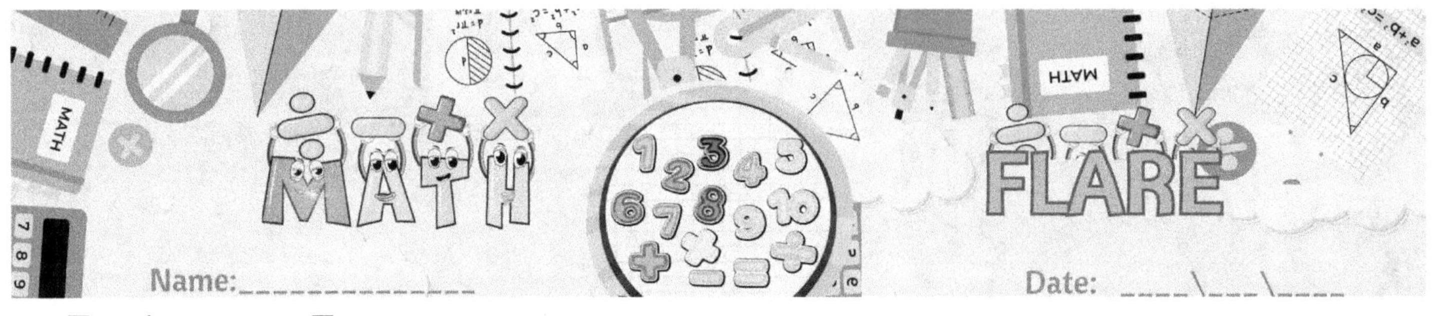

Evaluating Equations

Evaluate each expression when: $x = 1$

1. $(3x)^1 =$

2. $3x - 5 =$

3. $8 \div x + 5 =$

4. $x + 6 =$

5. $5x - x =$

6. $(10 + 6x) + (4x - 1) - (2 + 8x) =$

7. $(x + 7) \div 2 =$

8. $6 + (5x + 7) =$

9. $7 + 4x =$

10. $8(2 - x) =$

Evaluating Equations

Evaluate each expression when: x = 1

1. $\dfrac{x}{1} + 4 =$

2. $x \div 1 =$

3. $x - 1 =$

4. $4(10x - 5) + 3(4 + x) =$

5. $3x - 5 =$

6. $\dfrac{x}{1} =$

7. $5x + 9 =$

8. $7x - 6 + 10x =$

9. $5 + x =$

10. $9x + x =$

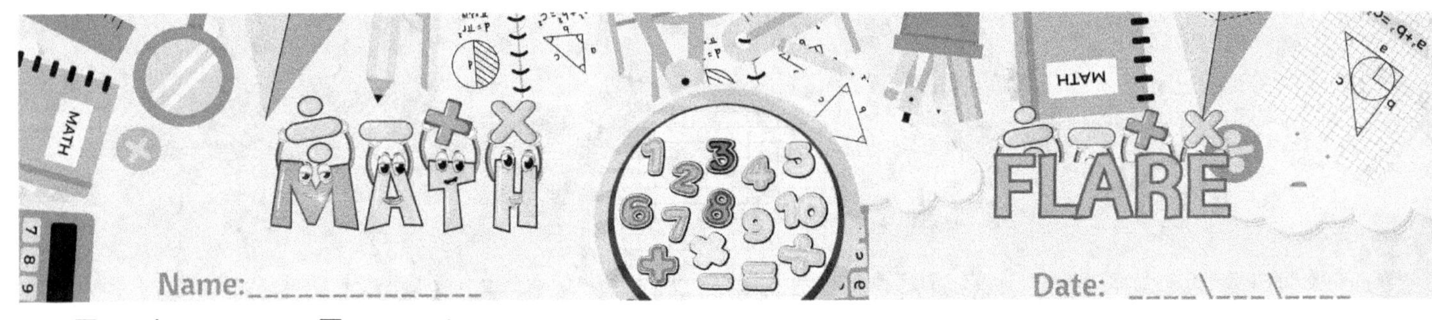

Evaluating Equations

Evaluate each expression when: x = 3

1. $6x + 5 - 10x =$

2. $x \div 3 =$

3. $5 \div (x + 2) =$

4. $3 + \dfrac{x}{1} =$

5. $5x + 1 =$

6. $10x + 9 =$

7. $8x + 8 =$

8. $5 + (3x + 6) =$

9. $7x^1 + 5x^1 =$

10. $\dfrac{9 + x}{x + 9} =$

Evaluating Equations

Evaluate each expression when: x = 5

1. $10 \div x + 7 =$

2. $10^1 + x^1 =$

3. $x + 10 =$

4. $9x - 3 + 8x =$

5. $(9x)^1 =$

6. $5x + 6 - 3x =$

7. $x + 9 =$

8. $5 + x =$

9. $5x - 4 + 2x =$

10. $x - 3 =$

Evaluating Equations

Evaluate each expression when: x = 2

1. $7x + x - 2 =$

2. $1 - x =$

3. $9x + 3 - 3x =$

4. $10 - x =$

5. $9x - x =$

6. $(8x)(x) =$

7. $x + 8 =$

8. $8 + x =$

9. $x + 5 =$

10. $x^1 + x - 6 =$

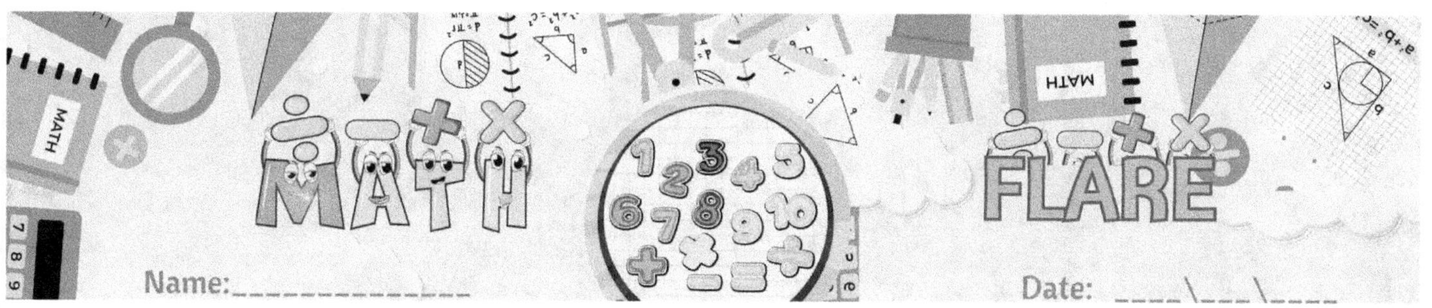

Verbal Algebra Expressions

1. Three times a number increased by 8 is 41. Find the number.

2. The quotient of a number and nine increased by 2 is 4. What is the number?

3. Four times a number is 0. What is the number?

4. The quotient of a number and seven is 1. Find the number.

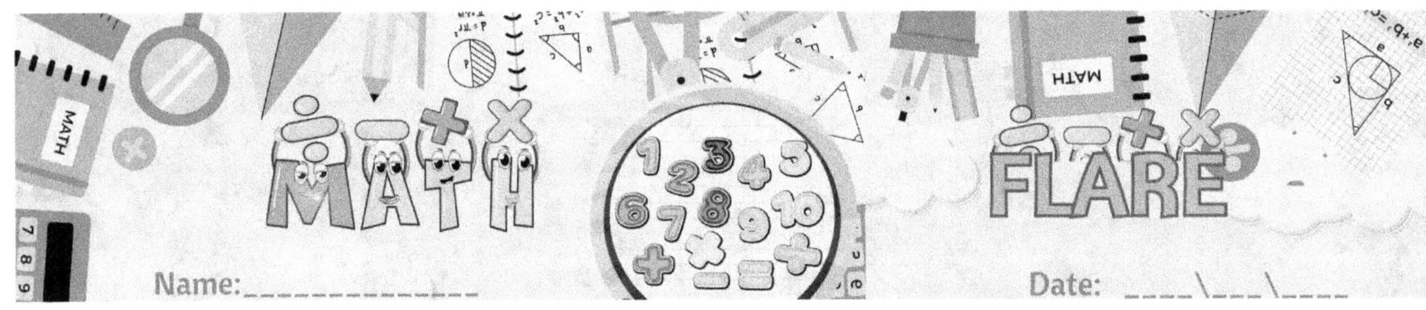

5. The difference of two numbers is 61. The larger number is 5 more than nine times the smaller number. What are the numbers?

6. The sum of two numbers is 11. The difference of the same two numbers is three. Find the numbers.

7. Eighteen more than the second of three consecutive even integers is the same as the difference between the third and six times the first. Find the numbers.

8. The product of six and some number is equal to the sum of that number and 30. What is the number?

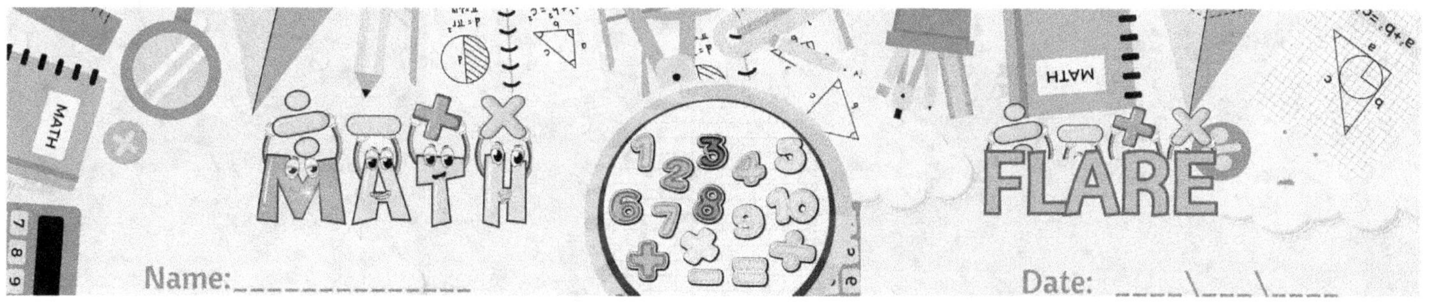

9. The sum of two consecutive numbers is 11. What are the numbers?

10. The sum of a number and nine is 10. Find the number.

11. Ten times a number diminished by 3 is 107. Find the number.

12. The sum of two numbers is 17. One number is three less than the other. Find the numbers.

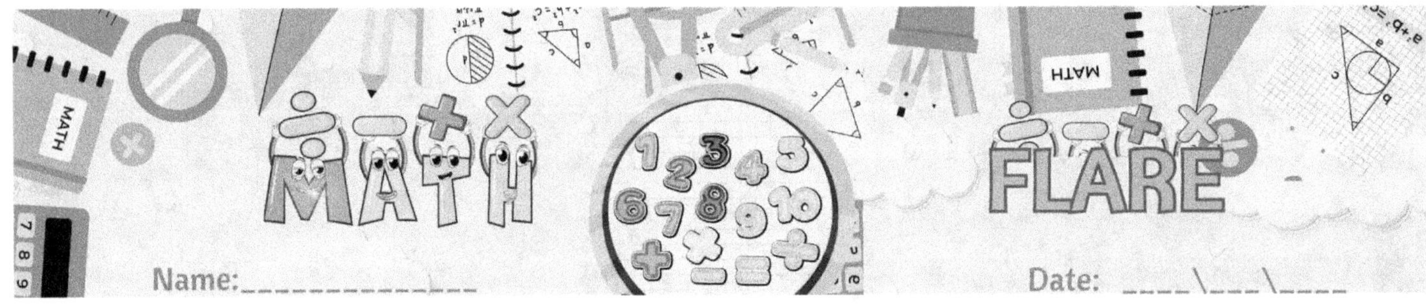

13. One-half of a number diminished by 1 is 8. Find the number.

14. The sum of three numbers is 62. The largest number is nine times the smallest, and the smallest is seven less than the middle number. Find the numbers.

15. Six is equal to the quotient of a number and 4. Find the number.

16. The difference of a number and nine is equal to 7. What is the number?

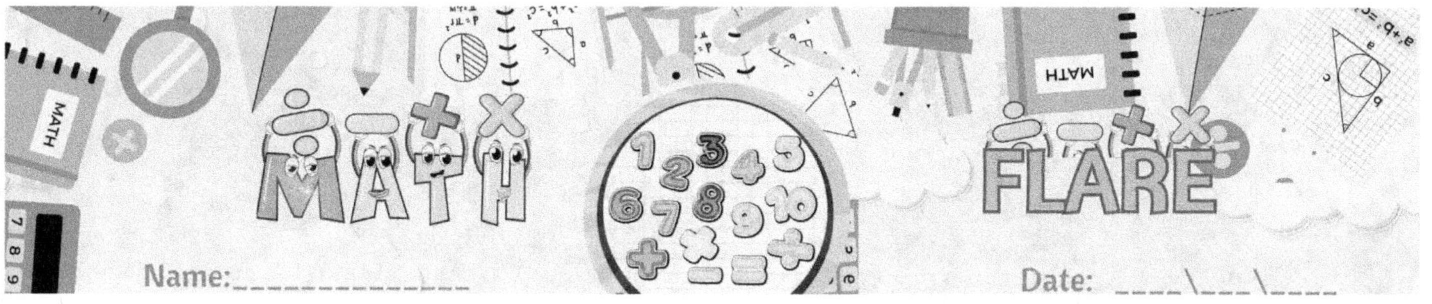

17. The difference of two numbers is 48. The larger number is 6 more than seven times the smaller number. What are the numbers?

18. One-half of a number decreased by 1 is 0. Find the number.

19. Twice a number is 2. What is the number?

20. If the product of eight and a number is increased by 1, the result is 57. Find the number?

21. The sum of a number and four is 8. Find the number.

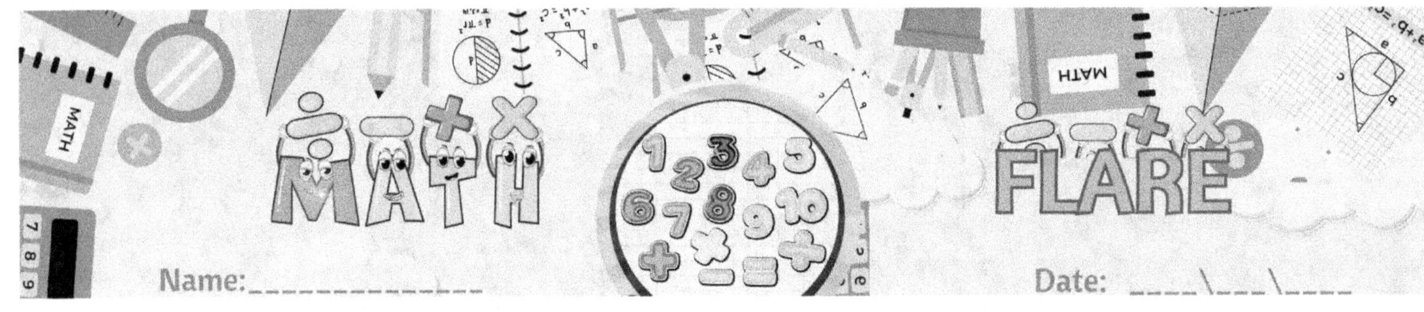

22. Four more than six times a number is 76. What is the number?

23. One less than twice a number is 15. Find the number.

24. Nine more than a number is 11. What is the number?

25. Six more than nine times a number is 33. What is the number?

26. The greater of two numbers is 7 less than six times the smaller number. Their sum is 42. Find the numbers.

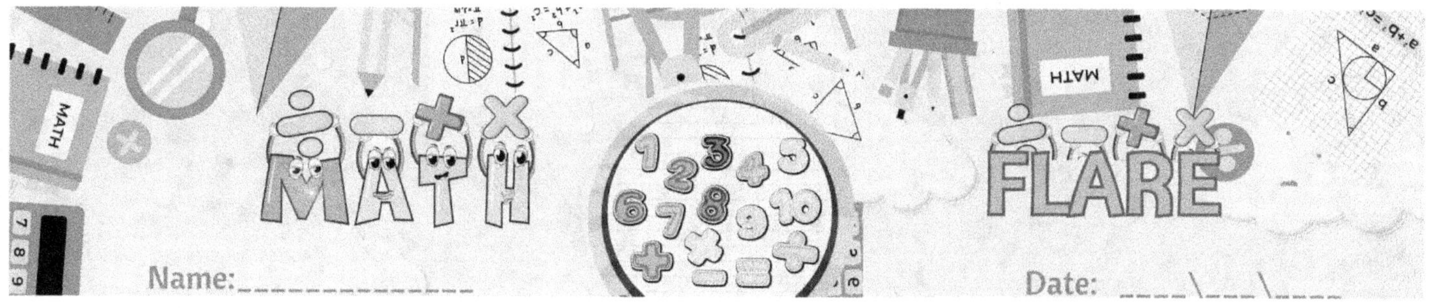

27. Find two consecutive odd integers such that six times the larger decreased by the smaller is 27.

28. One less than three times a number is 32. Find the number.

29. Four more than nine times a number is equal to the number increased by 60. What is the number?

30. 32 is equal to the product of eight and some number. Find the number.

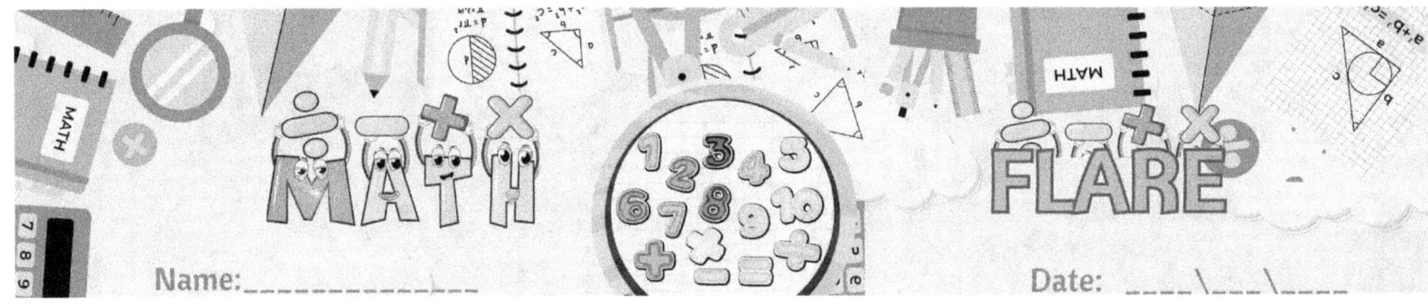

31. Five times a number equals 8 less than nine times the number. What is the number?

32. The product of nine and some number is equal to the sum of that number and 56. What is the number?

33. Three times a number equals 15 less than six times the number. What is the number?

34. The sum of two numbers is 64. The larger number is seven times the smaller number. What are the numbers?

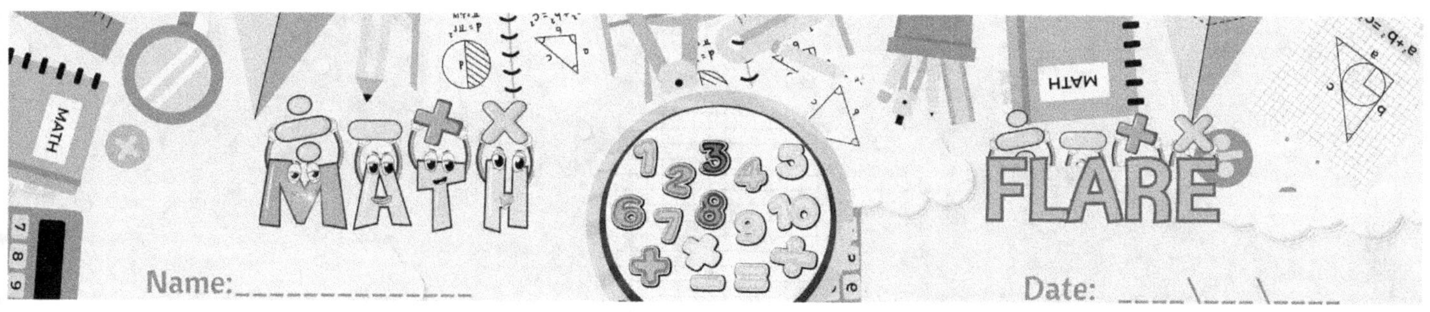

35. One-half of a number increased by 1 is 2. What is the number?

36. 27 is equal to the product of nine and some number. Find the number.

37. The sum of four consecutive even numbers is 36. What are the numbers?

38. One of two numbers is one-half of the other number. The sum of the numbers is 3. Find the numbers.

39. The sum of the largest and six times the smallest of three consecutive numbers is equal to 37. Find the numbers.

40. The sum of two numbers is 22. One number is ten less than the other. Find the numbers.

41. The sum of two numbers is 35. The larger number is four times the smaller number. What are the numbers?

42. The sum of two numbers is 19. One number is five less than the other. Find the numbers.

Chapter. 02

Linear Equation

Standard Linear Functions

A linear equation is an algebraic equation that represents a straight line when graphed on a coordinate plane. It consists of variables raised to the power of 1 (i.e., no exponents higher than 1) and constant coefficients.

The general form of a linear equation in one variable x is:

$$ax + b = 0$$

Where a and b are constants, and x is the variable.

Let's solve the linear equation:

$$-2x + 9 = 5$$

- **Isolate the variable term:** We want to isolate the term containing x on one side of the equation. To do this, we'll move the constant term to the other side. Subtract 9 from both sides:

$$-2x + 9 - 9 = 5 - 9$$

$$-2x = -4$$

- **Divide by the coefficient of the variable:** To solve for x, divide both sides by the coefficient of x, which is -2:

$$\frac{-2x}{-2} = \frac{-4}{-2}$$

$$x = 2$$

Graphing Linear Equation

Graphing a linear equation involves plotting the points that satisfy the equation on a coordinate plane and connecting them to form a straight line. Linear equations are equations of the form $y = mx + b$, where m represents the slope of the line, and b represents the y-intercept, the point where the line intersects the y-axis.

To graph a linear equation:

1. Identify the slope (m) and y-intercept (b) from the equation.

2. Plot the y-intercept $(0, b)$ as a point on the y-axis.

3. Use the slope to find additional points on the line. The slope represents the change in y for every unit change in x.

4. Connect the points to form a straight line.

For example, to graph the equation:

$$y = \frac{9}{4}x - 8$$

1. **Identify the slope and y-intercept:** The slope is $\frac{9}{4}$, and the y-intercept is -8.

2. **Plot the y-intercept:** Plot the point $(0, -8)$.

3. **Use the slope to plot additional points:** the slop is $\frac{9}{4}$ to find another point. we will move up 9 units and 4 units to the right from the y-intercept to find another point.

4. **Draw the line:** Once we have at least two points, we can draw a straight line.

We can continue this process to plot more points and extend the line further if needed.

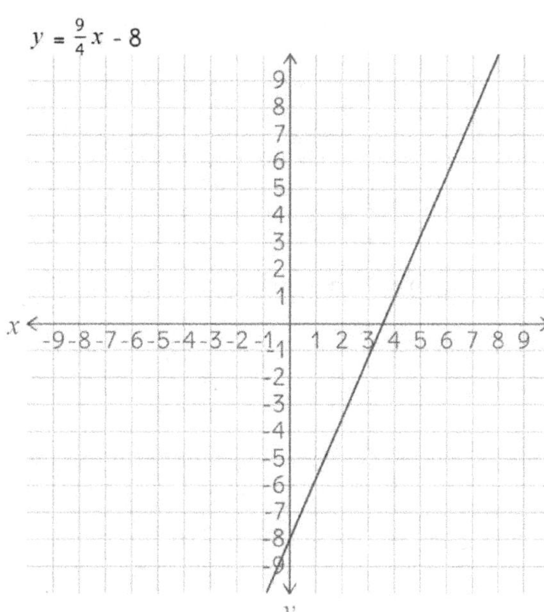

y = \frac{9}{4}x - 8

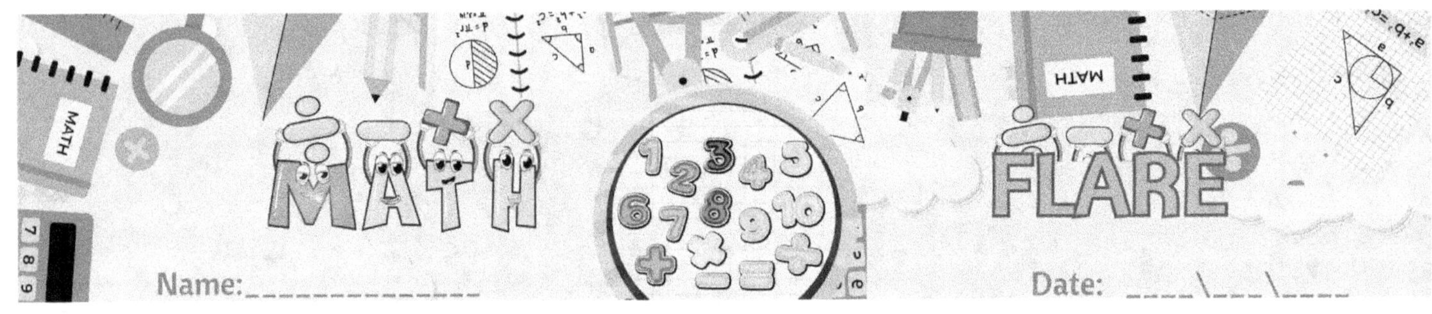

Standard Linear Equations

1. $10x + 1 = -39$

2. $3x + 7 = -11$

3. $10x + 8 = 68$

4. $-9x + 3 = -87$

5. $1x + 7 = 8$

6. $-3x + 3 = -27$

7. $-6x + 10 = 40$

8. $-1x + 9 = 1$

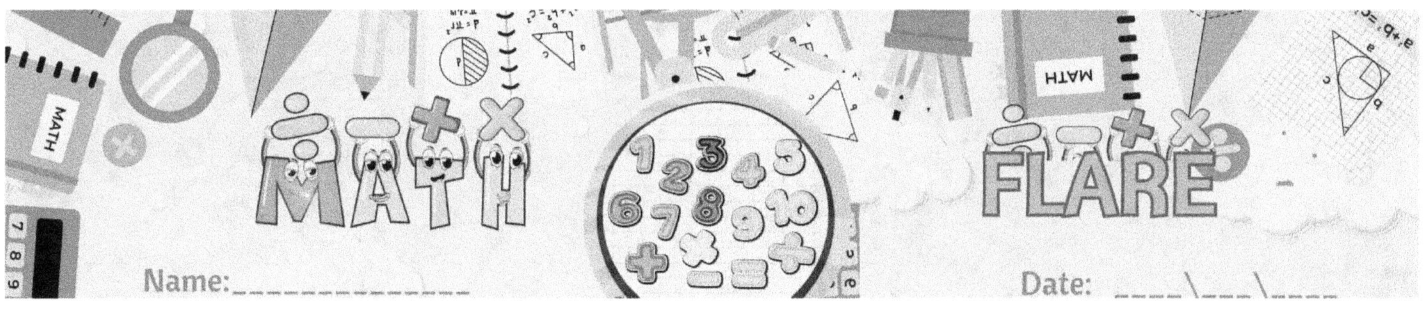

9. -10x + -6 = 24

13. 1x + -10 = 0

10. 2x + 10 = 18

14. -8x + -4 = 52

11. -10x + 8 = -22

15. 5x + -2 = 13

12. 10x + 2 = -88

16. 1x + -5 = -6

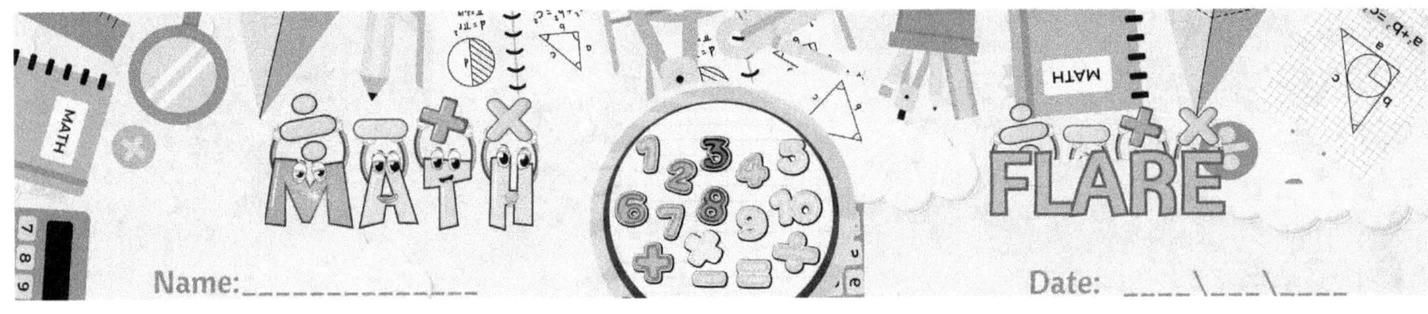

17. -7x + 0 = -14

21. 9x + -9 = -18

18. -8x + 7 = -17

22. -5x + -4 = 11

19. 10x + 3 = -57

23. -9x + 6 = -57

20. 7x + 0 = -14

24. 1x + 6 = -3

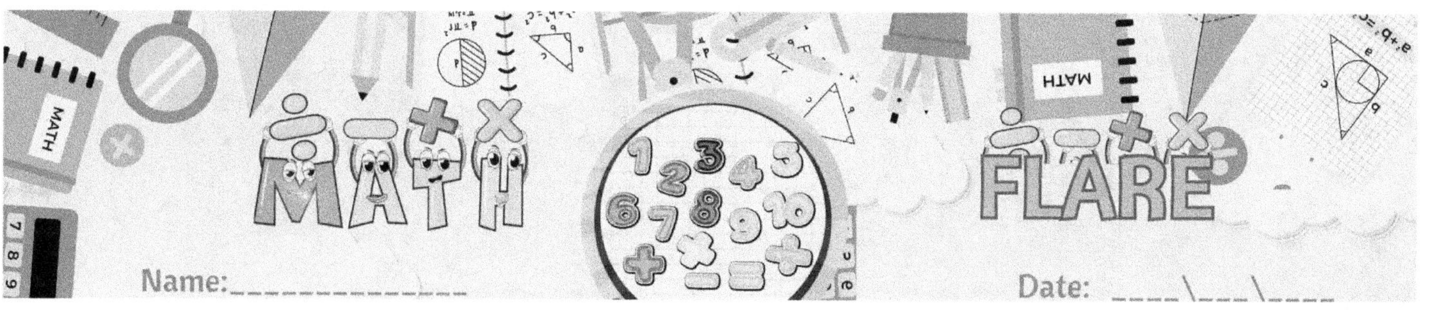

25. 10x + 8 = -12

29. -5x + 7 = -13

26. -8x + -2 = 54

30. 6x + -7 = -19

27. 8x + 1 = 1

31. -9x + 7 = -65

28. -4x + -5 = -9

32. -4x + 7 = 39

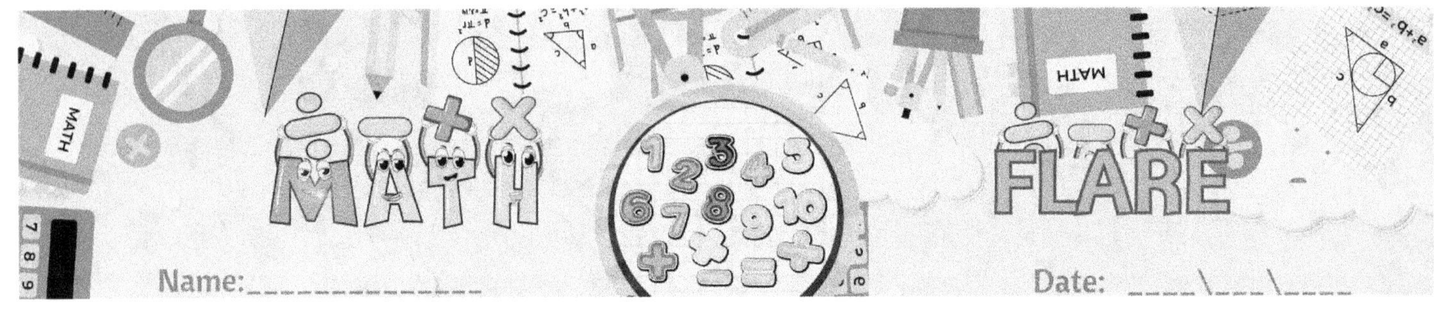

33. -2x + -8 = 8

37. 2x + 7 = 17

34. -6x + 1 = 7

38. 5x + -7 = 23

35. -10x + 5 = 45

39. -7x + -3 = 32

36. 5x + -5 = -15

40. -1x + 0 = 8

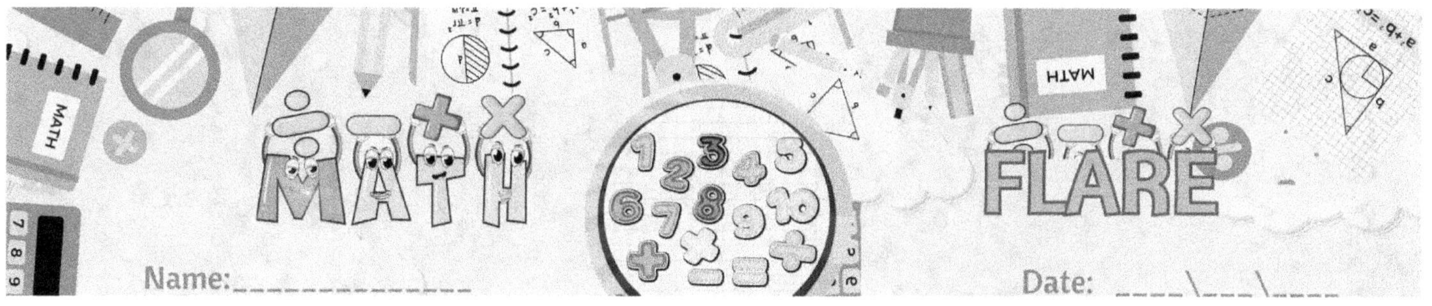

41. -7x + 7 = -21

45. -8x + 6 = -10

42. 5x + -6 = 24

46. -10x + 7 = -63

43. 8x + -3 = 5

47. -5x + -4 = 6

44. -5x + 8 = 8

48. -2x + -9 = 5

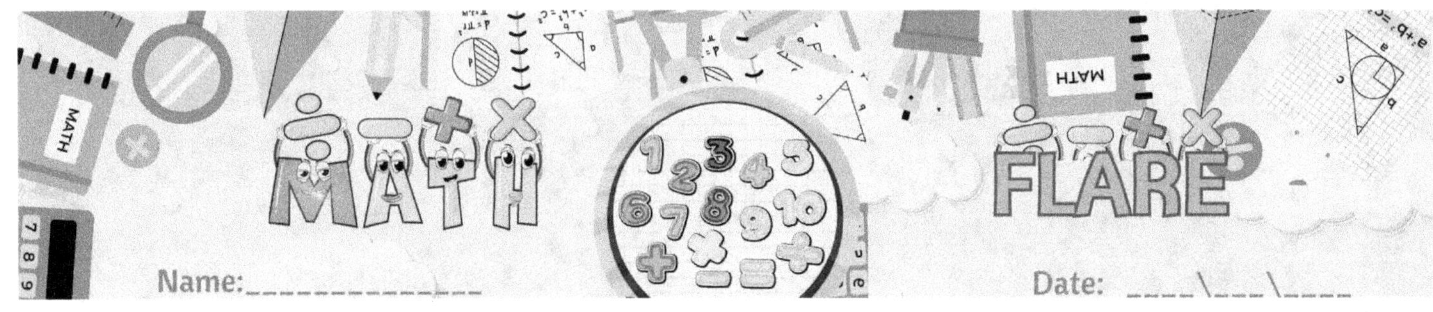

Graphing Linear Equations

1. $y = \dfrac{-7}{4}x - 4$

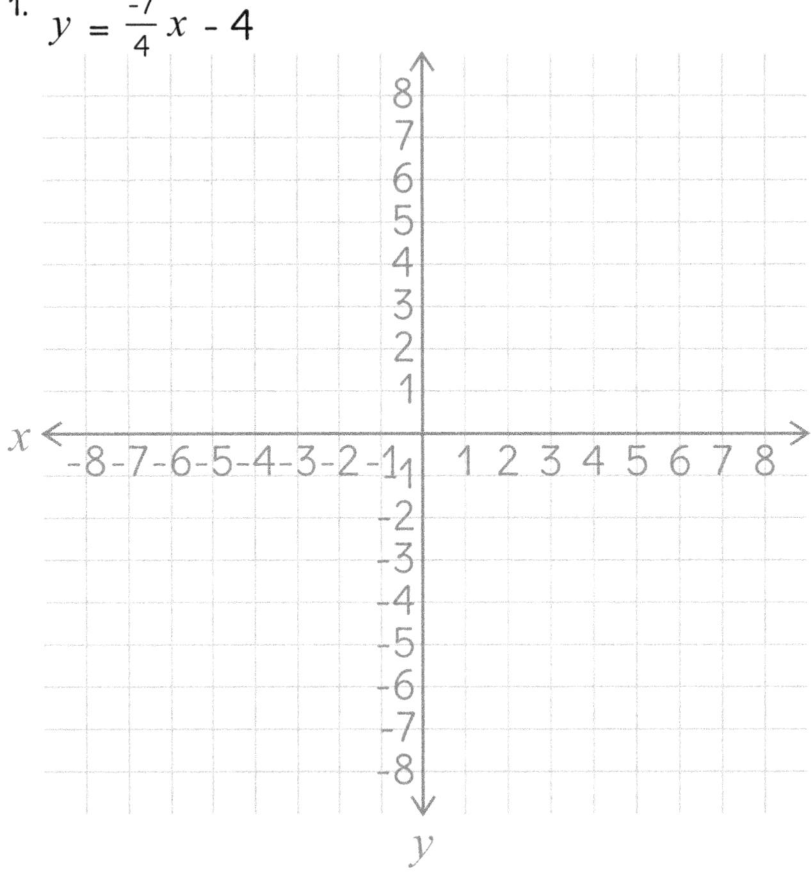

2. $y = \dfrac{-5}{2}x + 3$

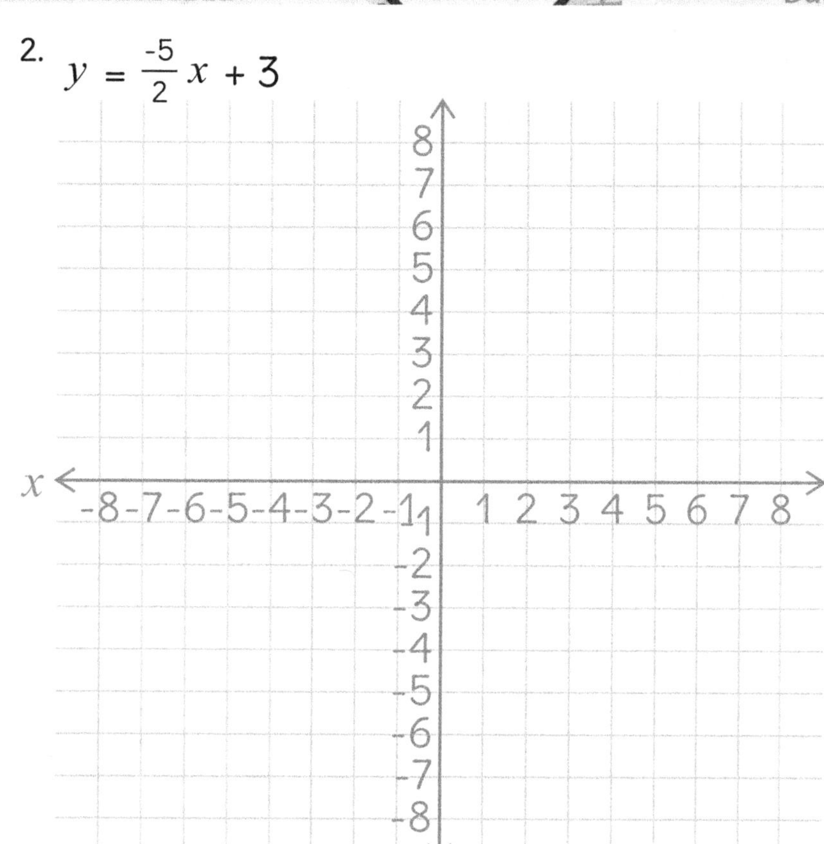

Name:________________ Date: ______________

3. $y = \dfrac{-3}{4}x - 4$

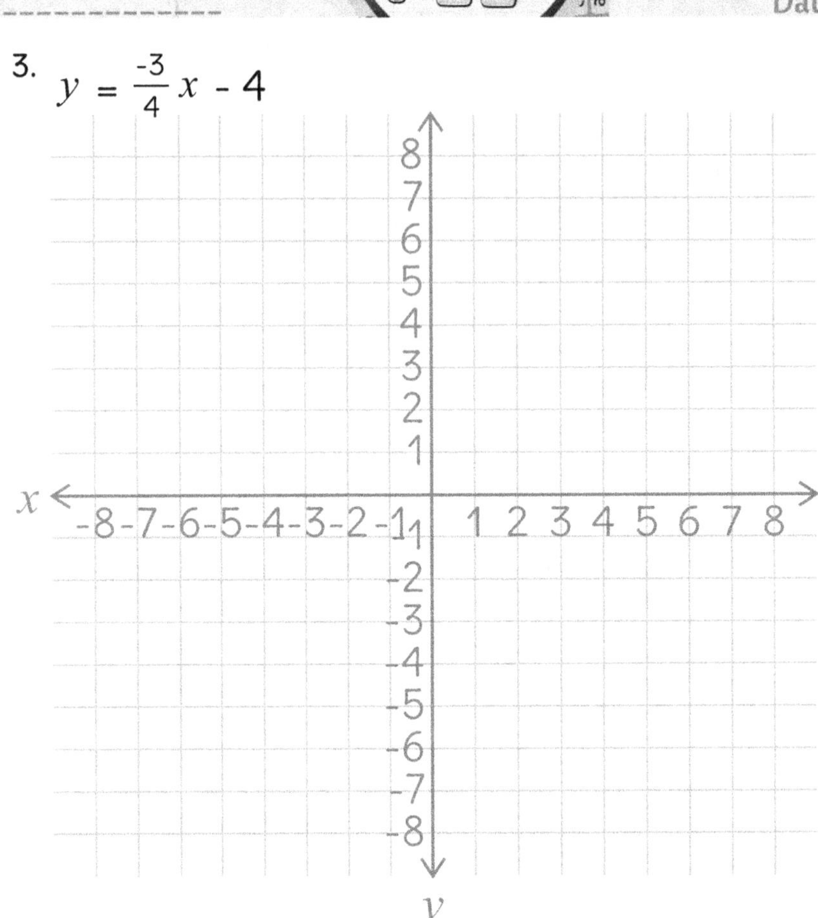

4. $y = \dfrac{-5}{4}x + 6$

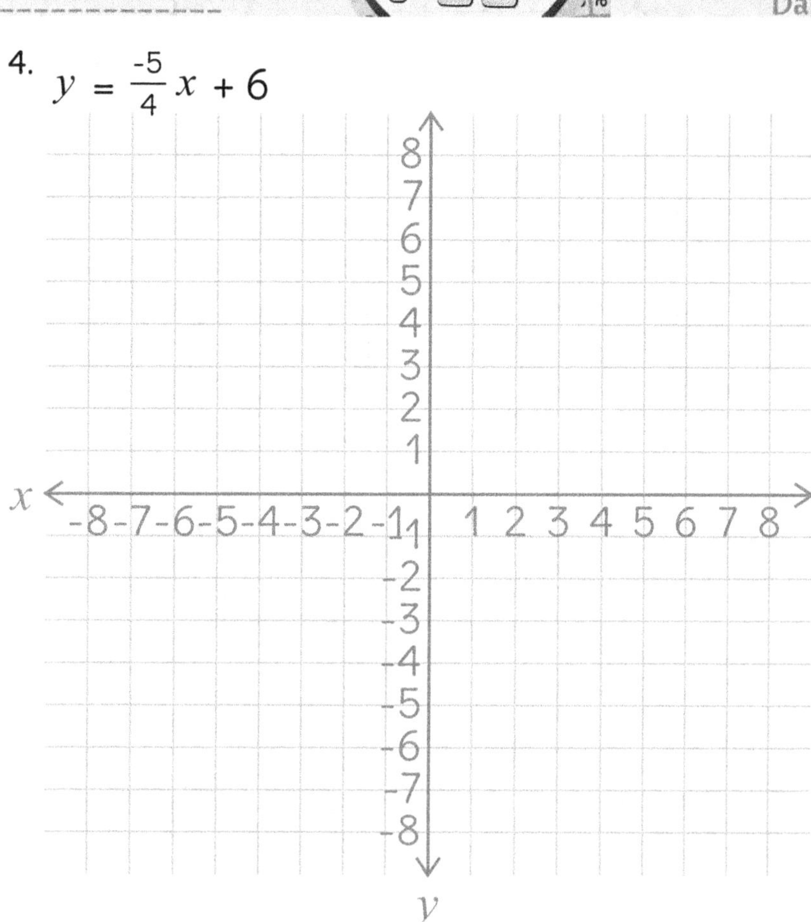

5. $y = \dfrac{5}{4}x - 5$

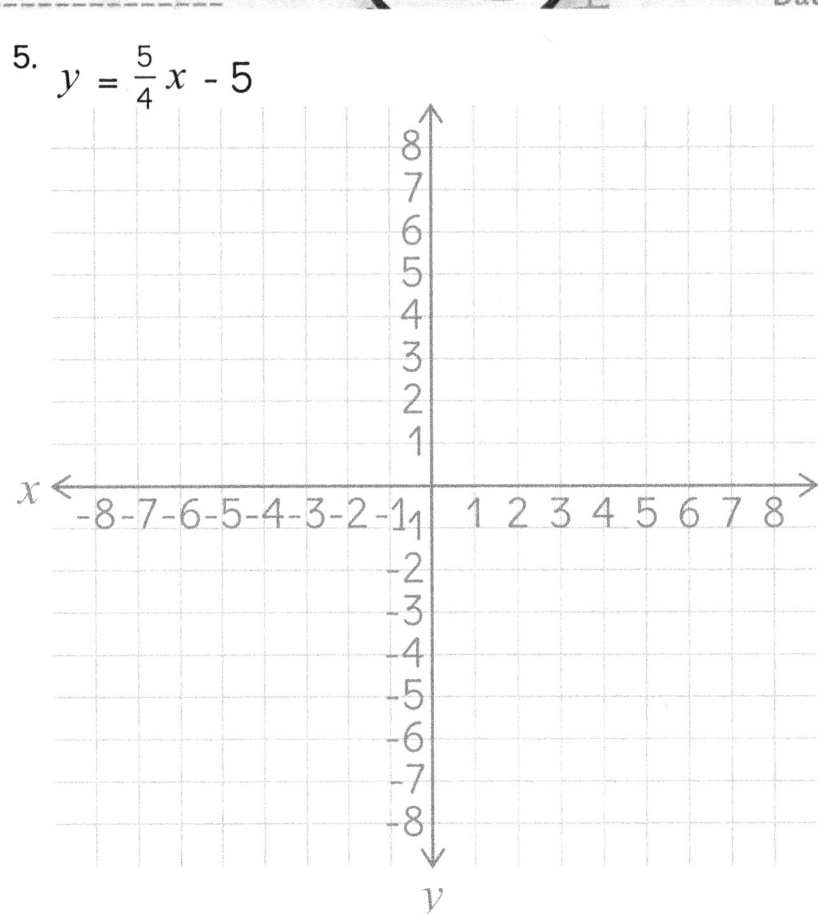

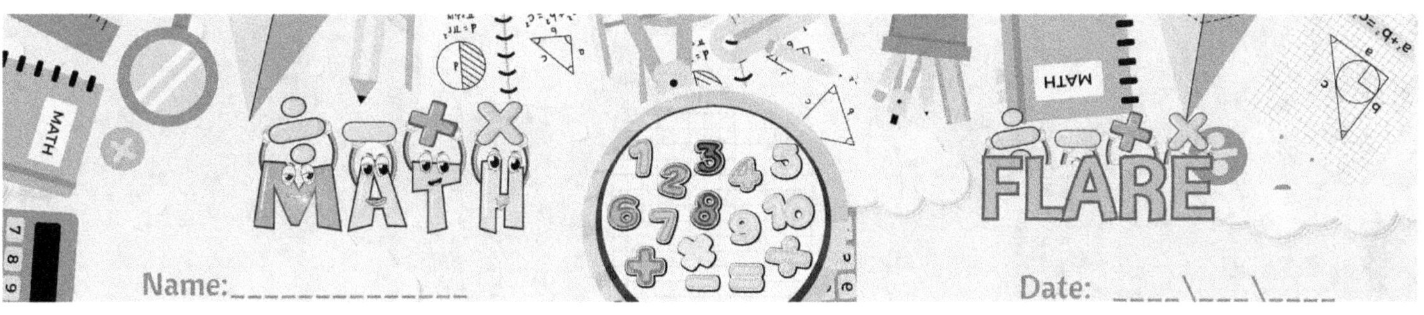

6. $y = x + 7$

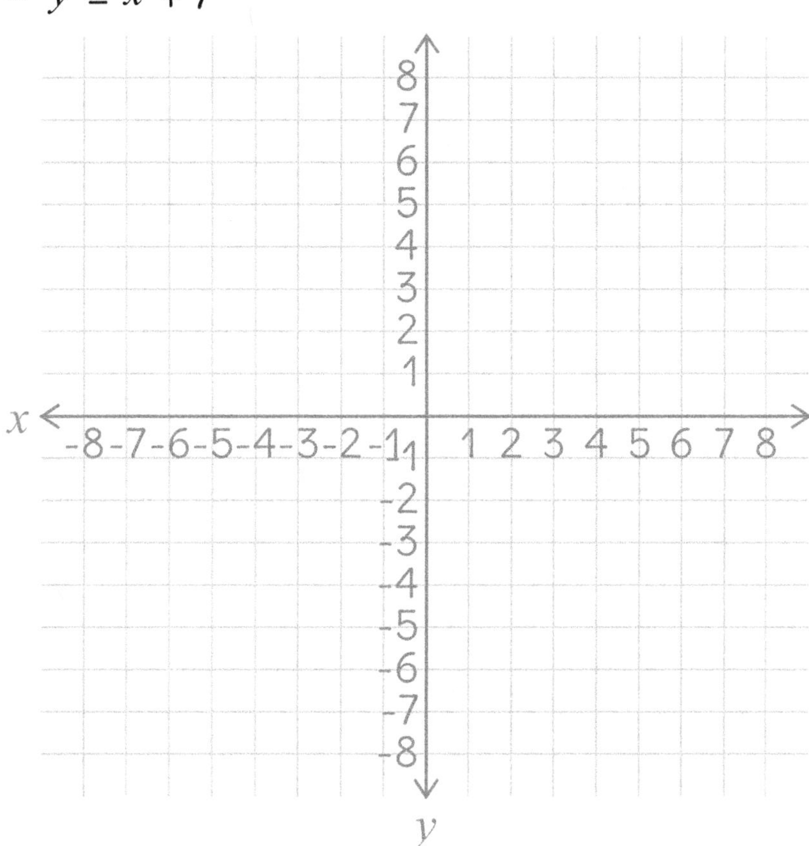

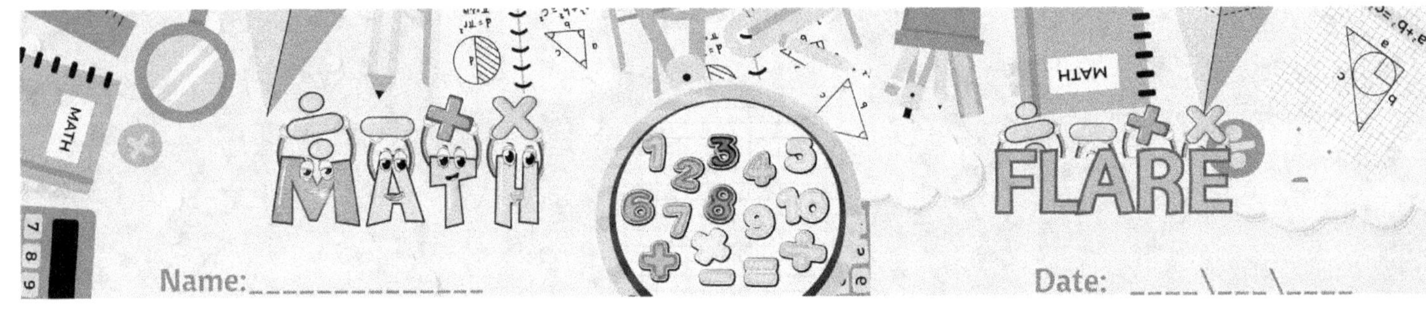

7. $y = \dfrac{-5}{2}x + 2$

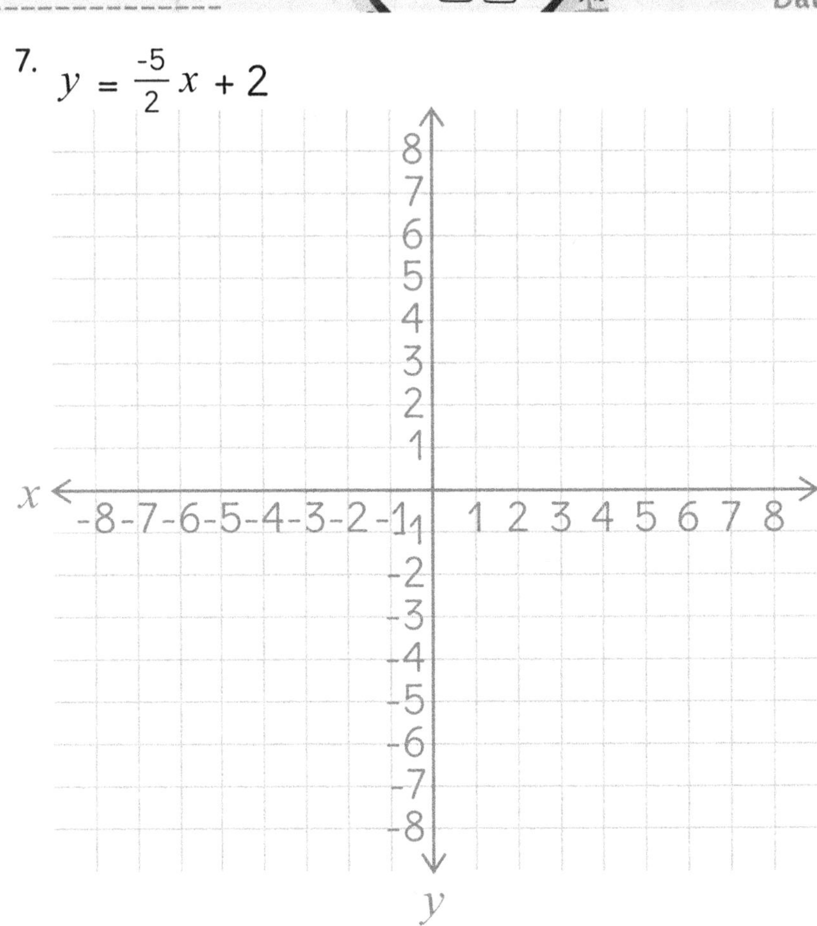

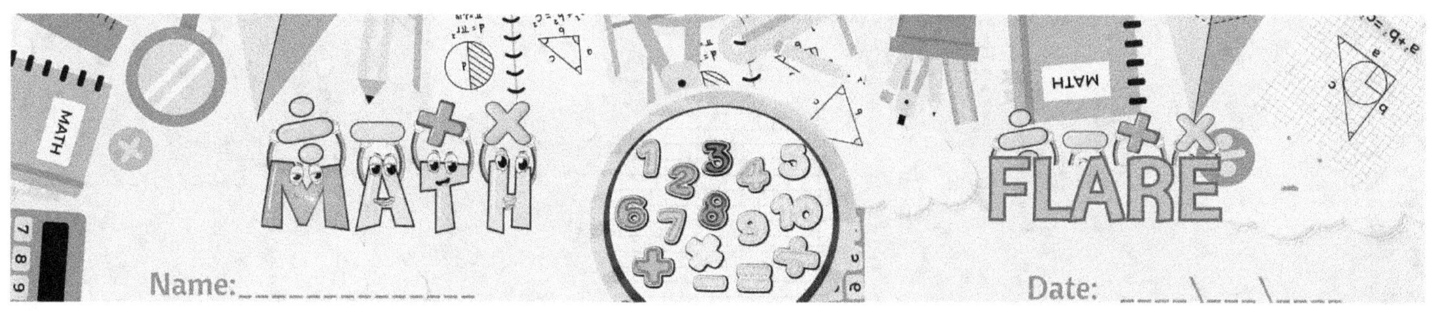

8. $y = \dfrac{3}{2}x + 7$

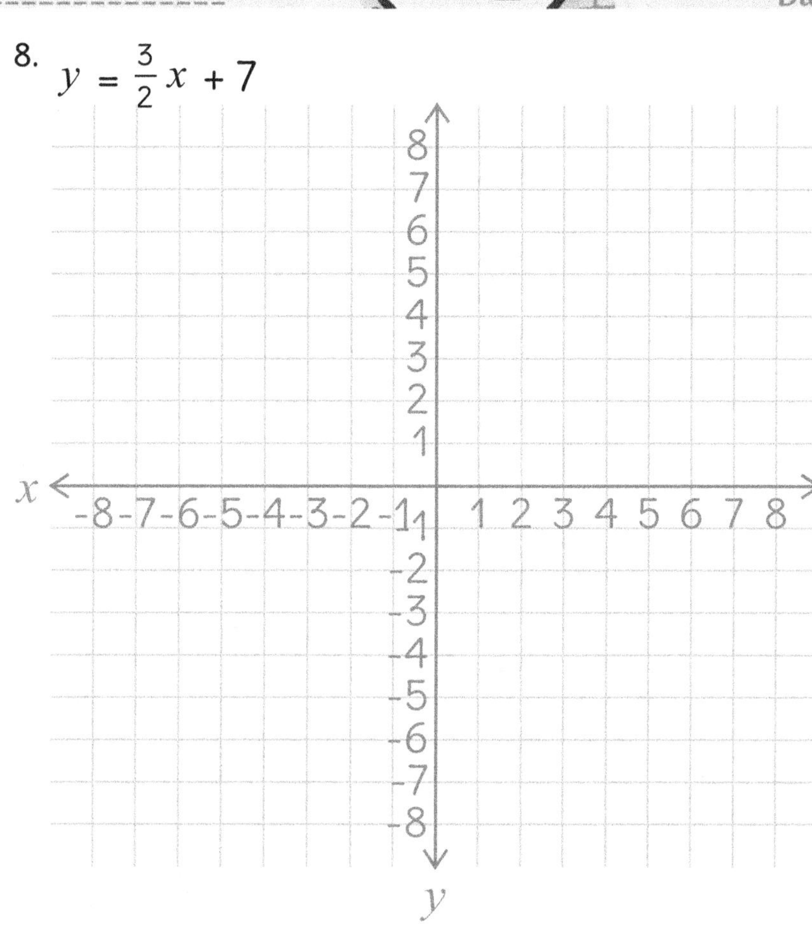

9. $y = \dfrac{7}{4}x - 8$

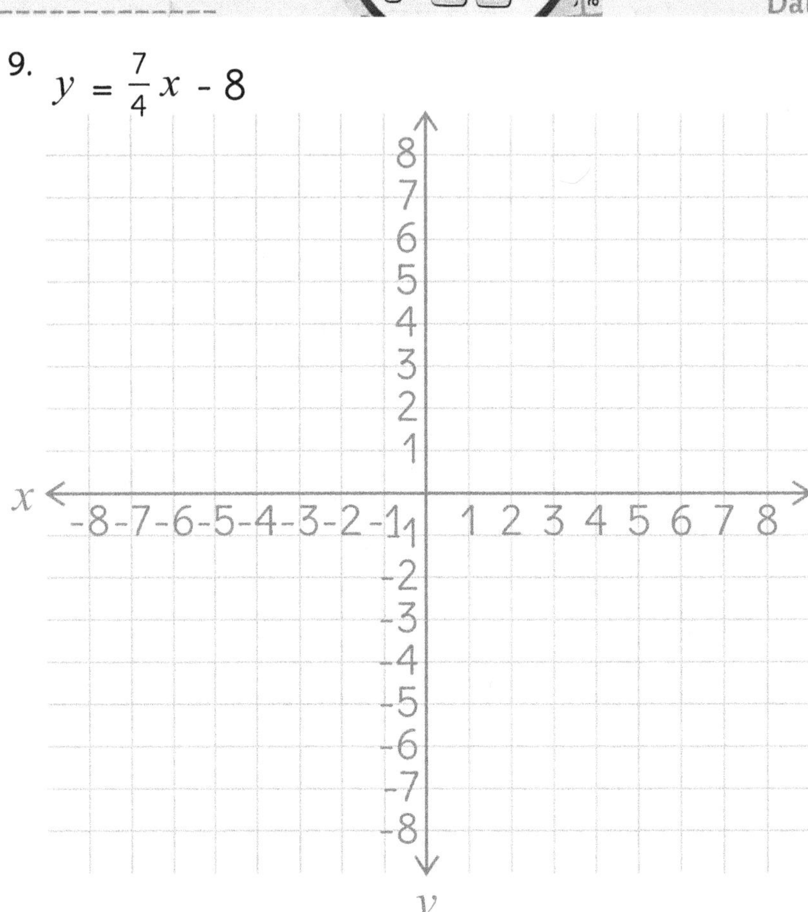

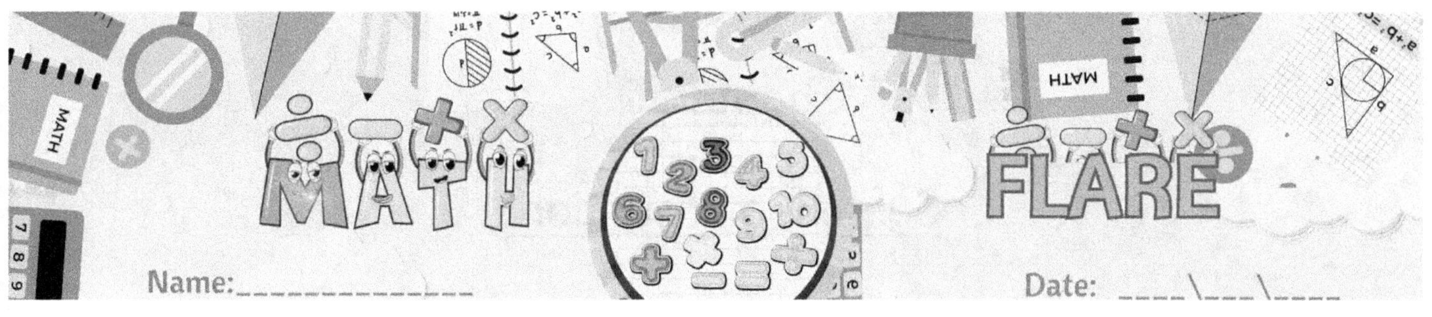

10.
$$y = \frac{5}{4}x - 4$$

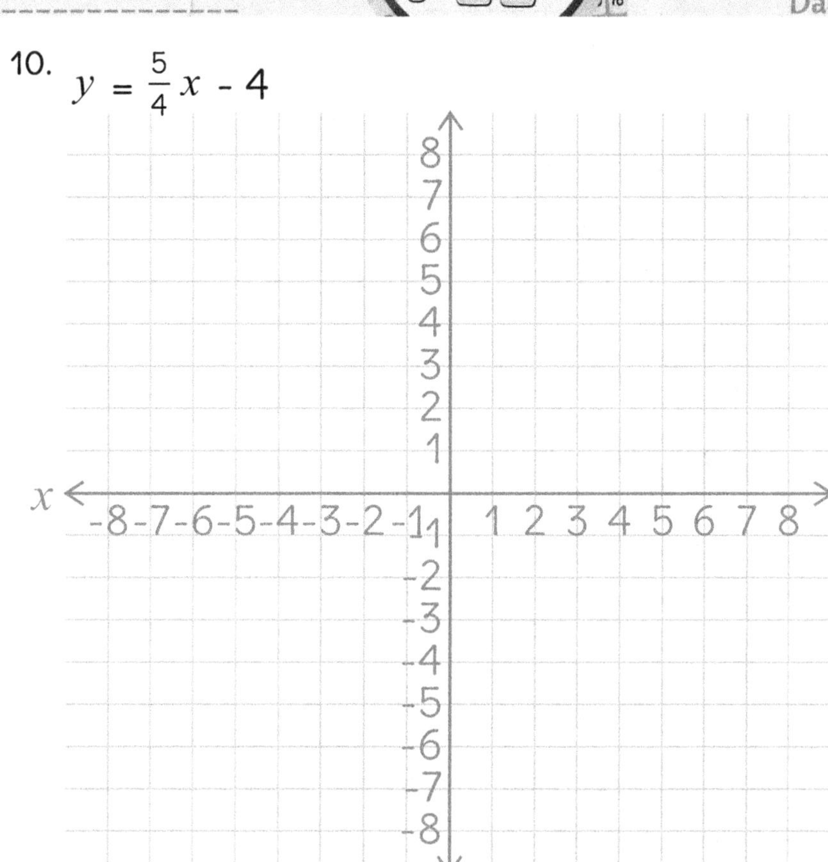

Chapter. 03

System of Equations

A system of equations is a collection of two or more equations involving the same set of variables. The solution to a system of equations is the set of values for the variables that satisfy all the equations simultaneously.

Solving by Elimination:

To solve a system of equations by elimination, we manipulate the equations to eliminate one of the variables.

Given the system:

$$4x + 5y = 6$$

$$10x + 6y = 8$$

Step 1: Multiply each equation by a constant such that the coefficients of one of the variables become equal or multiples of each other.

Let's try to eliminate the variable x.

- Multiply the first equation by 5 and the second equation by -2:

$$20x + 25y = 30$$

$$-20x - 12y = -16$$

Step 2: Add the two equations together to eliminate the variable x.

$$(20x - 20x) + (25y - 12y) = 30 - 16$$

$$13y = 14$$

Step 3: Solve for y:

$$y = \frac{14}{13} = 1.077$$

Step 4: Substitute the value of y into one of the original equations to solve for x. Let's use the first equation:

$$4x + 5\left(\frac{14}{13}\right) = 6$$

$$4x + \frac{70}{13} = 6$$

$$4x = 6 - \frac{70}{13}$$

$$4x = \frac{78 - 70}{13}$$

$$4x = \frac{8}{13}$$

$$x = \frac{2}{13} = 0.154$$

the solution to the system of equations is x = 0.154 and y = 1.077.

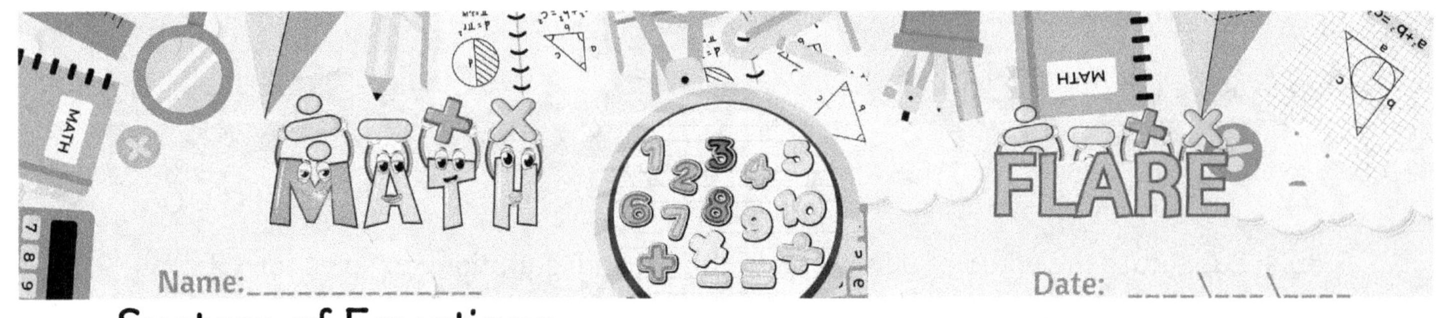

System of Equations

1. $10x + 4y = 4$

   $7x + 10y = 2$

2. $7x + 8y = 7$

   $9x + 6y = 6$

3. $1x + 8y = 3$

   $5x + 1y = 6$

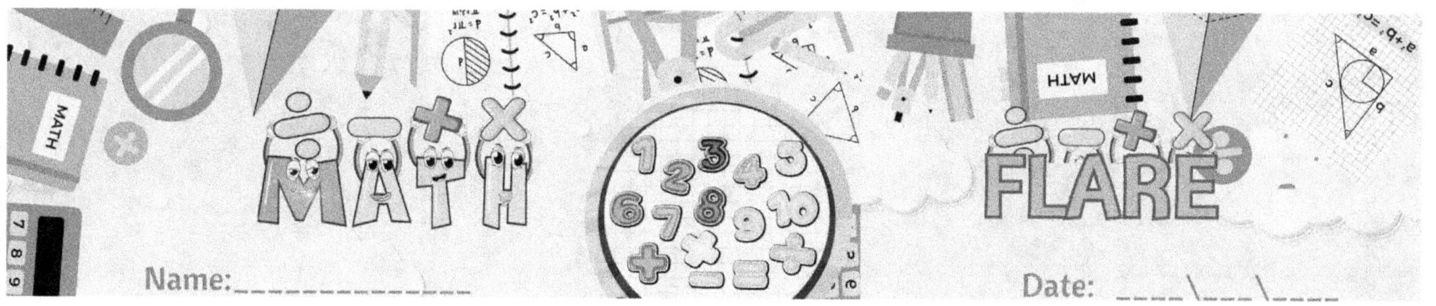

4. $4x + 7y = 10$

   $3x + 6y = 3$

5. $3x + 4y = 6$

   $10x + 2y = 1$

6. $10x + 1y = 6$

   $2x + 6y = 10$

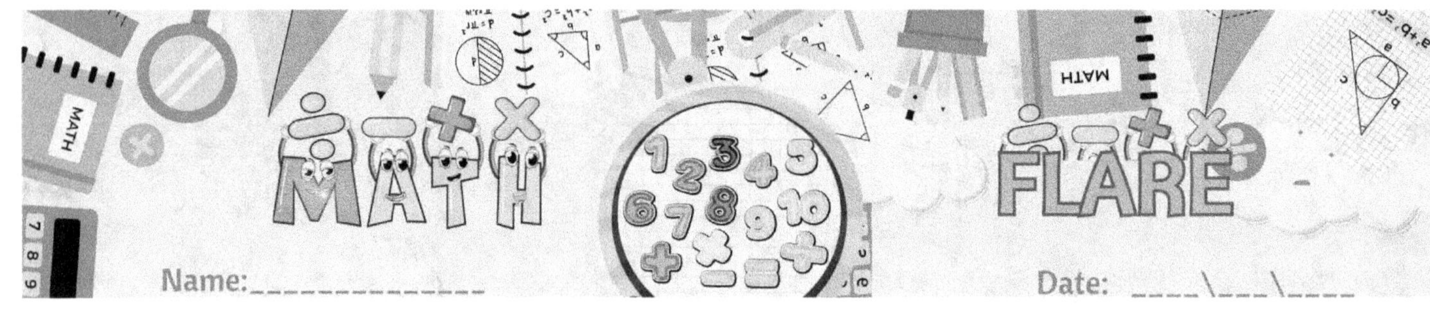

7. $2x + 9y = 8$

   $9x + 7y = 4$

8. $3x + 1y = 4$

   $6x + 3y = 4$

9. $5x + 9y = 9$

   $4x + 8y = 2$

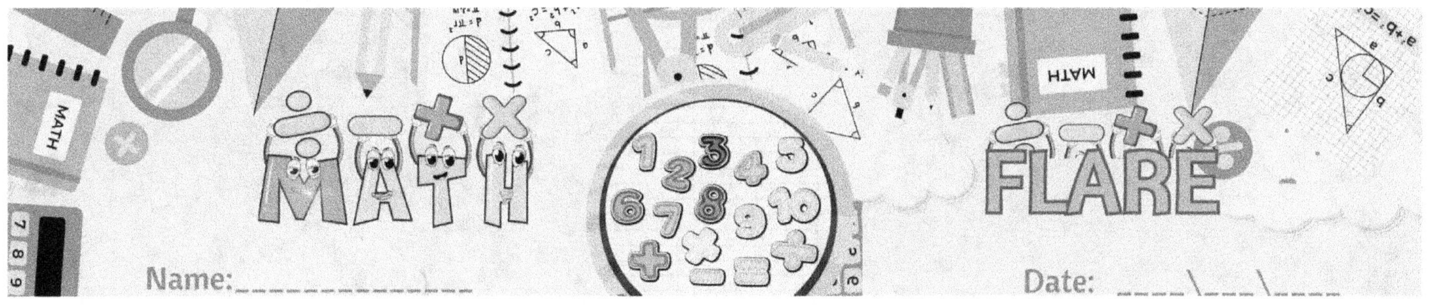

10. $4x + 3y = 5$

    $6x + 2y = 5$

11. $3x + 1y = 4$

    $3x + 6y = 4$

12. $8x + 8y = 10$

    $6x + 9y = 9$

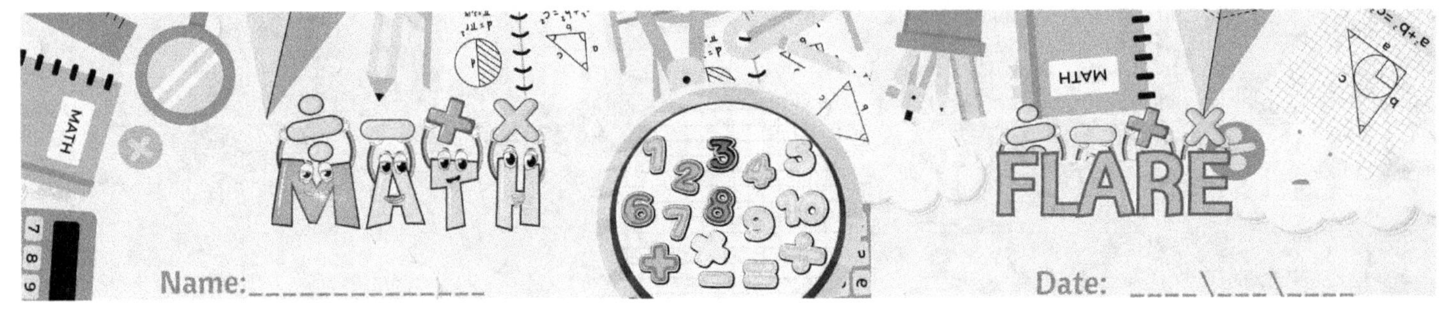

13. 8x + 10y = 1

    6x + 4y = 1

14. 1x + 6y = 10

    3x + 1y = 9

15. 10x + 9y = 8

    5x + 1y = 7

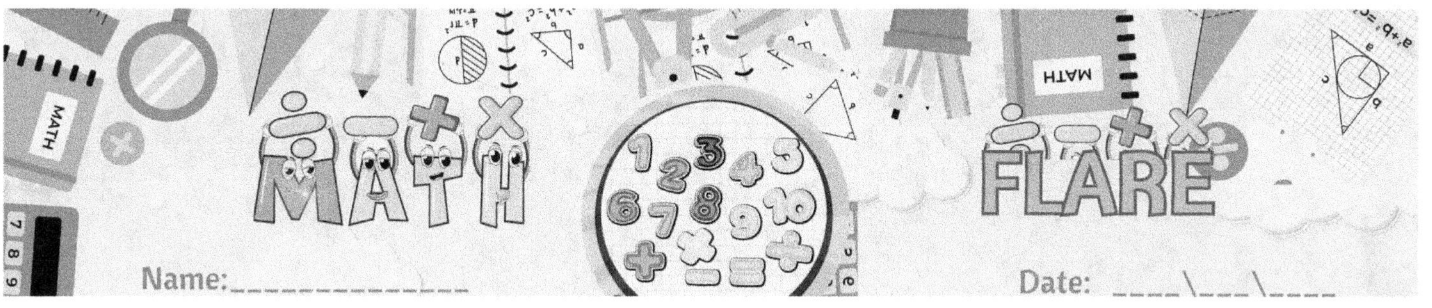

16. $10x + 7y = 4$

$1x + 9y = 7$

17. $6x + 4y = 6$

$8x + 3y = 2$

18. $3x + 5y = 4$

$7x + 10y = 7$

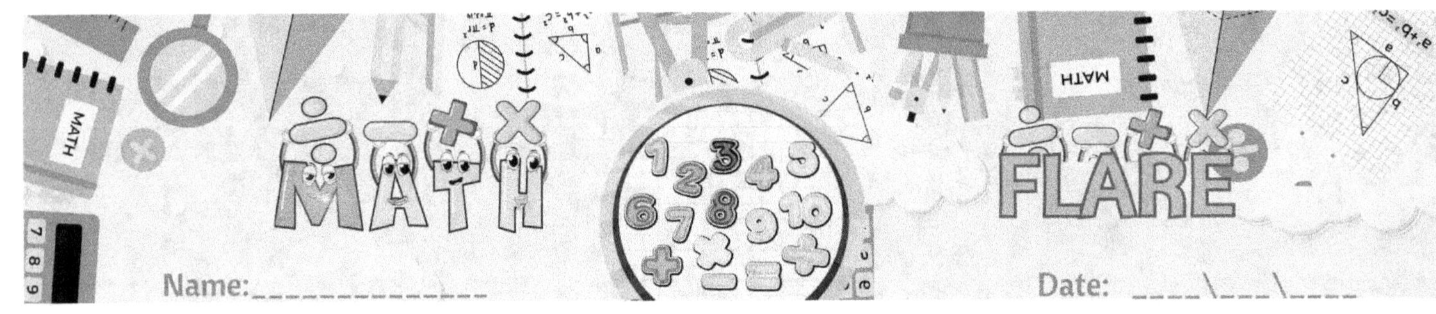

19. $2x + 2y = 3$

   $3x + 6y = 8$

20. $10x + 5y = 7$

   $4x + 5y = 6$

21. $7x + 3y = 3$

   $9x + 1y = 6$

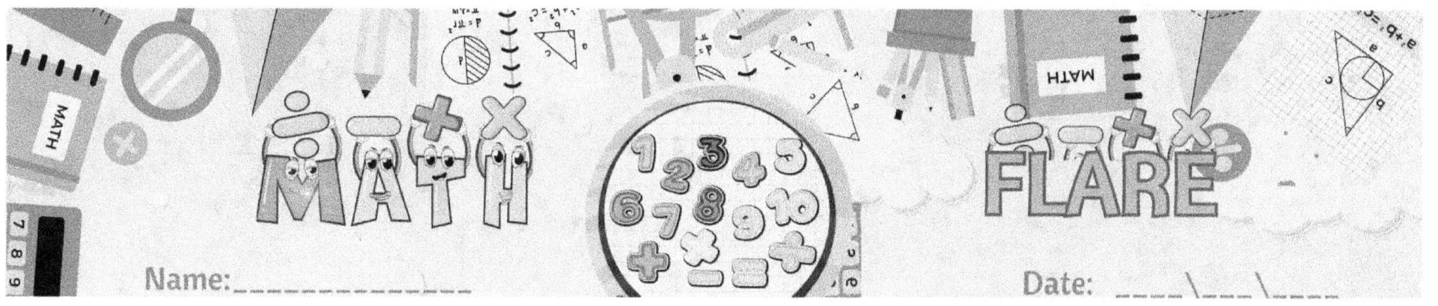

22. $7x + 9y = 1$

   $4x + 1y = 3$

23. $3x + 8y = 7$

   $10x + 2y = 5$

24. $1x + 2y = 3$

   $4x + 10y = 2$

25. $10x + 7y = 2$

 $5x + 3y = 5$

26. $9x + 9y = 7$

 $9x + 7y = 6$

27. $8x + 6y = 7$

 $9x + 5y = 5$

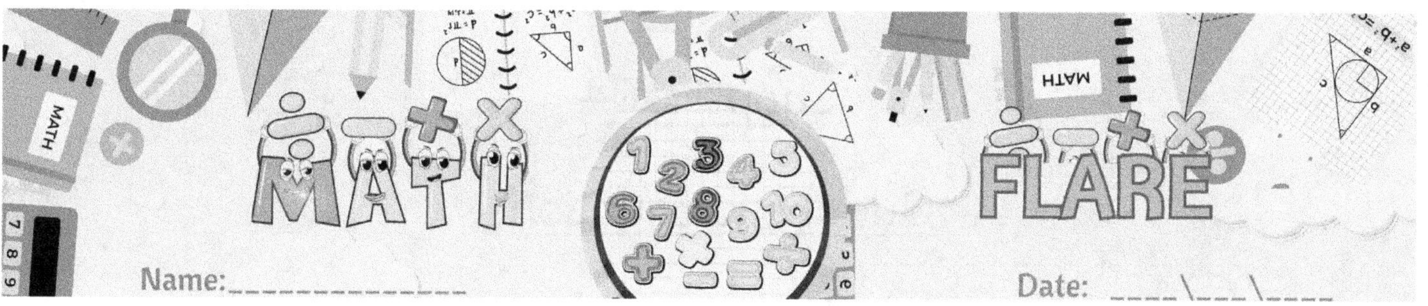

28. $8x + 3y = 7$

   $7x + 8y = 3$

29. $4x + 7y = 5$

   $4x + 5y = 2$

30. $10x + 3y = 3$

   $7x + 2y = 7$

Chapter. 04

Quadratic Equations

A quadratic equation is a polynomial equation of the second degree, meaning it can be written in the form:

$$ax^2 + bx + c = 0$$

where a, b, and c are constants, and x is the variable being solved for. The solutions to a quadratic equation are the values of x that make the equation true.

Now, let's solve the quadratic equation $11x^2 - 1 = 0$ and understand it step by step using quadratic formula.

1. **Identify the coefficients:**

    In the equation $11x^2 - 1 = 0$,

    $$a=11, b=0, \text{ and } c=-1.$$

2. **Apply the quadratic formula:**

    The quadratic formula states that for an equation $ax^2 + bx + c = 0$, the solutions for x are given by:

    $$x = \frac{-b \pm \sqrt{b^2 - 4ac}}{2a}$$

    Plugging in the values a=11, b=0, and c=−1 into the quadratic formula, we get:

    $$x = \frac{-0 \pm \sqrt{0 - 4(11)(-1)}}{2(11)}$$

3. Simplify inside the square root:

$$0^2 - 4(11)(-1) = 0 - (-44) = 44$$

4. Plug in the simplified values:

$$x = \frac{\pm \sqrt{44}}{22}$$

5. Simplify the square root:

Since 44 is not a perfect square, we can write it as $\sqrt[2]{11}$

$$x = \frac{\pm \sqrt[2]{11}}{22}$$

6. Simplify further if possible:

We can simplify $\sqrt[2]{11}$ to $\sqrt{11}$ by canceling out the common factor:

$$x = \frac{\pm \sqrt{11}}{11}$$

7. Final solution:

So, the solutions to the equation are:

$$x = \frac{\sqrt{11}}{11} \text{ and } x = \frac{-\sqrt{11}}{11}$$

or

$$(x = 0.302, \text{ and } x = -0.302)$$

These are the roots of the quadratic equation. They represent the points where the graph of the quadratic equation intersects the x-axis.

Let's solve another equation:

$$-4p^2 + 6p - 6 = 0$$

$$p = \frac{-b \pm \sqrt{b^2 - 4ac}}{2a}$$

where $a = -4$, $b = 6$, and $c = -6$.

Let's plug these values into the quadratic formula:

$$p = \frac{-6 \pm \sqrt{6^2 - 4(-4)(-6)}}{2(-4)}$$

First, let's simplify inside the square root:

$$6^2 - 4\,(-4)\,(-6)$$

$$= 36 - 96 = -60$$

So, we have:

$$p = \frac{-6 \pm \sqrt{-60}}{-8}$$

We can simplify the square root of −60 by factoring out −1:

$$\sqrt{-60}$$

$$= \sqrt{-1 \times 60}$$

$$= \sqrt{-1} \times \sqrt{60}$$

$$= i\sqrt{60}$$

So, we have:

$$p = \frac{-6 \pm i\sqrt{60}}{-8}$$

Simplify:

$$\sqrt{60} \text{ to } \sqrt{4 \times 15} = 2\sqrt{15}$$

$$p = \frac{-6 \pm i \times 2\sqrt{15}}{-8}$$

Now, divide both the numerator and denominator by −2 to simplify:

$$p = \frac{3 \pm i\sqrt{15}}{4}$$

So, the solutions to the equation are:

$$p = \frac{3 + i\sqrt{15}}{4} \text{ and } p = \frac{3 - i\sqrt{15}}{4}$$

This equation -4p² + 6p - 6 = 0 has no real solutions.

When a quadratic equation has no real solutions, it means that the solutions are not real numbers, but rather complex numbers. In this case, the solutions involve the imaginary unit i because the discriminant ($b^2 - 4ac$) is negative, which results in taking the square root of a negative number when applying the quadratic formula.

In mathematics, such equations are said to have "no real roots" or "no real solutions." They are also sometimes referred to as having "complex roots" or "complex solutions." Complex numbers include a real part and an imaginary part, and they are often written in the form $a + bi$, where a and b are real numbers and i is the imaginary unit, defined as $i = \sqrt{-1}$.

Let's solve another equation:

$$12x^2 + 6x - 2 = 0$$

$$x = \frac{-b \pm \sqrt{b^2 - 4ac}}{2a}$$

where $a = 12$, $b = 6$, and $c = -2$.

Let's plug these values into the quadratic formula:

$$x = \frac{-6 \pm \sqrt{6^2 - 4(12)(-2)}}{2(12)}$$

First, let's simplify inside the square root:

$$6^2 - 4(12)(-2)$$

$$= 36 - (-96)$$

$$= 36 + 96$$

$$= 132$$

So, we have:

$$X = \frac{-6 \pm \sqrt{132}}{24}$$

Now, let's simplify the square root of 132:

$$X = \frac{-6 \pm \sqrt{4 \times 33}}{24}$$

$$X = \frac{-6 \pm 2\sqrt{33}}{24}$$

$$X = \frac{-6 \pm \sqrt{33}}{12}$$

So, the solutions to the equation are:

$$X = \frac{-6 + \sqrt{33}}{12} \text{ and } X = \frac{-6 - \sqrt{33}}{12}$$

or (x = 0.229, and x = -0.729)

Let's solve a quadratic equation where the right side is a number, instead of 0.

$$-8n^2 + 6n + 30 = 7$$

To solve the equation, we first need to bring all terms to one side to set the equation equal to zero:

$$-8n^2 + 6n + 30 - 7 = 0$$

Simplify:

$$-8n^2 + 6n + 23 = 0$$

Now, to solve for n, we can use the quadratic formula:

$$n = \frac{-b \pm \sqrt{b^2 - 4ac}}{2a}$$

where $a = -8$, $b = 6$, and $c = 23$.

Plugging these values into the formula, we get:

$$n = \frac{-6 \pm \sqrt{6^2 - 4(-8)(23)}}{2(-8)}$$

$$n = \frac{-6 \pm \sqrt{36 + 736}}{-16}$$

$$n = \frac{-6 \pm \sqrt{772}}{-16}$$

Now, let's simplify the square root of 772. We can factor out 4:

$$\sqrt{772} = \sqrt{4 \times 193} = 2\sqrt{193}$$

So, our equation becomes:

$$n = \frac{-6 \pm 2\sqrt{193}}{-8}$$

So, the solutions to the equation are:

$$n = \frac{-3 + \sqrt{193}}{-8} \text{ and } n = \frac{-3 - \sqrt{193}}{-8}$$

or

$(n = -1.362, \text{ and } n = 2.112)$

Quadratic Equations

1. $4n^2 - 12n - 1 = 0$

2. $5m^2 - 4m - 9 = 0$

3. $4p^2 + 6p - 88 = 0$

4. $-9r^2 - r + 18 = 0$

5. $m^2 - 16 = 0$

6. $3b^2 - 8b + 2 = 0$

7. $2r^2 + 7r + 4 = 0$

8. $-2n^2 + 3n + 21 = 0$

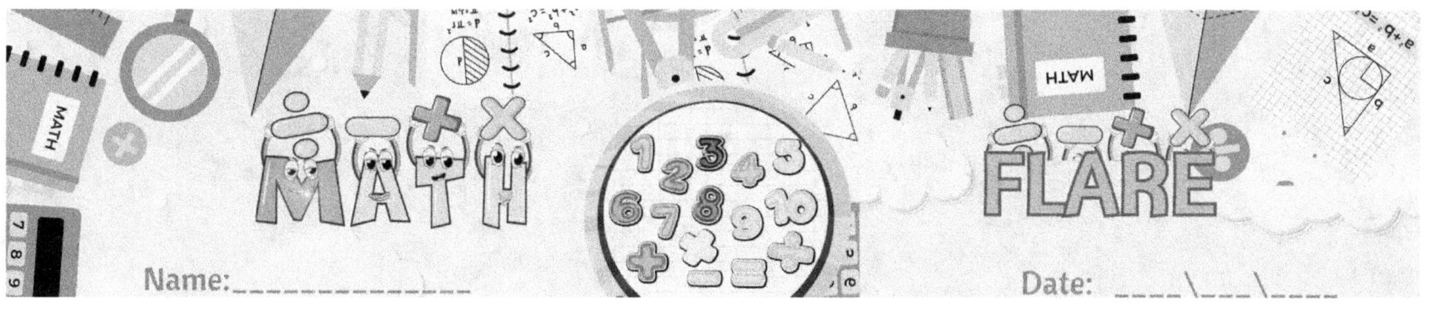

9. $-6v^2 + 7v + 33 = 0$

13. $2b^2 - 6b - 56 = 0$

10. $-10a^2 - a - 2 = 0$

14. $5n^2 + 5n - 1 = 0$

11. $2n^2 - 6n + 4 = 0$

15. $m^2 + 6m + 5 = 0$

12. $-5n^2 + 10n + 24 = 0$

16. $-6v^2 + 54 = 0$

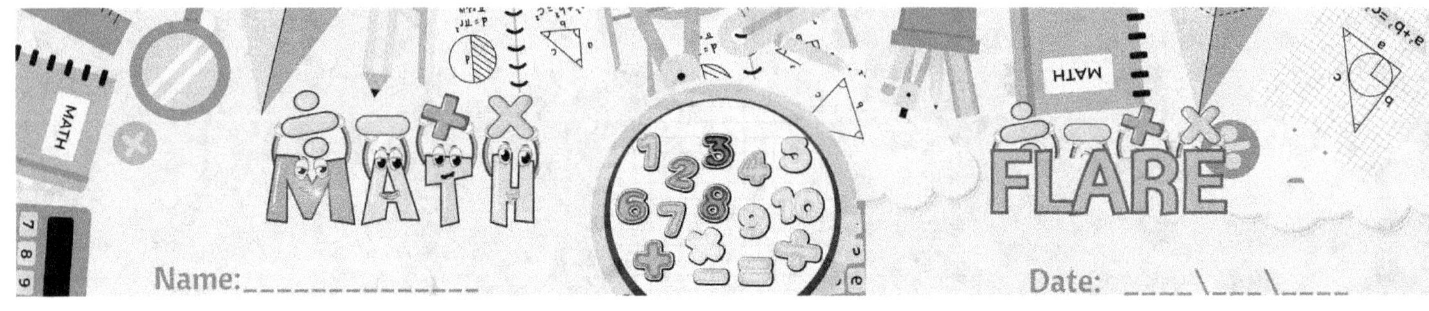

17. $-4a^2 + 3a + 85 = 0$

21. $-10n^2 + 2n + 20 = 0$

18. $-x^2 + 25 = 0$

22. $-5x^2 - 3x + 54 = 0$

19. $3x^2 - 6x - 19 = 0$

23. $-3b^2 + 5b + 12 = 0$

20. $12m^2 + 8m - 3 = 0$

24. $-3n^2 - 7n + 7 = 0$

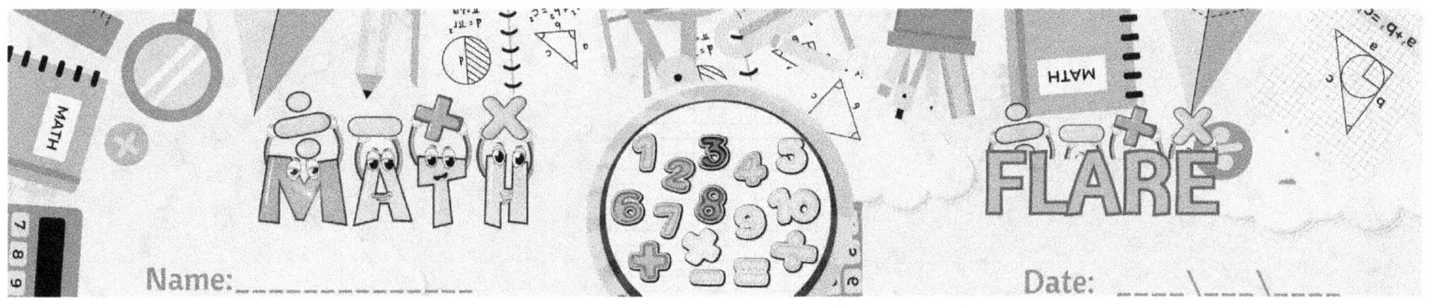

25. $-p^2 + 4p + 21 = 0$

29. $3x^2 + 6x - 9 = 0$

26. $b^2 - 11b - 42 = 0$

30. $3x^2 + 9x + 6 = 0$

27. $-9r^2 + 9r - 1 = 0$

31. $-6r^2 + 10 = 4$

28. $6r^2 + 10r - 10 = 0$

32. $-2v^2 - 4v + 58 = -12$

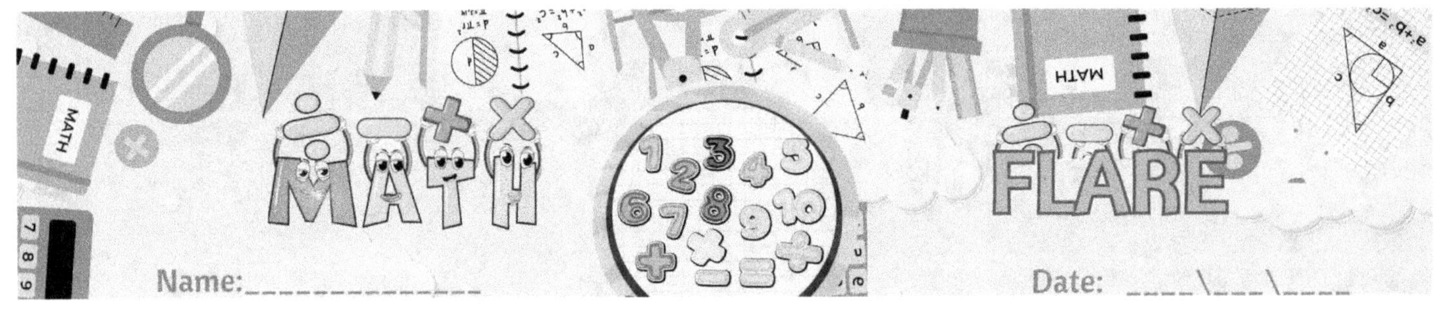

33. $6a^2 - 8a - 40 = -10$

37. $-10a^2 - 10a + 30 = 8$

34. $-6x^2 - 9x + 16 = 10$

38. $-3v^2 - 2v - 6 = 5$

35. $-9k^2 + 2k + 6 = 5$

39. $-8x^2 + 9x + 11 = -4$

36. $10m^2 - 5m + 14 = 11$

40. $12n^2 - 28 = -10$

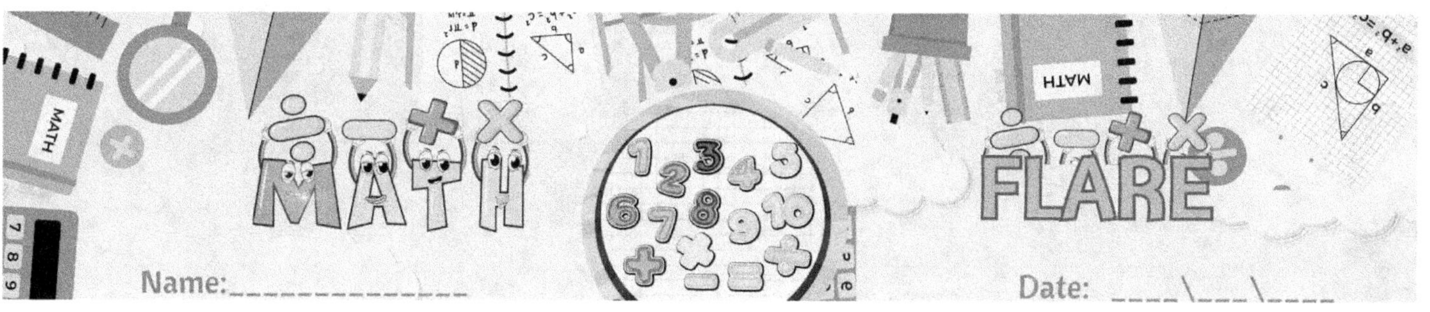

41. $-4x^2 = -4$

45. $-2x^2 + 101 = 3$

42. $-5v^2 + v + 12 = -10$

46. $4m^2 - 111 = -11$

43. $-2b^2 + b - 5 = -8$

47. $n^2 - 10n - 30 = -6$

44. $-2b^2 + 6b - 1 = -9$

48. $2k^2 + 4k - 14 = 2$

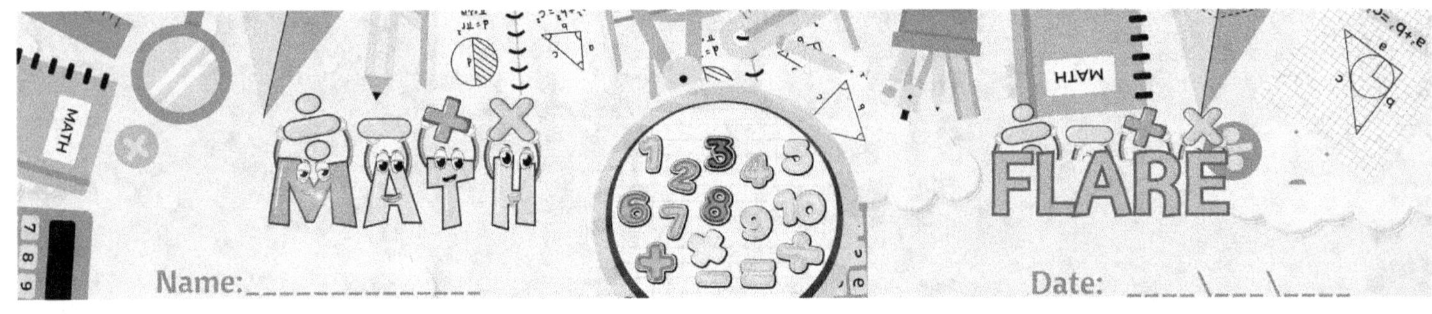

49. $6b^2 + 9b + 2 = 8$

53. $-2a^2 + 15 = 7$

50. $4n^2 - 11n - 47 = -9$

54. $-k^2 + 29 = 4$

51. $7p^2 - 12p - 10 = -5$

55. $6k^2 - 106 = -10$

52. $-5n^2 - 5n + 23 = 11$

56. $5n^2 - 8n - 20 = -5$

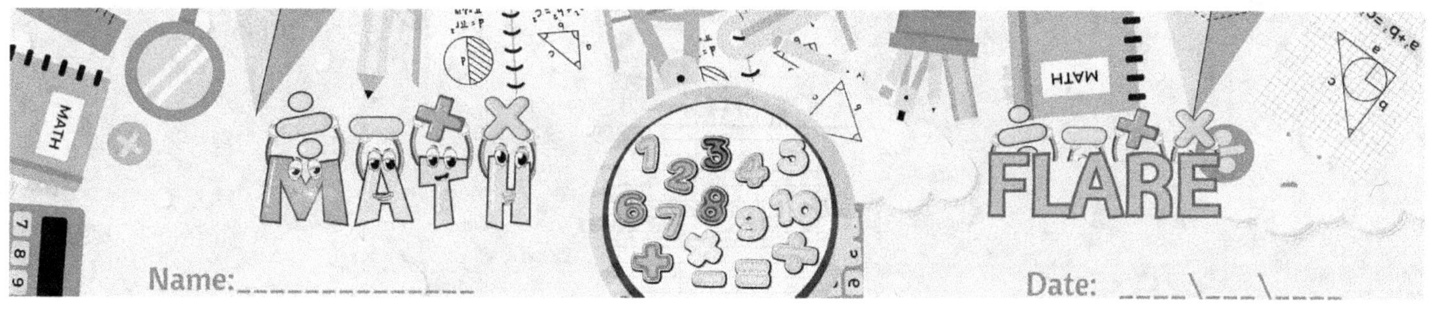

57. $-r^2 + 12r - 29 = -5$

58. $4n^2 + 8n - 36 = -4$

59. $9r^2 + 2r = -12$

60. $-8v^2 - 7v + 20 = 6$

Chapter. 05

Polynomials

A polynomial is an algebraic expression consisting of one or more terms, where each term is a constant, a variable, or a product of constants and variables raised to whole number exponents.

Examples of polynomials include:

- $(7v^2 + 2v^4) + (8v^2 + 4v^4)$
- $(2v + 4v^2 + 2) - (5v - 4v^4 - 6v^2)$
- $(7x - 5y)(2x - 6y)$
- $(6x^2 + 4xy + 6y^2)(8x^2 + 3xy + 3y^2)$
- $\dfrac{2x^3 + 8x^2 + 2x}{2x^2}$

Operations on Polynomials

Addition of Polynomials:

- To add polynomials, simply combine like terms.
- Like terms are terms that have the same variable(s) raised to the same power(s).
- For example, to add $3x^2 + 2x$ and $5x^2 - 7x$, group the like terms: $3x^2 + 5x^2$ and $2x - 7x$, then add each group separately.

Subtraction of Polynomials:

- To subtract polynomials, distribute the negative sign and then add.
- For example, to subtract $x^2 - 2x$ from $4x^2 + 3x$, distribute the negative sign to each term in the second polynomial: $-(x^2 - 2x)$, then add each term separately.

<u>Multiplication of Polynomials:</u>

- To multiply polynomials, use the distributive property and then combine like terms.

- For example, to multiply $(x + 2)(3x - 4)$, distribute each term in the first polynomial to each term in the second polynomial, then combine like terms.

<u>Division of Polynomials:</u>

- Division of polynomials involves dividing one polynomial by another. It can be done using long division or synthetic division.

Let's solve the expression:

$$(7x^2 - 7x) - (x - 2x^2)$$

Step 1: Distribute the Negative Sign:

Distribute the negative sign in the second polynomial:

$$(7x^2 - 7x) - x + 2x^2$$

Step 2: Combine Like Terms:

$$(7x^2 + 2x^2) + (-7x - x)$$

Step 3: Perform addition and subtraction of coefficients:

$$9x^2 - 8x$$

Let's perform the multiplication of polynomials:

$$(5u + 2v)(8u^2 - uv - 3v^2)$$

We can distribute each term in the first polynomial $(5u + 2v)$ to every term in the second polynomial $(8u^2 - uv - 3v^2)$.

1. Multiply $5u$ by each term in the second polynomial:

$$5u \cdot 8u^2 = 40u^3$$
$$5u \cdot (-uv) = -5u^2v$$
$$5u \cdot (-3v^2) = -15uv^2$$

2. Multiply $2v$ by each term in the second polynomial:

$$2v \cdot 8u^2 = 16u^2v$$

$$2v \cdot (-uv) = -2uv^2$$

$$2v \cdot (-3v^2) = -6v^3$$

Combine the like terms:

$$40u^3 - 5u^2v - 15uv^2 + 16u^2v - 2uv^2 - 6v^3$$

Combine the like terms involving u and v.

$$40u^3 + (16u^2v - 5u^2v) + (-15uv^2 - 2uv^2) - 6v^3$$

$$40u^3 + 11u^2v - 17uv^2 - 6v^3$$

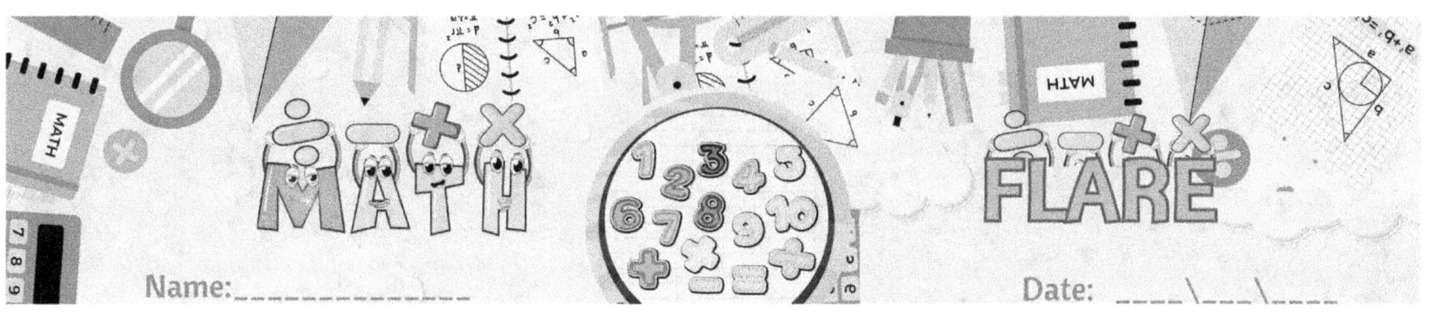

Polynomials: Addition and Subtraction

1. $(5 + 6x^3) + (x^3 + 7)$

2. $(5b^4 - 8b) - (4b^4 + 5b)$

3. $(8k^3 - 3k^2) - (5k^3 + 6k^2)$

4. $(3 + 8p) + (p - 7)$

5. $(5 - 6b^2) + (5b^2 - 7b^3)$

6. $(5x^2 - 4x^3) - (3x^2 - 7x^3)$

7. $(x^3 - 2x^2) + (8x^3 + x^2)$

8. $(6k^3 - 8k^2) + (k^3 + 4k^2)$

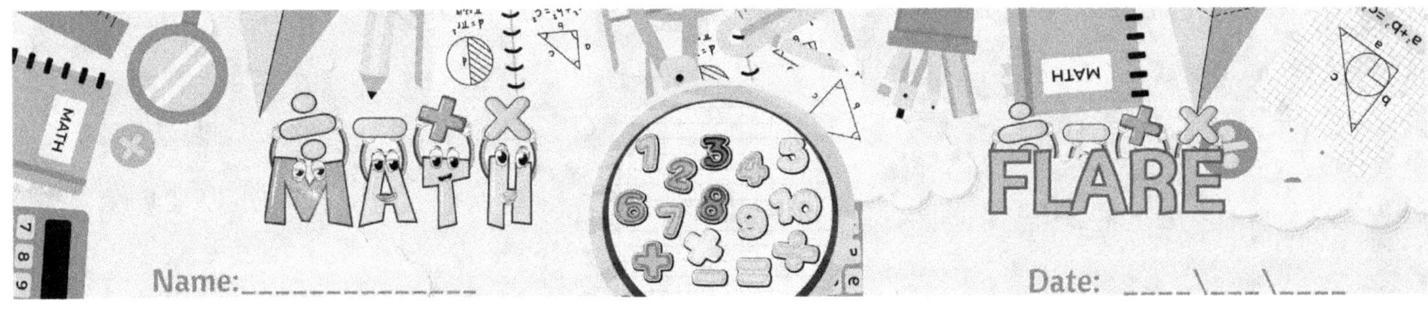

9. $(7b^4 + 3b^3) + (6b^4 + 8b^3)$

13. $(7p^3 - 4p^4) + (6p^3 - 4p^4)$

10. $(7n^3 + 7n^2) + (7n - 7n^2)$

14. $(3x - 3x^3) + (5x^3 + 8x)$

11. $(8p^3 - 7p^4) + (8p^4 + 7p^3)$

15. $(k^4 + k^3) - (6k^3 + k^4)$

12. $(2x^4 + 3x^2) + (5x^4 + 2)$

16. $(4v^2 + 6v^3) + (7v^3 - 6v^2)$

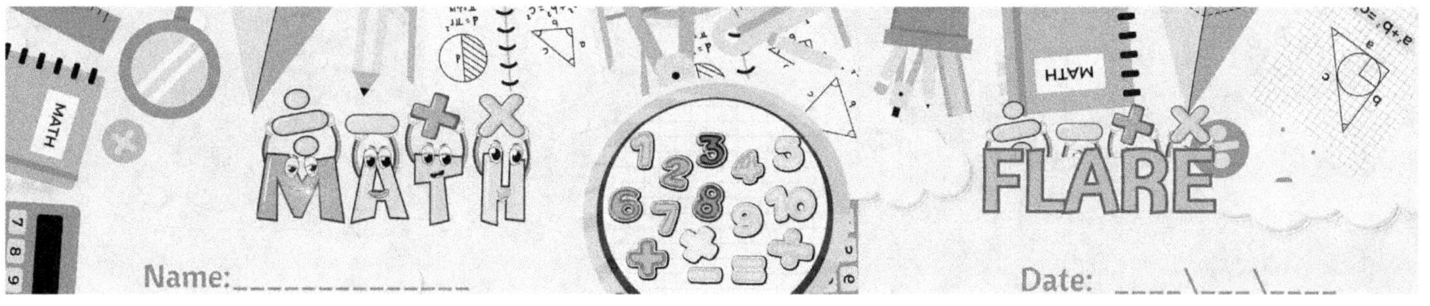

17. $(2 - 7v^4) + (2 - 4v^4)$

21. $(7x - 7) - (6x + 6)$

18. $(2p^2 + 4) + (6 + 8p^2)$

22. $(3x^3 + 8x^2) - (6x^3 - 8x^2)$

19. $(6r - r^2) - (8r^2 + 7r)$

23. $(4x^4 - 3x^3) - (5x^4 - 5x^3)$

20. $(6a^3 - 8a^4) - (2a^3 + 6a^4)$

24. $(8n + 3n^2) - (3n^2 - 2n)$

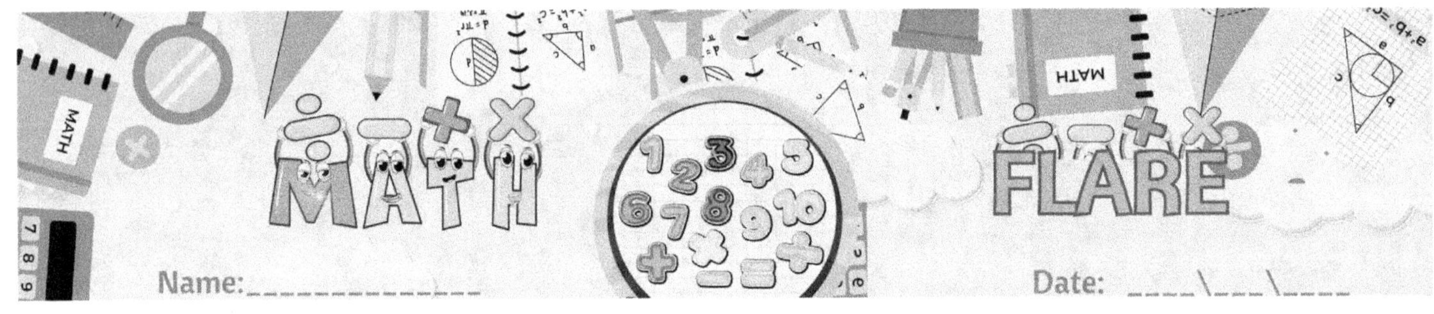

25. $(5x^4 - x^3) + (2x^4 - 6x^3)$

26. $(5 + a^3) - (1 + 7a^3)$

27. $(7x^3 + 6x^4) - (3x^3 - 3x^4)$

28. $(8x^2 + 3) - (6x^2 + 2)$

29. $(6b^4 + 2) - (8b^4 + 4)$

30. $(x^4 - 7x^2) - (2x^4 - 2x^2)$

31. $(7x^4 + 5x) + (7x + 2 - x^4)$

32. $(4n^4 + 3) - (8 + 5n^4 - 2n)$

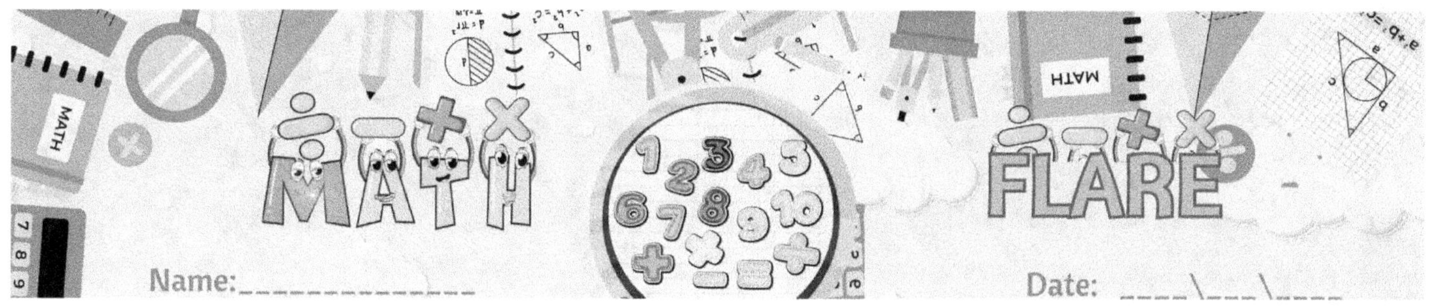

33. $(7x^3 + 6x^4) + (3x^2 - x^3 - 2x^4)$

37. $(6 - 6n^4) + (4n + 4 - 7n^4)$

34. $(5r + 4r^2) + (6r^2 - 1 - 5r)$

38. $(7r - 7r^2) - (5r^4 - 4r^2 - 8r)$

35. $(7p^3 - 3p^4) - (4p^3 + p^4 + 4p^2)$

39. $(7 - 4p) - (5p + p^3 - 7)$

36. $(3n^4 - n^2) + (6n^2 + 8n^4 - 5n^3)$

40. $(7b^3 - 5b) - (b^3 - 5b^2 - 6b)$

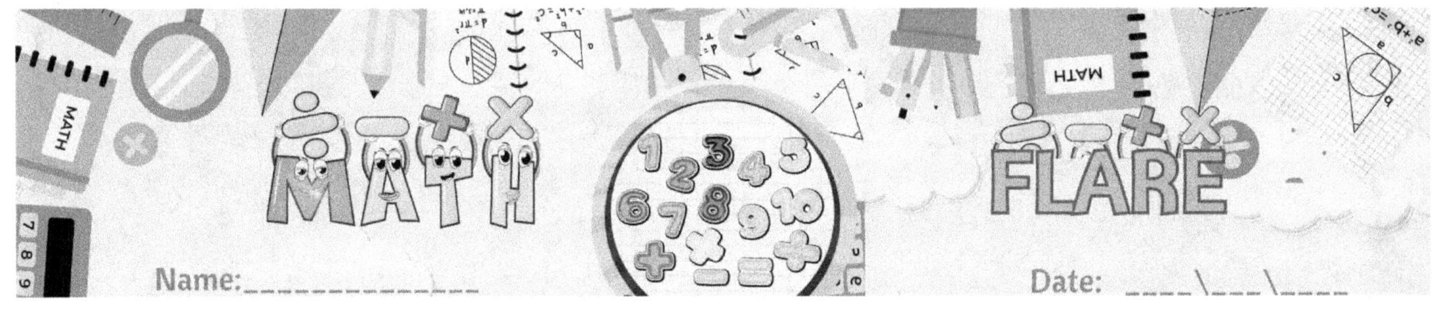

41. $(1 + x^3) + (x^3 + 1 + 6x^2)$

45. $(2b^2 + 4) - (7b^4 + 4b^2 - 3)$

42. $(5x^3 + 6) - (7 - 4x + 2x^3)$

46. $(8r + 2r^3) - (3r + 4r^2 - r^3)$

43. $(6b^4 + 6) + (5 - 7b^3 - 2b^4)$

47. $(4n + 4n^2) + (5n^3 - 8n - n^2)$

44. $(5n + 5n^4) + (6n - 5 - 2n^4)$

48. $(4 + 4m^3) - (4 - 8m^3 - 3m^2)$

49. $(4a + a^4) - (a^4 - 3 - 3a)$

53. $(2m^4 - 5) - (2m^4 - 3 - 5m^3)$

50. $(2 + 5n^4) + (2n^4 + 2n - 5)$

54. $(8 - 6x^2) - (8x^2 + 6 - x^3)$

51. $(8v^4 - 5v^3) + (7 + 5v^4 - 3v^3)$

55. $(5r^4 + r) + (8r^4 + 3r^3 + 5r)$

52. $(n^3 + 8n) + (2n - 8n^3 + 1)$

56. $(6n^2 - 7n) + (3 - 5n + 5n^2)$

57. $(4x^3 - 6x^4) - (2x^4 + x^2 - 6x^3)$

59. $(5 - p^3) + (p^3 - 6p^4 + 1)$

58. $(1 + x) + (3 + x^4 + 6x)$

60. $(4n^2 - 3n) - (7n - 7n^3 - 2n^2)$

61. $(3b^3 + 4b + 3b^4) + (7b^3 - b - 3b^4)$

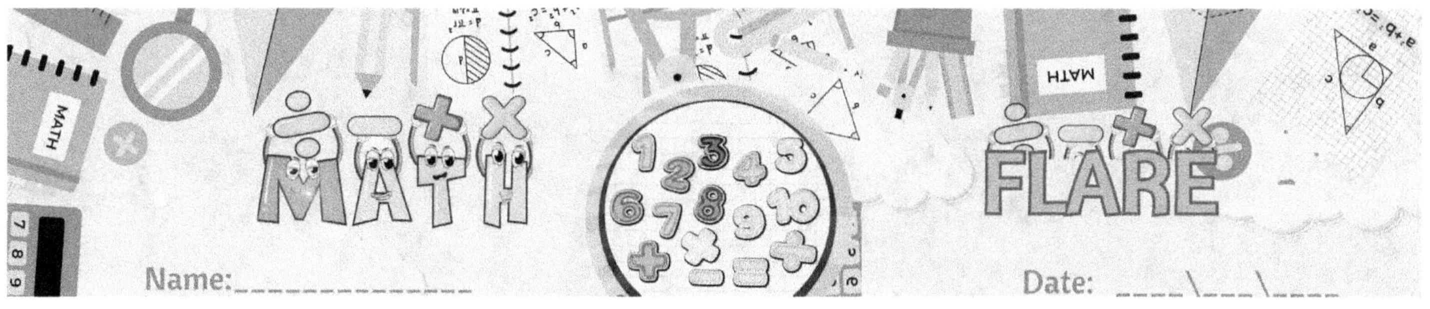

62. $(7n^4 + 2 - 4n^3) + (4 + 7n^3 - 8n^4)$

63. $(2x^4 + 5x^3 + x^2) - (x^3 - x^4 - 7)$

64. $(4b^4 + 2b^3 + 2b) - (7b^4 - 6b + 3b^3)$

65. $(5x^4 - 1 - 4x^3) - (7x^2 - 7x^4 - 3x^3)$

66. $(4b - b^3 - 8b^2) - (5b^3 + 6b^2 + 8b)$

67. $(6x^4 - x^3 + 5x) + (7x^4 + 6x - 6x^3)$

68. $(1 + 2k^3 - k) - (2k^4 + 5k^3 - 1)$

69. $(m^4 - 6m^3 - 5) + (6m^4 + 2m^3 - 8)$

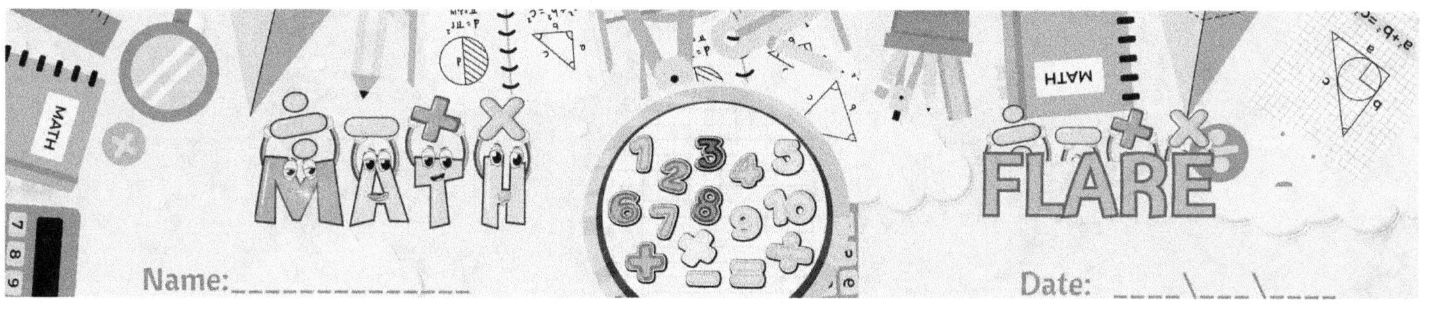

70. $(4n^3 - 3n^4 - 8n) - (5n^4 - 8n - 7n^3)$

71. $(8x - 3x^4 + 7x^2) + (2x^4 + x^3 - x)$

72. $(3x^4 - 7 - x) - (x^4 - 7x - 1)$

73. $(6x^2 - 6x^4 - 2) + (7 - 3x^2 + 7x^4)$

74. $(7p^2 - p^4 - 6p) - (2p^4 - 2p^2 + p)$

75. $(a - 7a^2 + a^3) + (2a^2 - 3a^3 - 5a)$

76. $(6b + 2b^3 - b^2) - (b^3 - 7b^2 + 3b)$

77. $(5n + 3n^4 - 8n^2) + (n - 6n^2 - 6n^4)$

78. $(6 + 2n^2 + 3n^4) + (3 + n^4 + 2n^2)$

79. $(5 - 5k - 8k^3) - (5k^3 + 2 - 6k)$

80. $(7v^3 + 3v^4 + 7v) - (8v^4 - 8v^3 + 8v)$

81. $(7m - 5m^4 + 5m^3) + (4m^3 + 4m - 6m^4)$

82. $(3n^4 - 3n + 6n^2) - (8n + 7n^2 + n^4)$

83. $(5b + 3b^3 + 4b^4) + (b - 6b^4 - 5)$

84. $(4x^3 - 1 - 6x) + (x + 6x^3 - 4)$

85. $(8v^4 + 7 - 7v^3) - (2v^2 + 5v^4 + 4v^3)$

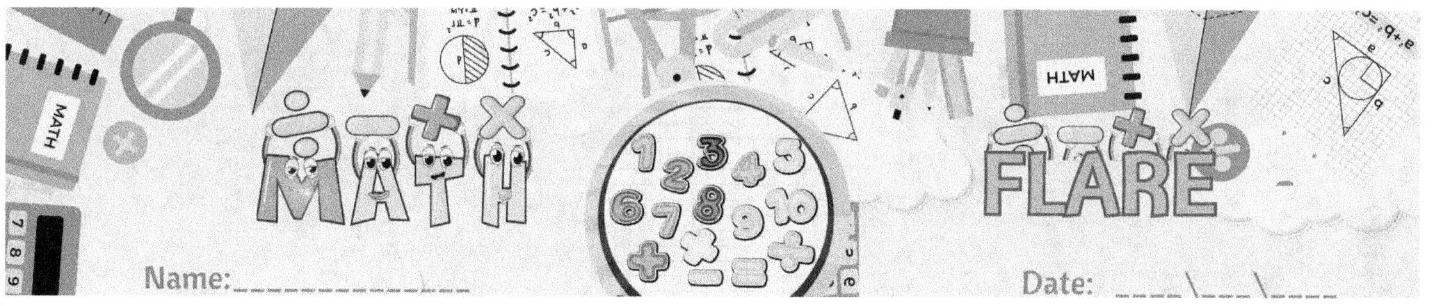

86. $(5 - 2x + 6x^2) + (2x^2 - 5x^4 - 8x)$

87. $(3n^2 + 8n^4 + 5n) + (7n + n^3 - 6n^2)$

88. $(4n^3 + 4n^2 - 4) - (8 + 8n^3 + 6n^2)$

89. $(1 + n^4 + 5n^3) + (n^3 - 6 + 2n^4)$

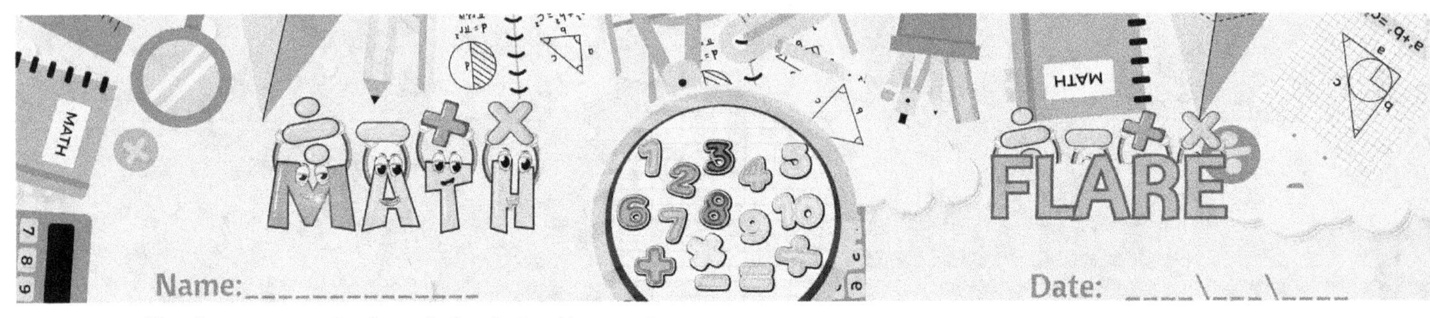

Polynomials: Multiplication

1. $(6x + 8y)(x - 6y)$

2. $(8a + 4b)(7a - 3b)$

3. $(4x - y)(5x + y)$

4. $(8m + 2n)(5m - 5n)$

5. $(7a + 8b)(a + 4b)$

6. $(8x - 3y)(8x + 2y)$

7. $(8x + 5y)(4x - 3y)$

8. $(4m - 7n)(2m - 6n)$

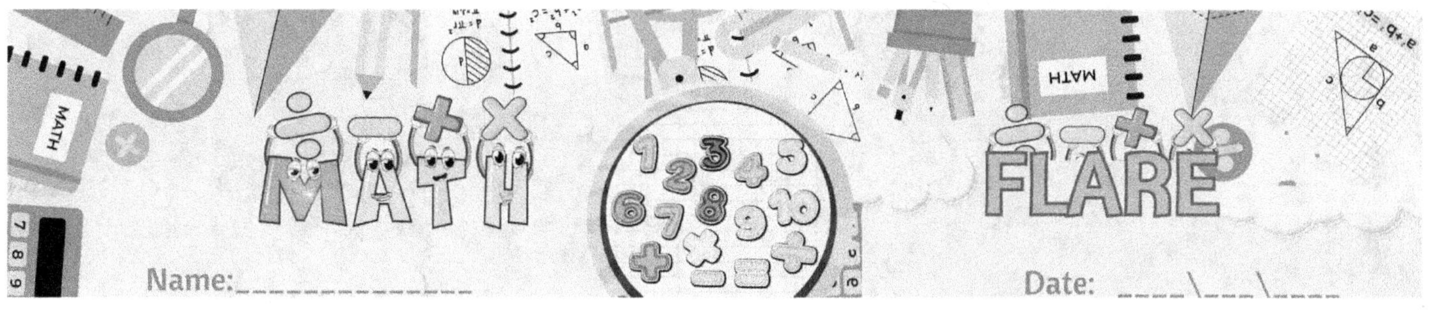

9. $(3u - 3v)(u + v)$

13. $(4x + 3y)(7x - 7y)$

10. $(7x - 3y)(3x + 3y)$

14. $(5a - 6b)(7a + 7b)$

11. $(5u + 5v)(u - 6v)$

15. $(8x - 7y)(4x + 7y)$

12. $(2m + 8n)(6m + 2n)$

16. $(2a + 7b)(4a - 8b)$

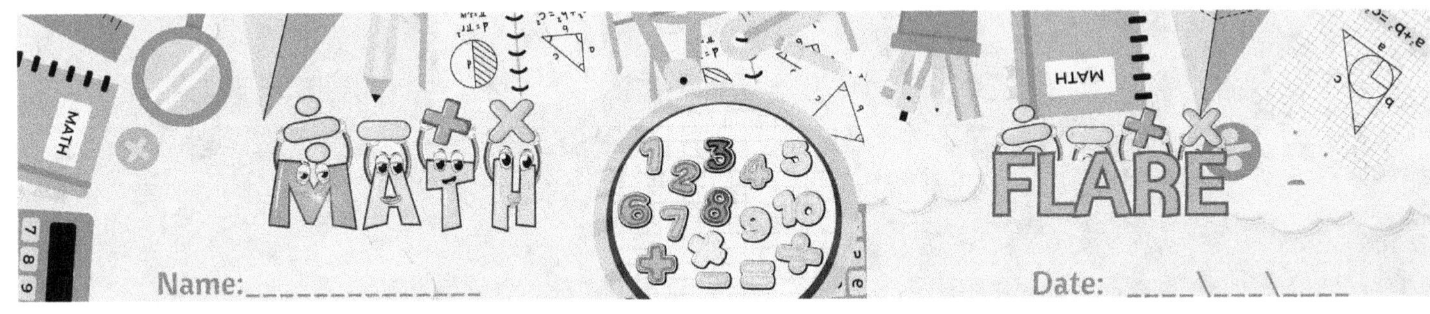

17. (5x - 4 y)(2x + 5 y)

21. (2x + 4 y)(7x + 3 y)

18. (8m - 5n)(2m - n)

22. (2x + 7 y)(x + 6 y)

19. (2x + 7 y)(7x - 4 y)

23. (8a - 7b)2

20. (6x - 6 y)(8x - 2 y)

24. (7x + 5 y)(2x - 6 y)

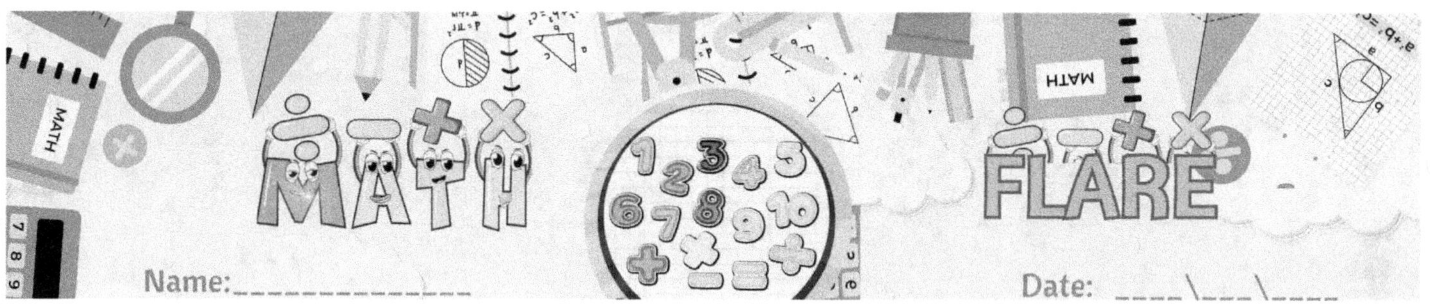

25. $(3u - 8v)(u - 6v)$

26. $(x + 7y)(x - 6y)$

27. $(4x - 5y)(7x + 8y)$

28. $(3m - 4n)(5m + 6n)$

29. $(6m - 3n)(4m + n)$

30. $(2a - 2b)(3a - 5b)$

31. $(8u + 6v)(u^2 + uv - 8v^2)$

32. $(7m - 3n)(2m^2 + 6mn - 3n^2)$

33. $(6x + 7y)(x^2 + xy - 6y^2)$

37. $(4x - 7y)(4x^2 - 5xy - y^2)$

34. $(x - 6y)(2x^2 + 2xy - 3y^2)$

38. $(7x - 3y)(2x^2 - 4xy - 5y^2)$

35. $(5m - 7n)(m^2 - 2mn + n^2)$

39. $(4x + y)(5x^2 + 5xy - 5y^2)$

36. $(6x + y)(4x^2 + 4xy - 5y^2)$

40. $(6x + 8y)(5x^2 - 2xy + 3y^2)$

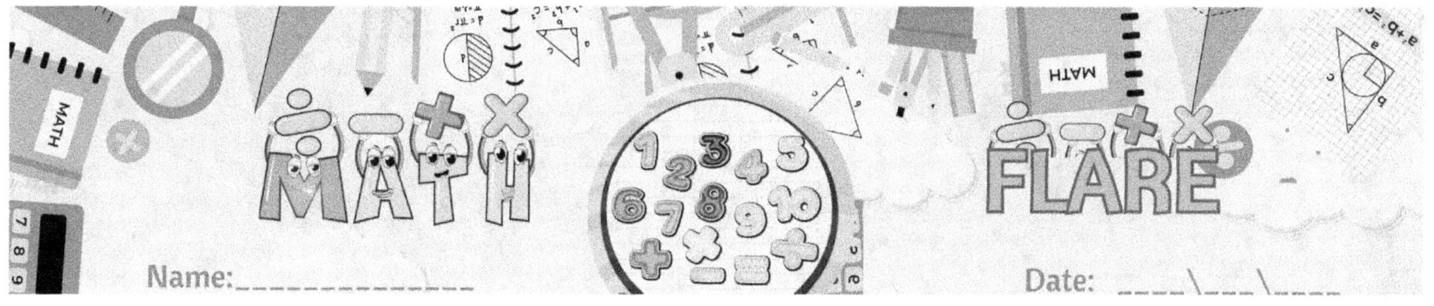

41. $(6x + 4y)(3x^2 + 4xy - 6y^2)$

45. $(8x - 7y)(4x^2 - 8xy + y^2)$

42. $(5x + 8y)(3x^2 + 5xy + 8y^2)$

46. $(2x + 4y)(7x^2 - 6xy - 6y^2)$

43. $(u - 3v)(3u^2 - uv - 6v^2)$

47. $(4x - 5y)(2x^2 - 7xy - 4y^2)$

44. $(4a - 6b)(a^2 - 4ab - 5b^2)$

48. $(2m - 6n)(7m^2 + 5mn - 3n^2)$

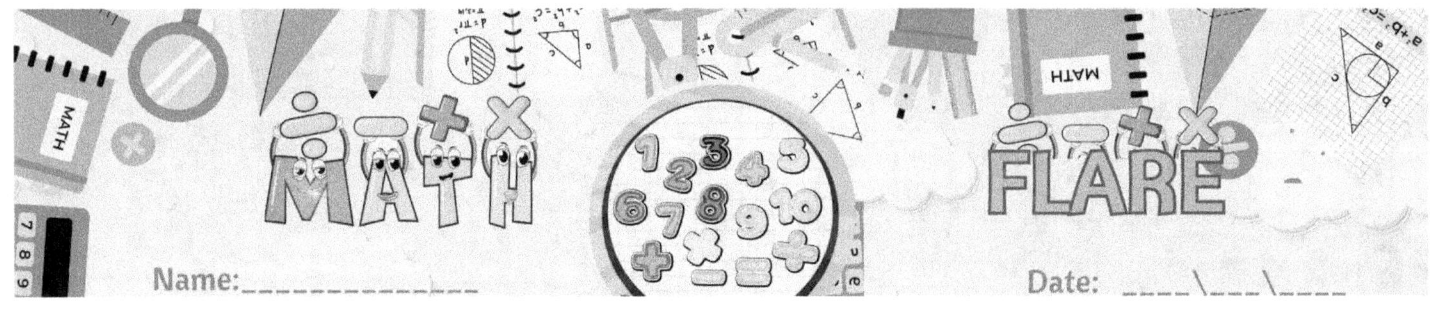

49. $(6x + 6y)(4x^2 - 4xy + 2y^2)$

53. $(8x + 6y)(8x^2 + xy + 2y^2)$

50. $(3a - 7b)(3a^2 + 3ab + 4b^2)$

54. $(x + 4y)(4x^2 + 8xy + 6y^2)$

51. $(x - y)(6x^2 - xy + 7y^2)$

55. $(3m - 7n)(2m^2 - 8mn - 6n^2)$

52. $(5a - 3b)(7a^2 + ab - 2b^2)$

56. $(x - 4y)(6x^2 - 3xy + 5y^2)$

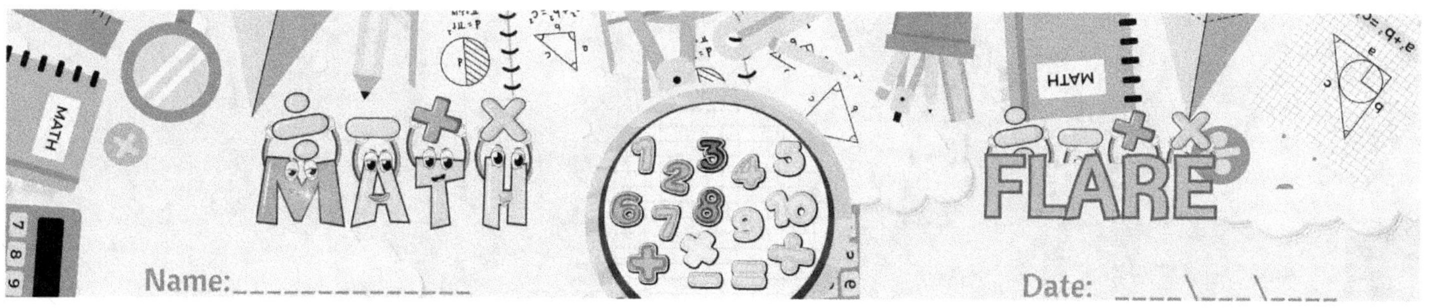

57. $(a - 2b)(7a^2 + 7ab - 8b^2)$

59. $(5x - 3y)(7x^2 - 4xy - 5y^2)$

58. $(4x - 6y)(3x^2 - 4xy + 6y^2)$

60. $(7u - 8v)(3u^2 + 2uv + v^2)$

61. $(2m^2 - 4mn - 5n^2)(m^2 - 7mn + 5n^2)$

62. $(2u^2 + 6uv - v^2)(u^2 + 4uv + v^2)$

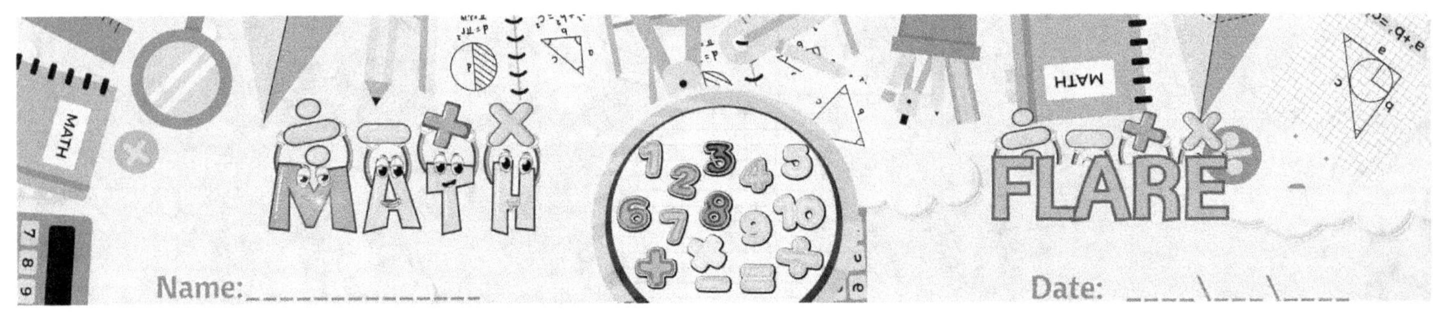

63. $(4u^2 - uv + 2v^2)(8u^2 + 5uv - 5v^2)$

64. $(x^2 - 2xy + 4y^2)(2x^2 - 5xy - 2y^2)$

65. $(2x^2 - 7xy - y^2)(2x^2 - 5xy - 7y^2)$

66. $(5x^2 - 8xy - 8y^2)(6x^2 - xy + 7y^2)$

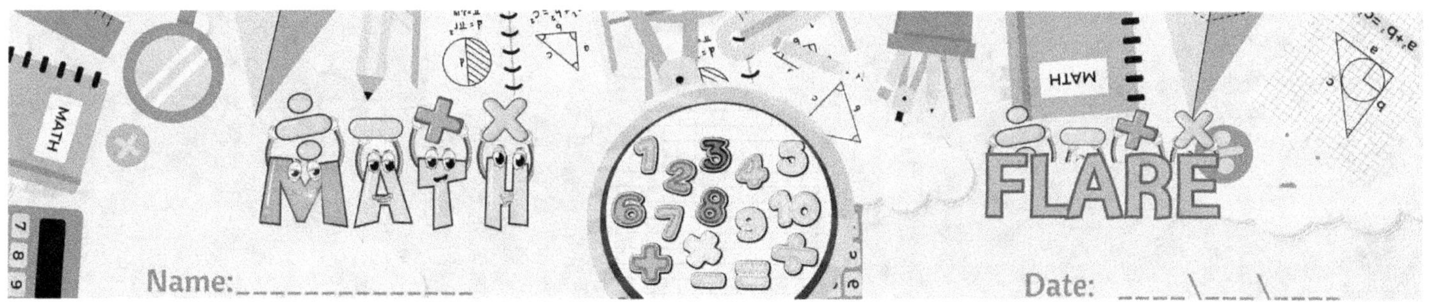

67. $(7a^2 + 7ab + 5b^2)(3a^2 - ab + 7b^2)$

68. $(2u^2 - 3uv + 7v^2)(4u^2 + 7uv + 8v^2)$

69. $(3a^2 - 2ab - 7b^2)(2a^2 + ab + 6b^2)$

70. $(7x^2 - 4xy - 2y^2)(8x^2 - 6xy + 6y^2)$

71. $(7m^2 - 4mn - 7n^2)(2m^2 + mn + 5n^2)$

72. $(2x^2 + 2xy + 5y^2)(x^2 + 8xy - 2y^2)$

73. $(5x^2 + 8xy + 4y^2)(7x^2 + 7xy - 6y^2)$

74. $(7x^2 + 3xy - y^2)(3x^2 - 8xy - 4y^2)$

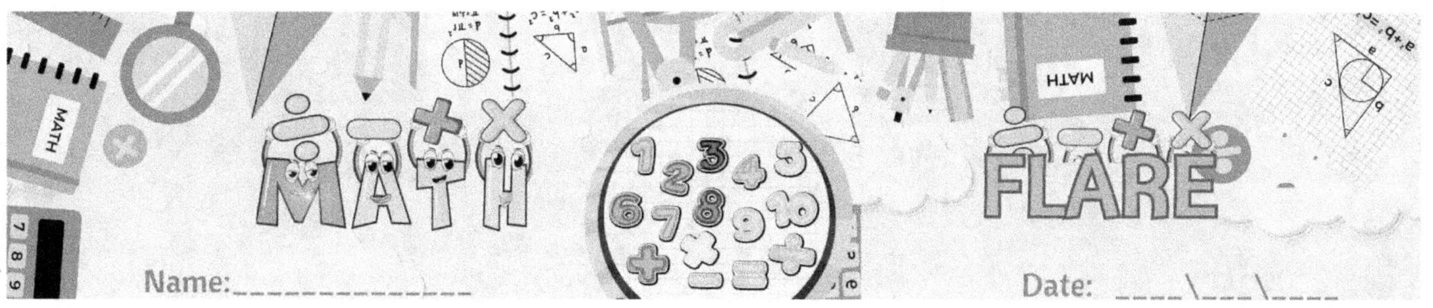

75. $(5m^2 - 4mn + 7n^2)(6m^2 + 4mn + n^2)$

76. $(7a^2 - 2ab + 8b^2)(6a^2 - 2ab - 4b^2)$

77. $(8x^2 + 2xy - y^2)(3x^2 - 2xy + 6y^2)$

78. $(4x^2 - 2xy - 4y^2)(7x^2 + 7xy - 4y^2)$

79. $(8a^2 + 6ab + 5b^2)(3a^2 - ab - b^2)$

80. $(8m^2 - 7mn - 8n^2)(8m^2 - 5mn + 4n^2)$

81. $(x^2 + 6xy - 4y^2)(x^2 + 5xy + 7y^2)$

82. $(x^2 + xy - y^2)(3x^2 - 7xy + y^2)$

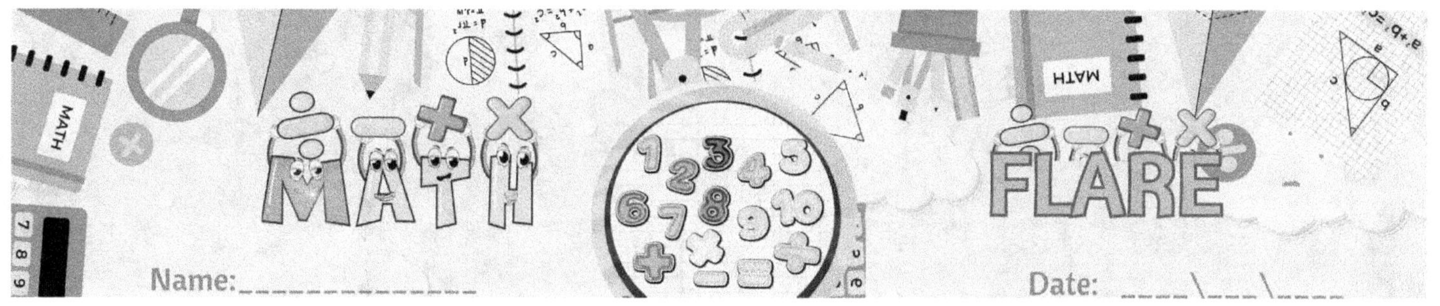

83. $(4x^2 + 4xy - 3y^2)(4x^2 - 2xy + 6y^2)$

84. $(2x^2 - 3xy + y^2)(2x^2 + 3xy + 8y^2)$

85. $(5u^2 + 4uv - 6v^2)(5u^2 - 5uv + 8v^2)$

86. $(7u^2 + 3uv - 2v^2)(8u^2 - 8uv - 6v^2)$

87. $(2x^2 + xy + 5y^2)(5x^2 + 8xy + 5y^2)$

88. $(8x^2 - 8xy - 6y^2)(5x^2 + xy + 8y^2)$

89. $(5x^2 + 7xy - 2y^2)(6x^2 - xy - 5y^2)$

90. $(6x^2 - 2xy - 5y^2)(7x^2 - 2xy + 3y^2)$

Chapter. 06

<u>Geometry</u>

<u>Area and Perimeter</u>

The area of a shape represents the amount of space it occupies. The perimeter of a shape is the total distance around its outer edge.

Area of Rectangle

For a square, since all four sides are equal, we only need to know the length of one side to find its area. We can calculate the area of a square by multiplying the length of one side by itself (squared). So, if the length of one side of the square is 's', then the area (A) is given by:

$$A = s \times s$$

4 in

4 in

$$A = 4 \times 4$$

$$A = 16$$

Perimeter of Rectangle

For a square, since all four sides are equal, we can find the perimeter by adding up the lengths of all four sides. If 's' represents the length of one side, then the perimeter (P) is given by:

$$P = 4 \times s$$

$$P = 4 \times 4$$

$$P = 16$$

Area of Triangle:

The area of a triangle represents the amount of space enclosed within its three sides. The formula for calculating the area of a triangle depends on the type of triangle. For a general triangle, we use the formula:

$$A = \frac{1}{2} \times \text{base} \times \text{height}$$

Where:

- *A* represents the area of the triangle.

- The base is the length of any one side of the triangle.

- The height is the perpendicular distance from the base to the opposite vertex.

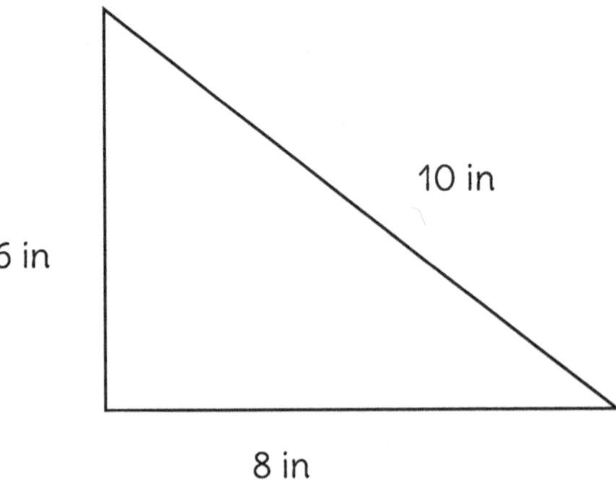

$$A = \frac{1}{2} \times \text{base} \times \text{height}$$

$$A = \frac{1}{2} \times 6 \times 8$$

$$A = \frac{1}{2} \times 48$$

$$A = 24$$

Perimeter of Triangle:

The perimeter of a triangle is the total length of its three sides. To find the perimeter, we simply add the lengths of all three sides together:

$$P = \text{side1} + \text{side2} + \text{side3}$$

$$P = 6 + 8 + 10$$

$$P = 24$$

Equilateral Triangle

An equilateral triangle is a triangle in which all three sides are equal in length. To find the area and perimeter of an equilateral triangle, we can use the following formulas:

- Area (A): $\frac{\sqrt{3}}{4} \times a^2$ where a is the length of one side of the equilateral triangle.
- Perimeter (P): $P = 3a$ where a is the length of one side of the equilateral triangle.

Let's solve a problem:

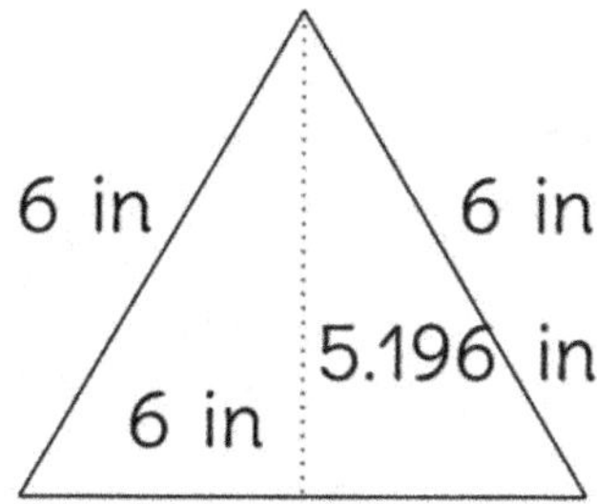

Area of Equilateral Triangle:

$$\text{Area (A): } \frac{\sqrt{3}}{4} \times (6)^2$$

$$\text{Area (A): } \frac{\sqrt{3}}{4} \times 36$$

$$\text{Area (A): } \frac{36\sqrt{3}}{4}$$

$$\text{Area (A): } \frac{36(1.73)}{4}$$

$$\text{Area (A): } \frac{62.35}{4}$$

$$\text{Area (A): } 15.59 \text{ in}^2$$

Perimeter of Equilateral Triangle:

$$P = 3a$$

$$P = 3(6) = 18$$

Isosceles Triangle

An isosceles triangle is a triangle with at least two sides of equal length. The angles opposite the equal sides are also equal.

Area of Isosceles Triangle

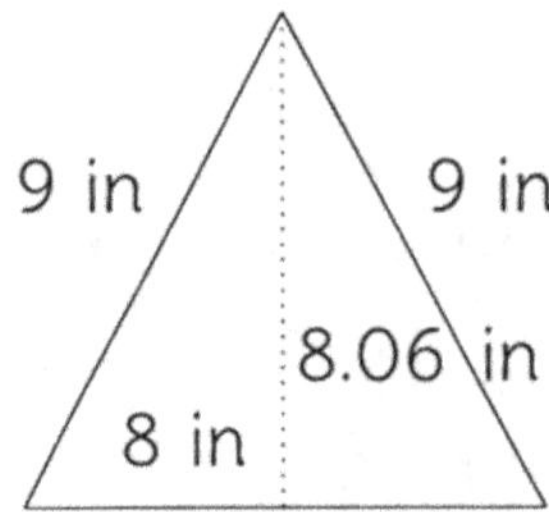

$$A = \frac{1}{2} \times \text{base} \times \text{height}$$

$$A = \frac{1}{2} \times 8 \times 8$$

$$A = \frac{1}{2} \times 64$$

$$A = 32$$

Perimeter of Isosceles Triangle

The perimeter of a triangle is the total length of its three sides. To find the perimeter, we simply add the lengths of all three sides together:

$$P = side1 + side2 + side3$$

$$P = 9 + 9 + 8$$

$$P = 26$$

Scalene Triangle

A scalene triangle is a triangle with no equal sides and no equal angles. The formula for finding various properties of a scalene triangle is as follows:

Area (A): The area of a scalene triangle can be calculated using Heron's formula, which is given by:

$$A = \sqrt{s(s-a)(s-b)(s-c)}$$

where s is the semi-perimeter of the triangle,

and a, b, and c are the lengths of its three sides.

Perimeter (P): The perimeter of a scalene triangle is the sum of the lengths of its three sides.

$$P = side1 + side2 + side3$$

Let's find the Area and Perimeter of a Scalene Triangle:

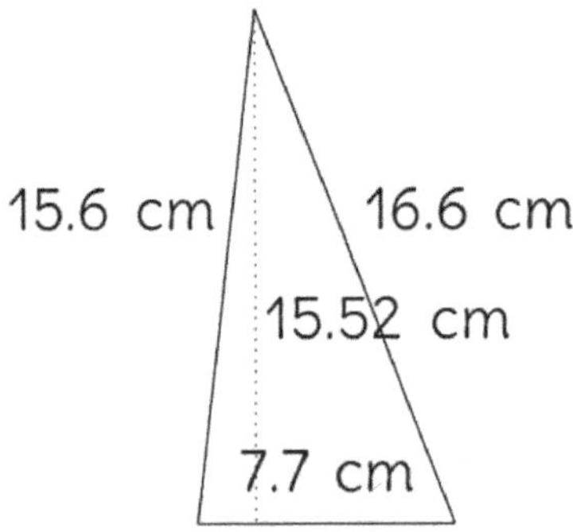

Area (A): First, we calculate the semi-perimeter (s):

$$S = \frac{a+b+c}{2} = \frac{15.6 + 16.6 + 7.7}{2} = \frac{39.8}{2} = 19.9 \text{ cm}$$

Heron's formula to find the area:

$$A = \sqrt{s(s-a)(s-b)(s-c)}$$

$$A = \sqrt{19.9\,(19.9 - 15.6)(19.9 - 16.6)(19.9 - 7.7)}$$

$$A = \sqrt{19.9 \times 4.3 \times 3.3 \times 12.2}$$

$$A = \sqrt{3445} \approx 59$$

Perimeter (P):

$$P = side1 + side2 + side3$$

$$P = 15.6 + 16.6 + 7.7$$

$$P = 39.8$$

Area and Perimeter of an L-shape

The L-shaped figure typically consists of two rectangles joined together to form an L-shape. To find the area and perimeter of an L-shaped figure, we will need to calculate the areas and perimeters of each rectangle and then combine them.

Area=Area of Rectangle 1 + Area of Rectangle 2

Perimeter=Perimeter of Rectangle 1 + Perimeter of Rectangle 2

Let's find the Area and Perimeter of an L-shape:

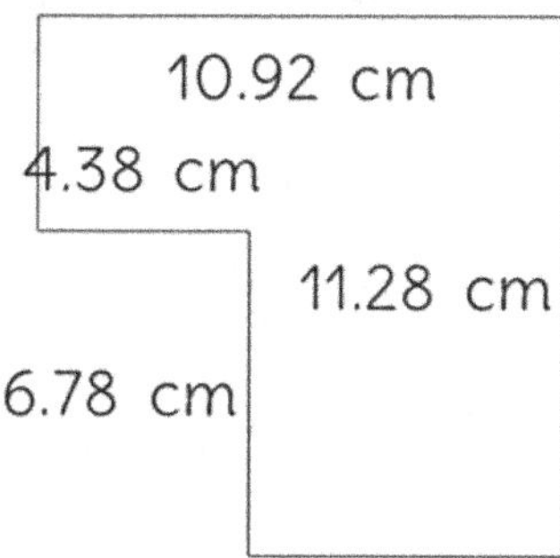

Area of L-Shape

$$Area\ 1 = 4.38 \times 4.5 = 19.7\ cm^2$$

$$Area\ 2 = 11.28 \times 6.54 = 73.7\ cm^2$$

$$Area = 19.7 + 73.7$$

$$Area = 93.481\ cm^2$$

Perimeter of L-Shape

$$P = 11.28 + 6.54 + 6.78 + 4.38 + 4.5 + 10.92$$

$$P = 44.4\ cm$$

Area and Perimeter of U-shape

U-shape is basically composed of three rectangles, we'll need to calculate the area and perimeter of each rectangle separately and then sum them up.

Area of the U-shape:

The total area (A) of the U-shape is the sum of the areas of the three rectangles:

$$A = A1 + A2 + A3$$

Perimeter of the U-shape: The total perimeter (P) of the U-shape is the sum of the perimeters of the three rectangles:

$$P = P1 + P2 + P3$$

Let's find the area and perimeter of the following U-shape:

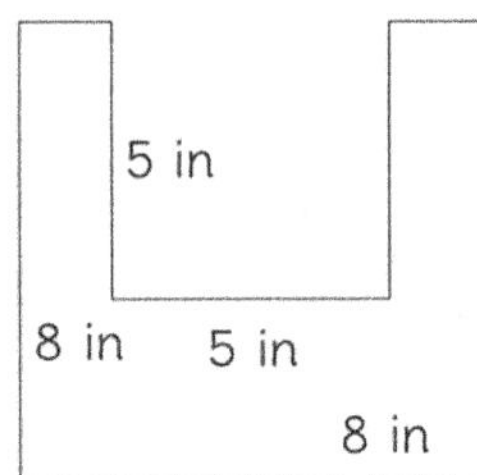

Area:

$$A1 = 8 \times 1.5 = 12 + A2 = 3 \times 5 = 15 + A3 = 8 \times 1.5 = 12$$

$$= 12 + 15 + 12$$

$$= 39 \text{ in}^2$$

Perimeter:

$$2 \times 8 + 2 \times 5 + 2 \times 8$$

$$= 16 + 10 + 16$$

$$= 42$$

Area and Perimeter of T-shape

The T-shape consists of two rectangles joined together to form a T-like structure.

Area of the T-shape:

To find the total area of the T-shape, we need to calculate the areas of both rectangles and then add them together.

$$\text{Area of Rectangle 1} = \text{Length} \times \text{Width}$$

Area of Rectangle 2 = Length × Width

Total Area = Area of Rectangle 1 + Area of Rectangle 2

The perimeter of the T-shape is the sum of the perimeters of the two rectangles, minus the length of the overlapping side:

Perimeter = 2(l1+w1) + 2(l2+w2) − (w1-w2)

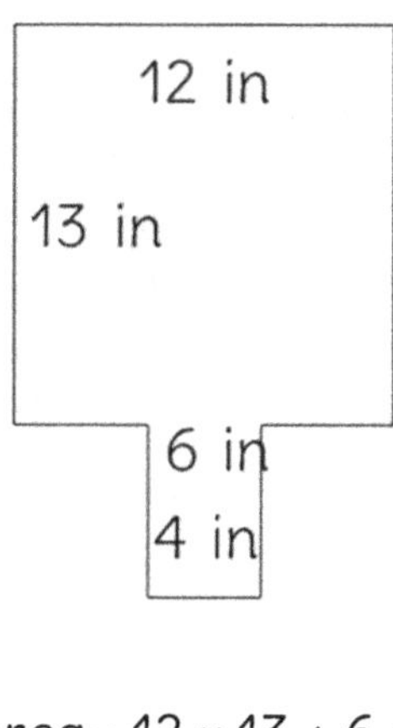

Area= 12 × 13 + 6 × 4

Area= 156 + 24

Area= 180 in²

Perimeter= 2(12+13) +2(6+4) − (12-4)

Perimeter=2(25) + 2(10) − 8

Perimeter= 50 + 20 − 8

Perimeter= 62 in²

Area and Perimeter of Parallelogram

A parallelogram is a four-sided polygon with opposite sides that are parallel and equal in length. To find the area and perimeter of a parallelogram, we use specific formulas based on its dimensions.

For example:

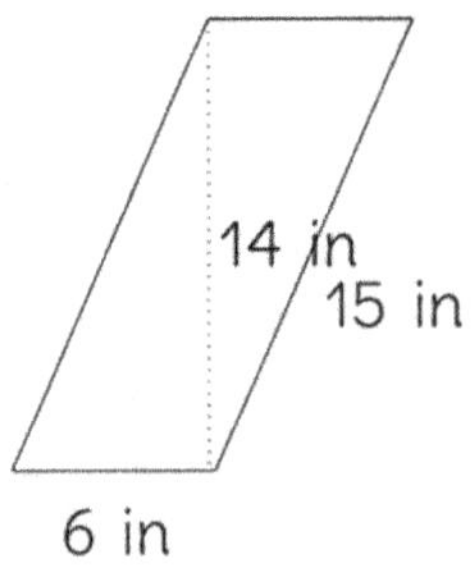

Let's denote:

- The length of one side of the parallelogram as $a = 15$.

- The length of an adjacent side (parallel to a) $b = 6$.

- The height of the parallelogram (perpendicular distance between the two parallel sides) as $h=14$

Area of Parallelogram

$$\text{Area} = \text{Base} \times \text{Height}$$

$$\text{Area} = 6 \times 14$$

$$\text{Area} = 84$$

Perimeter of Parallelogram

$$2(a + b)$$

$$= 2(15+6)$$

$$= 2(21)$$

$$= 42$$

<u>Area and Perimeter of Trapezoids</u>

A trapezoid is a quadrilateral with at least one pair of parallel sides. To find the area and perimeter of a trapezoid, we use specific formulas based on its dimensions.

For example:

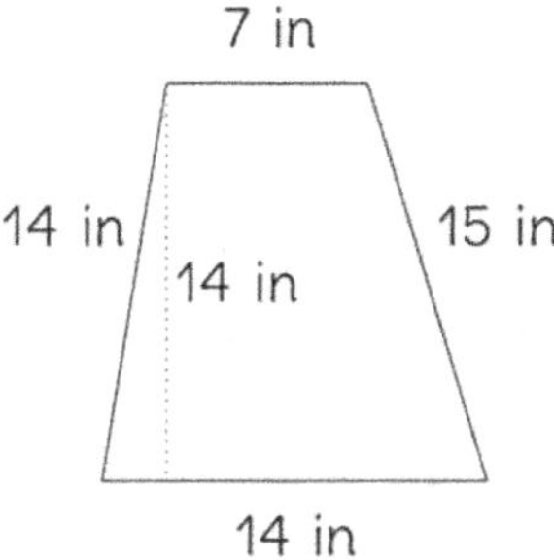

Let's denote:

- The lengths of the parallel sides of the trapezoid as $a = 7$ and $b = 14$.

- The lengths of the non-parallel sides as $c = 14$ and $d = 15$.

- The height of the trapezoid (the perpendicular distance between the parallel sides) as $h=14$.

Area of the Trapezoid:

The area of a trapezoid is given by the formula:

$$\text{Area} = \frac{1}{2} \times \text{Height} \times (\text{Sum of the lengths of the parallel sides})$$

$$\text{Area} = \frac{1}{2} \times h \times (a + b)$$

$$\text{Area} = \frac{1}{2} \times 14 \times (7 + 14)$$

$$\text{Area} = \frac{1}{2} \times 14 \times 21$$

$$\text{Area} = 147 \text{ in}^2$$

Perimeter of the Trapezoid:

$$\text{Perimeter} = 7 + 14 + 14 + 15$$

$$= 50 \text{ in}^2$$

Pythagorean Theorem

The Pythagorean Theorem is a fundamental principle in geometry that relates the lengths of the sides of a right triangle. It states that in any right triangle, the square of the length of the hypotenuse (the side opposite the right angle) is equal to the sum of the squares of the lengths of the other two sides.

$$a2 + b2 = c2$$

Let's use the Pythagorean Theorem to find the length of the hypotenuse (c) when $a=44$ and $b=78$.

$$c^2 = 44^2 + 78^2$$
$$c^2 = 1936 + 6084 \qquad c = \sqrt{8020}$$
$$c^2 = 8020 \qquad c \approx 89.554$$

Volume and surface Area

Volume refers to the amount of space occupied by a three-dimensional object. For shapes like cubes or rectangular prisms, we calculate volume by multiplying their length, width, and height.

To find the volume V of a rectangular prism, we use the formula:

$$Volume = length \ x \ width \ x \ height$$

Surface Area represents the total area covering all the faces of a three-dimensional object. For shapes like cubes or rectangular prisms, we find the surface area by summing the areas of all its faces.

The formula for surface area *SA* of a cube or rectangular prism is:

$$Surface\ Area\ =\ 2lw\ +\ 2lh\ +\ 2wh$$

Where: l is the length, w is the width, and h is the height of the object.

For example: Let's find the Volume and Surface Area of following rectangular prisms:

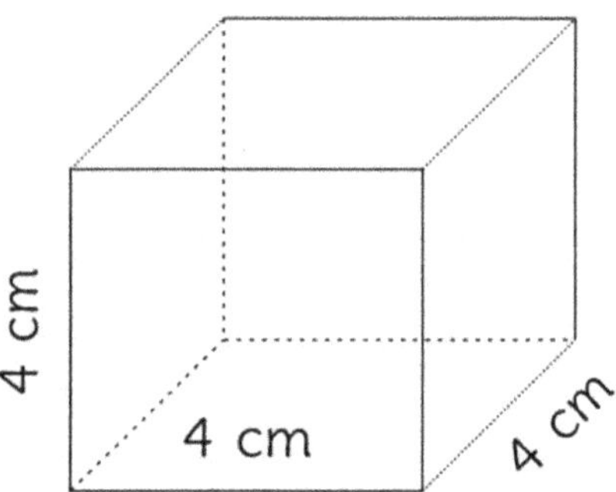

$$Volume\ =\ length\ \times\ width\ \times\ height$$

$$= 4 \times 4 \times 4$$

$$= 64\ cm^2$$

$$Surface\ Area\ =\ 2lw\ +\ 2lh\ +\ 2wh$$

$$= 2(4 \times 4) + 2(4 \times 4) + 2(4 \times 4)$$

$$= 32 + 32 + 32$$

$$= 96\ cm2$$

Different 3D objects have unique formulas for finding their volume and surface area. Here are some common ones:

1. Cube:

- Volume: $V = s^3$ (where s is the length of one side of the cube)

- Surface area: $SA = 6s^2$

2. Sphere:

- Volume: $V = (\frac{4}{3})\pi r^3$ (where r is the radius of the sphere)

- Surface area: $SA = 4\pi r^2$

3. Cone:

- Volume: $V = (\frac{1}{3})\pi r^2 h$ (where r is the radius of the base and h is the height of the cone)

- Surface area: $SA = \pi r^2 + \pi r \sqrt{(r^2 + h^2)}$

4. Cylinder:

- Volume: $V = \pi r^2 h$ (where r is the radius of the base and h is the height of the cylinder)

- Surface area: $SA = 2\pi r^2 + 2\pi rh$

5. Pyramid:

- Volume: $V = (\frac{1}{3})Bh$ (where B is the area of the base and h is the height of the pyramid)

- Surface area: $SA = B + \frac{1}{2}Pl$ (where P is the perimeter of the base and l is the slant height of the pyramid)

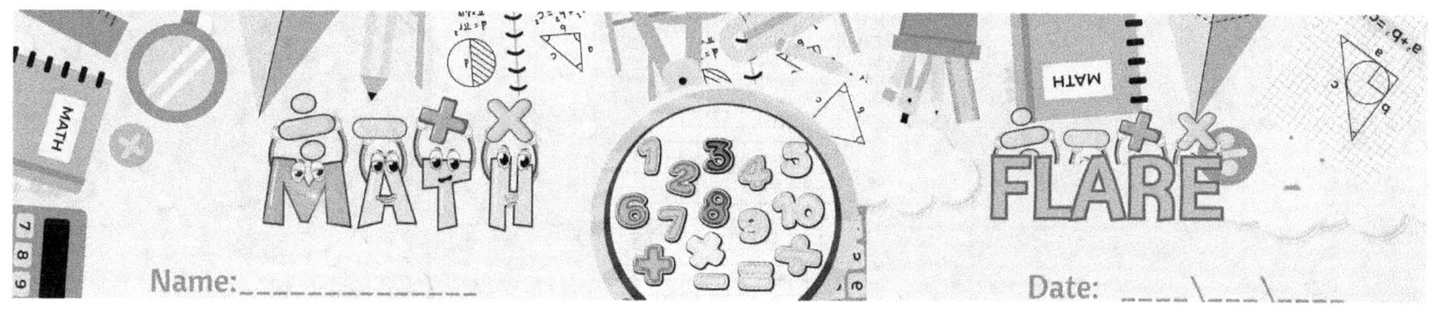

Area and Perimeter

1.

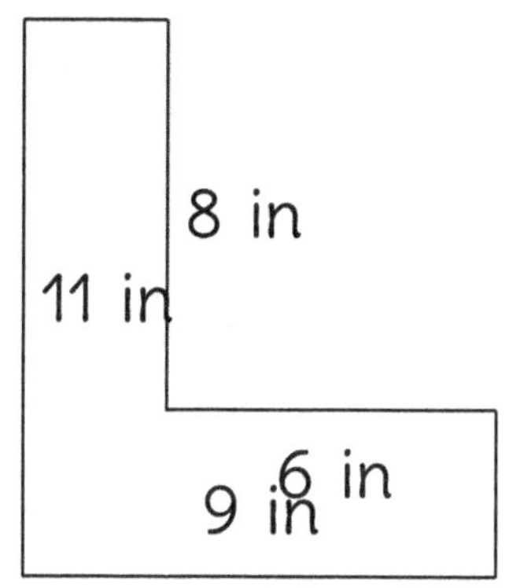

2.

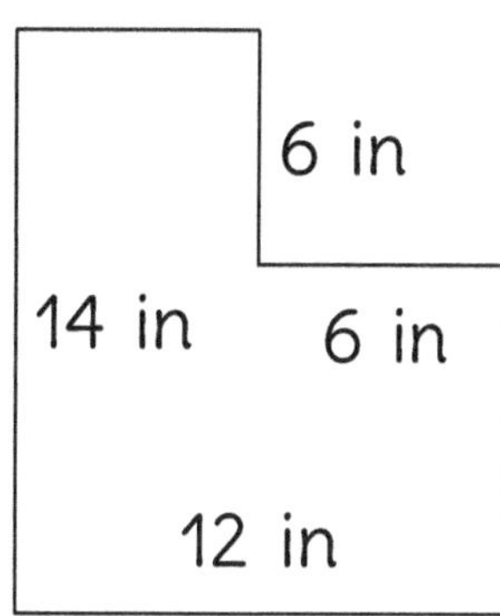

3.

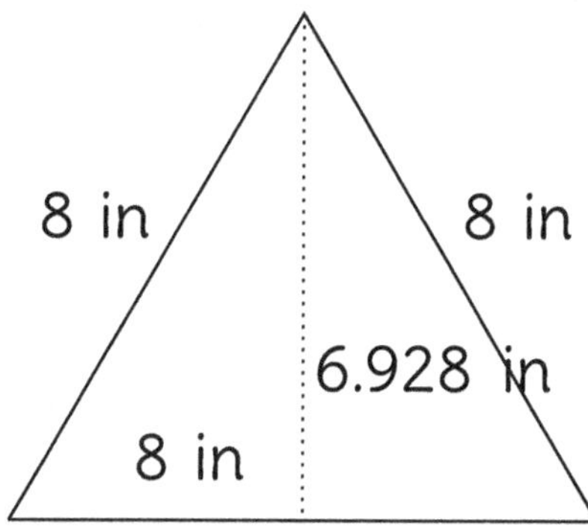

4.

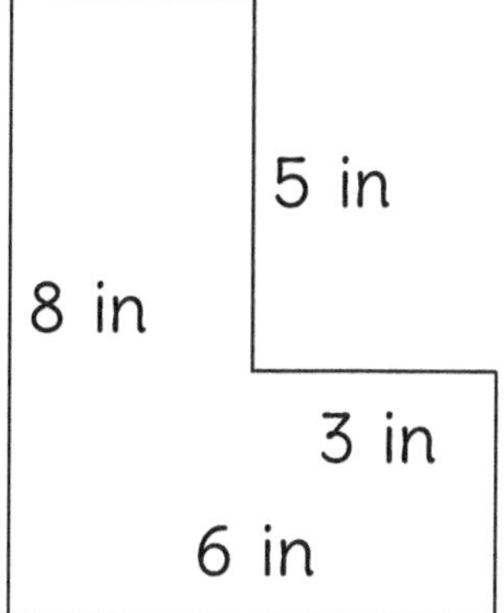

MATH FLARE
Name:
Date:

5.

6 in
11 in
7 in
10 in

6.

4 in
11 in
10 in
14 in

7.

7 in
8 in
8 in
7 in
12 in

8.

13 in
13 in
11.258 in
13 in

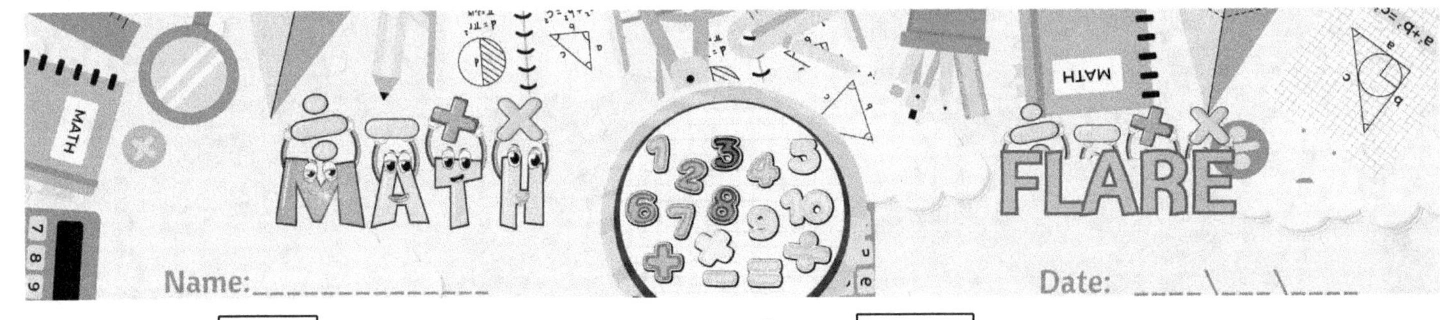

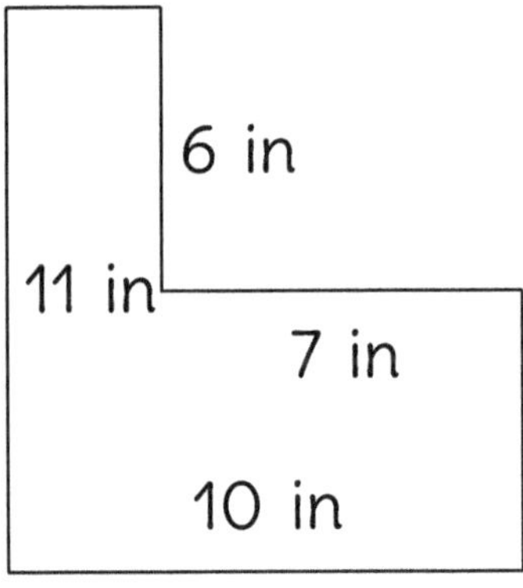

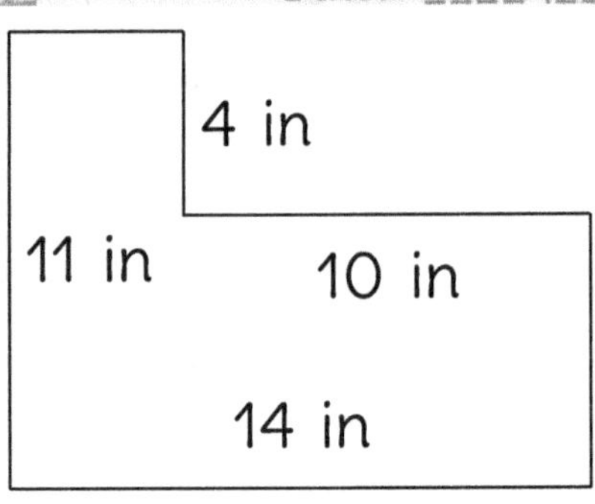

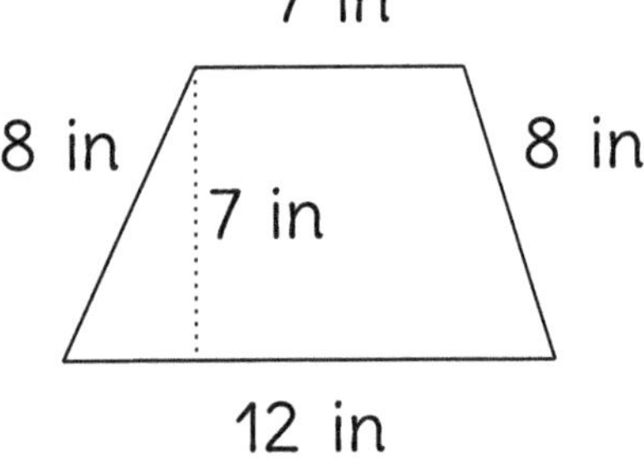

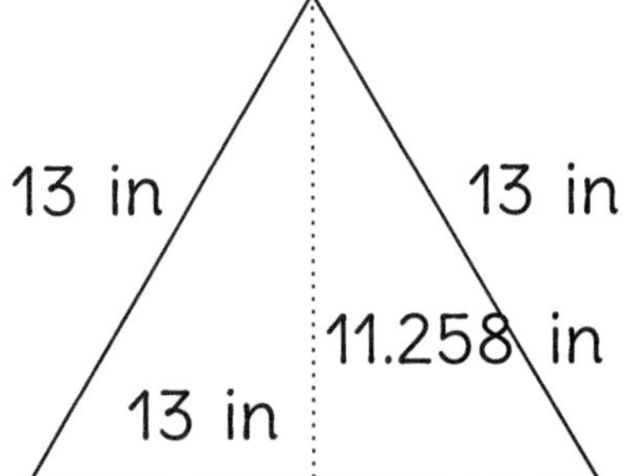

MATH
FLARE
MATH
Name:
Date:

9.

9 in
13 in
16 in
10 in

10.

17 in
16 in
16.24 in
7 in

11.

8 in
5 in
6 in
5 in
3 in

12.

4 in
4 in
11 in
15 in

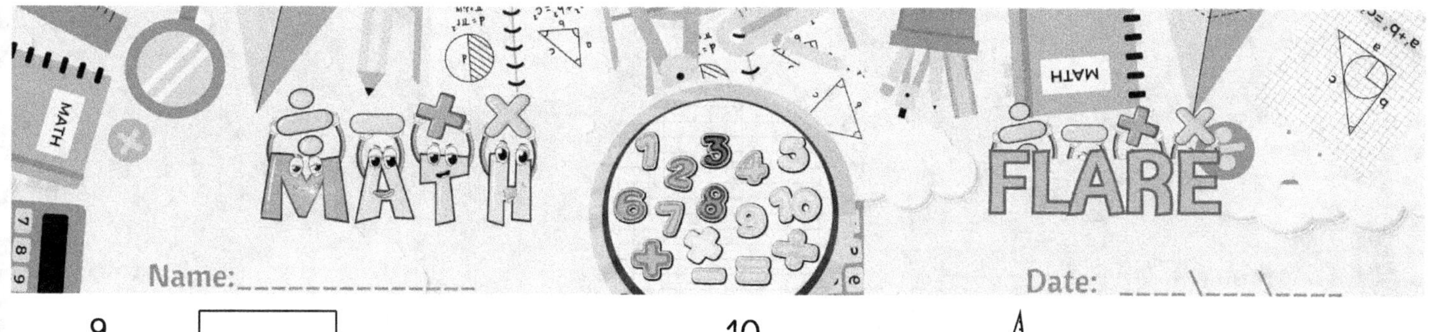

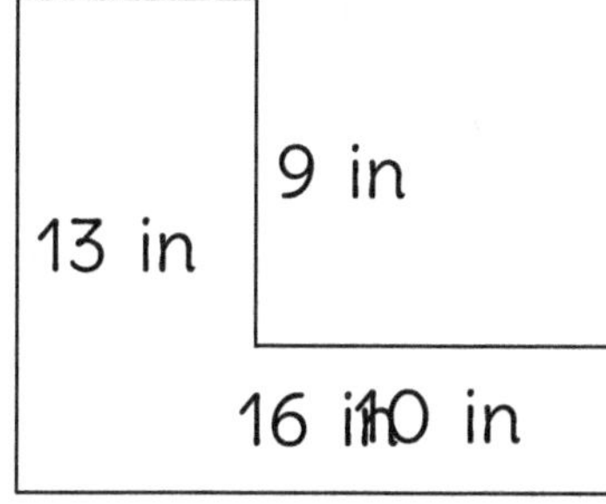

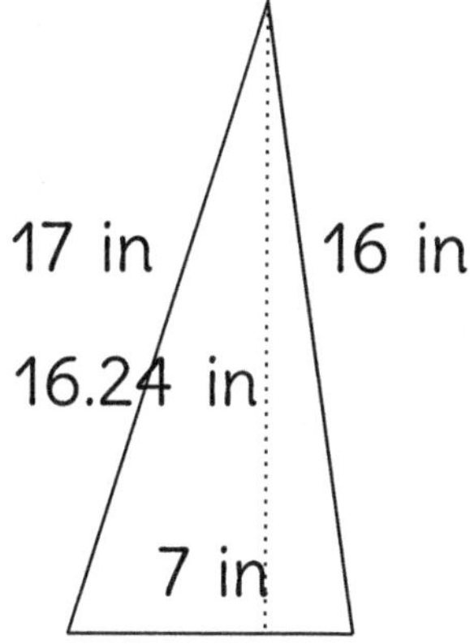

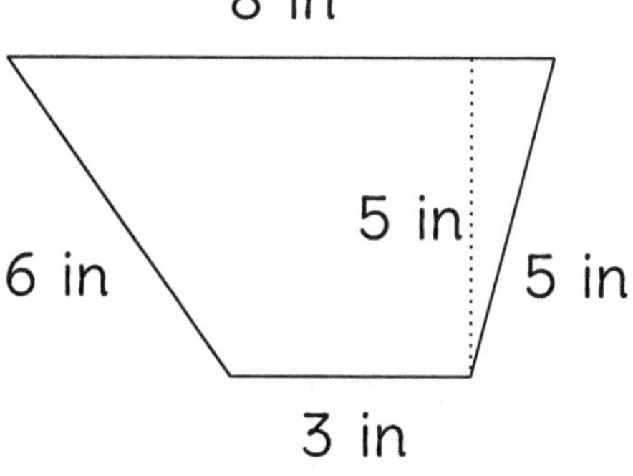

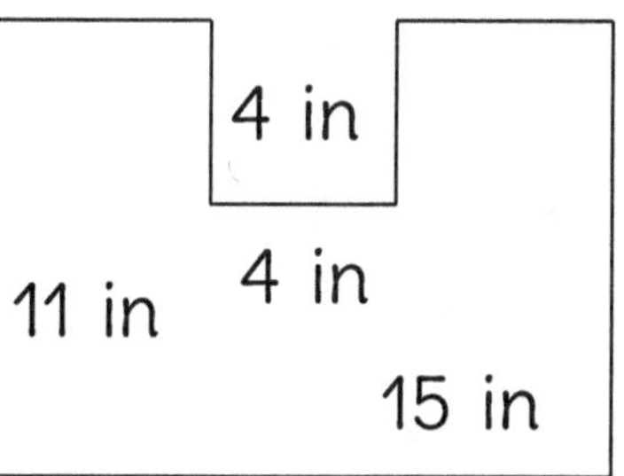

Name:
Date:

13.

11 in
7 in
3 in
7 in

14.

2 in
12 in
11 in
12 in
13 in

15.

3 in
7 in
6 in
7 in
9 in

16.

11 in
9 in
4 in
3 in

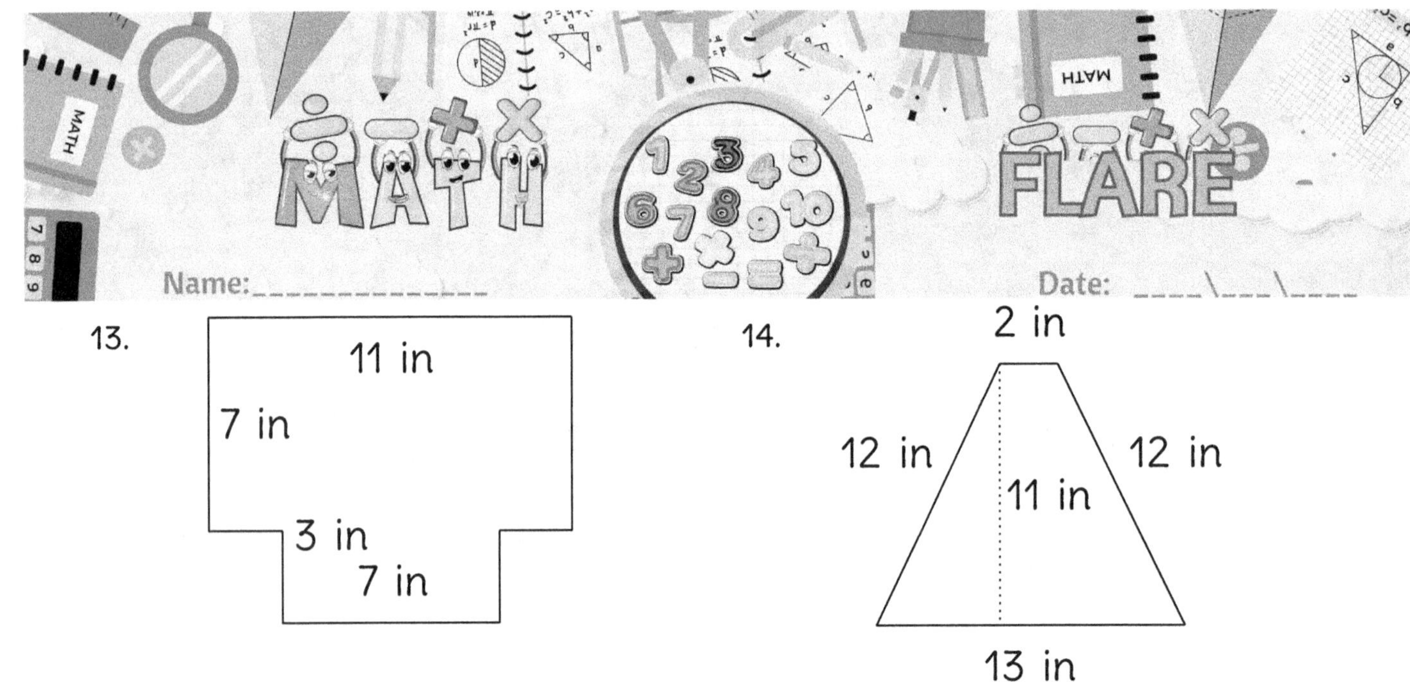

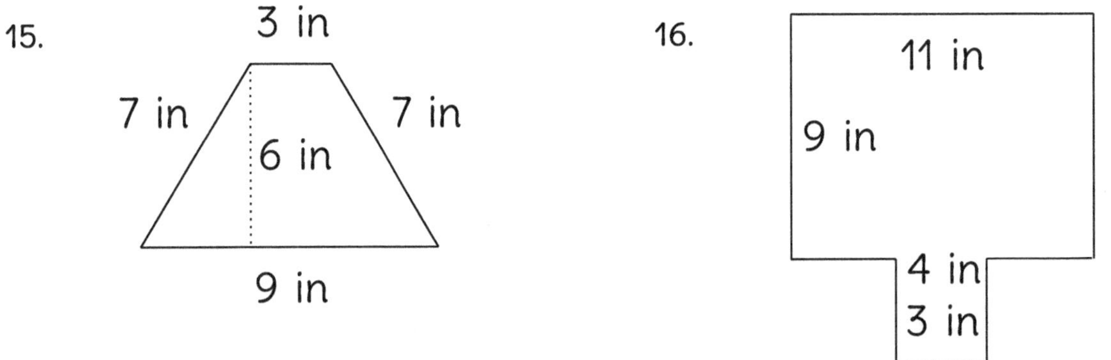

MATH
FLARE
Name:
Date:

17.

16 in
17 in
6 in

18.

6 in
7 in
4 in

19.

15 in
16 in
10 in

20.

11 in
11 in
6 in

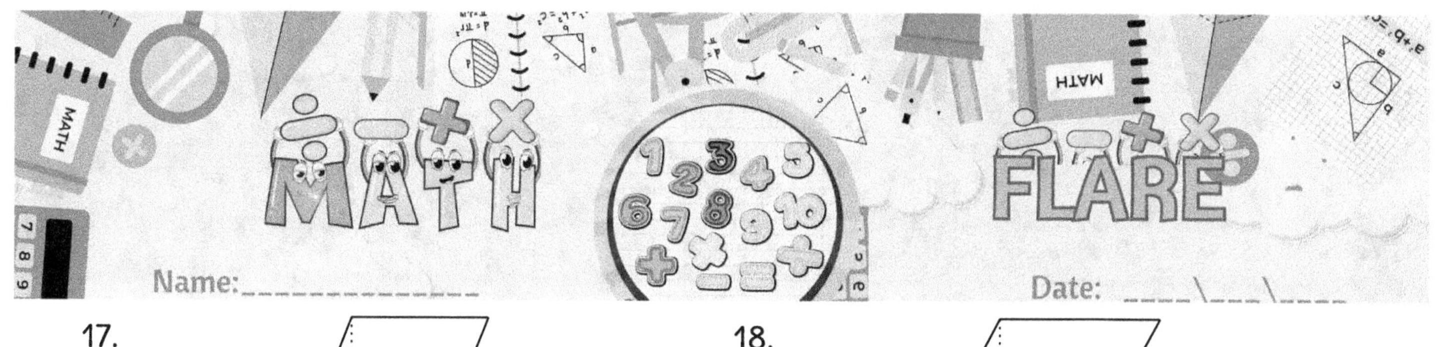

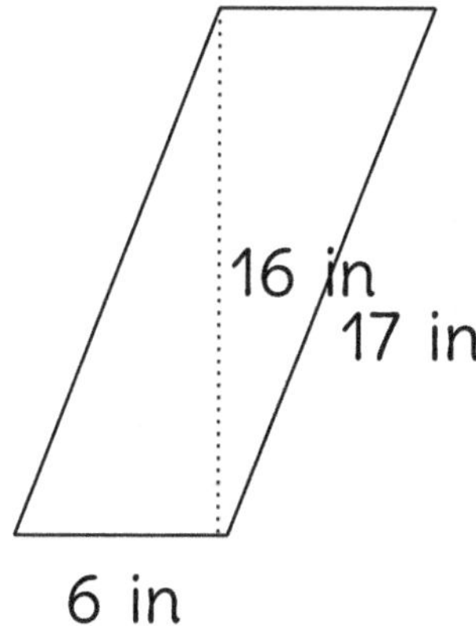

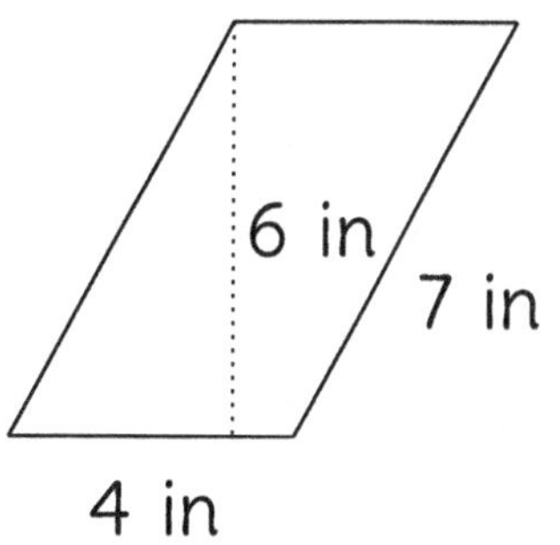

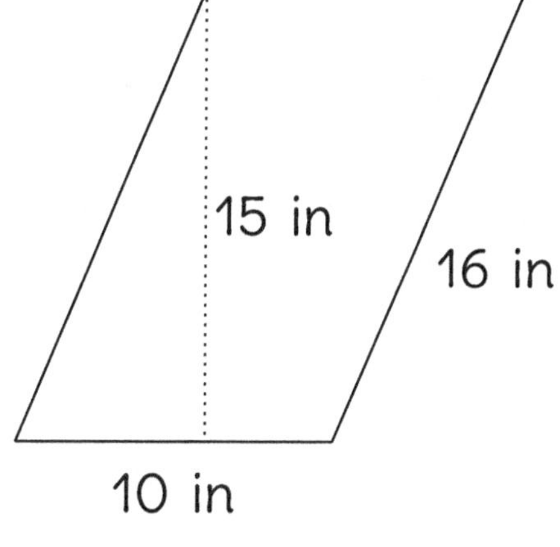

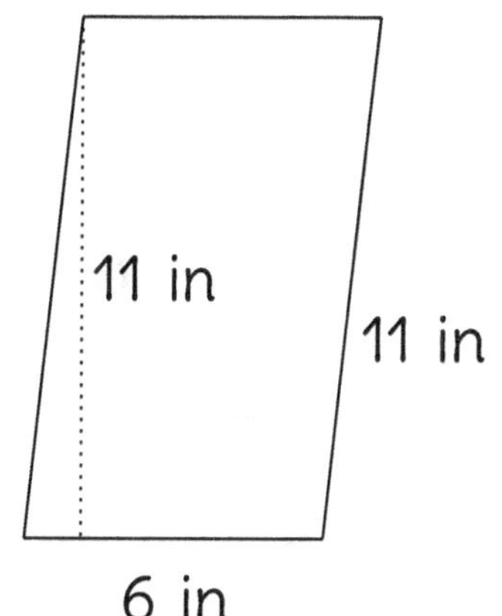

21.

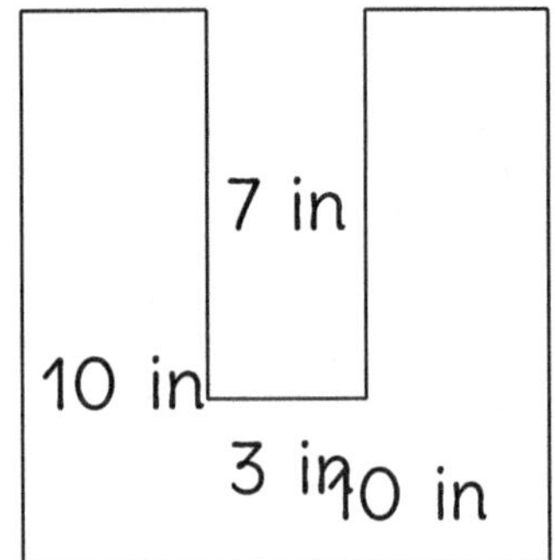

22.

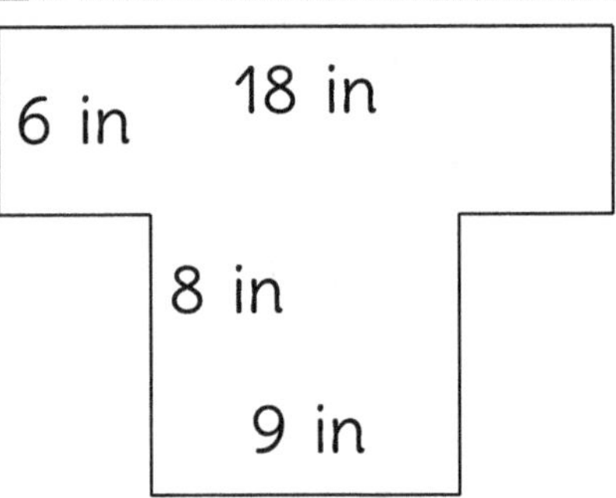

23.

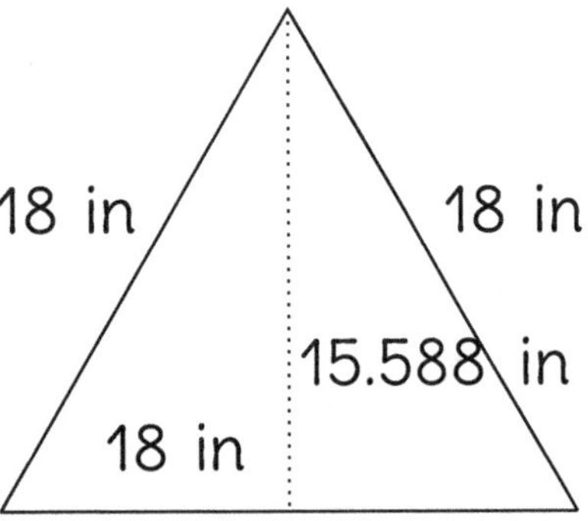

24.

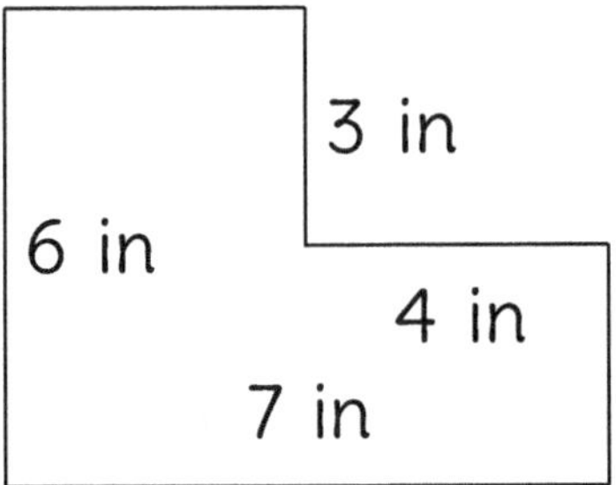

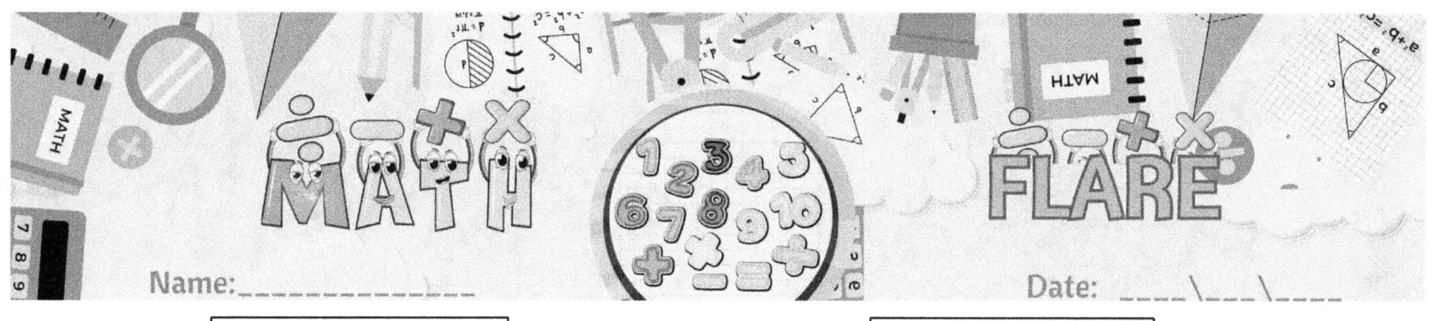

25.

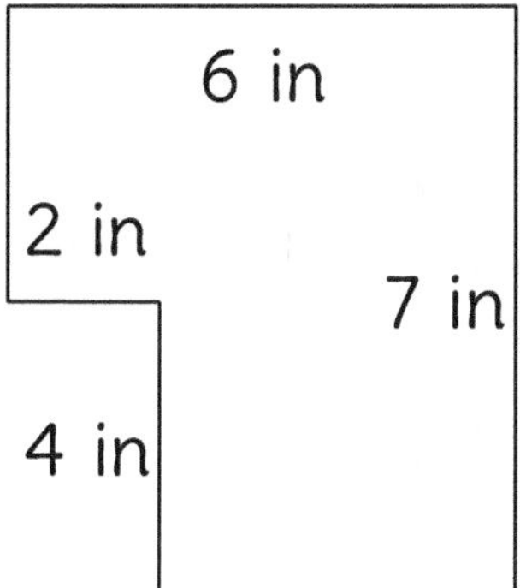

26.

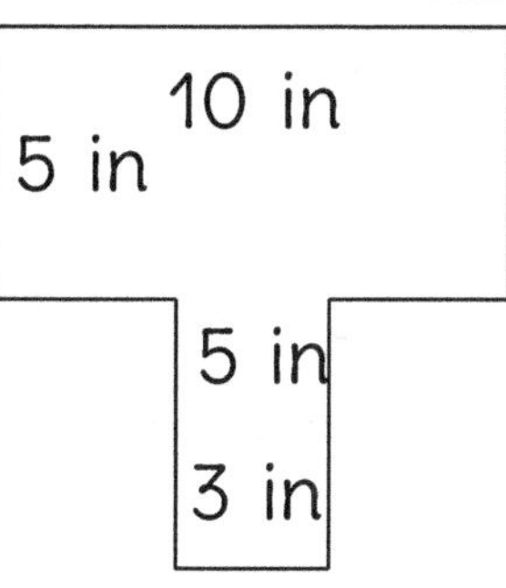

27.

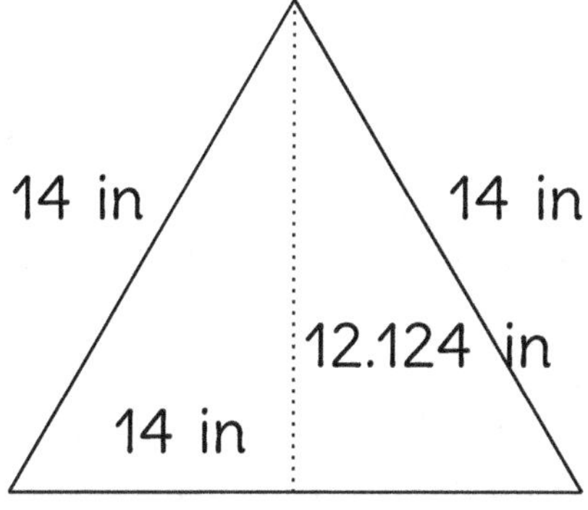

28.

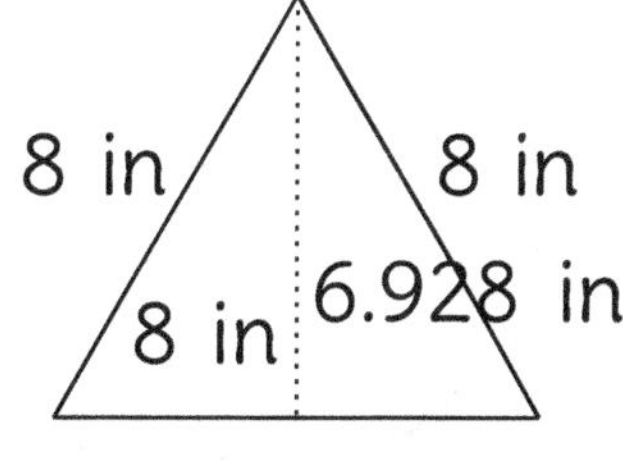

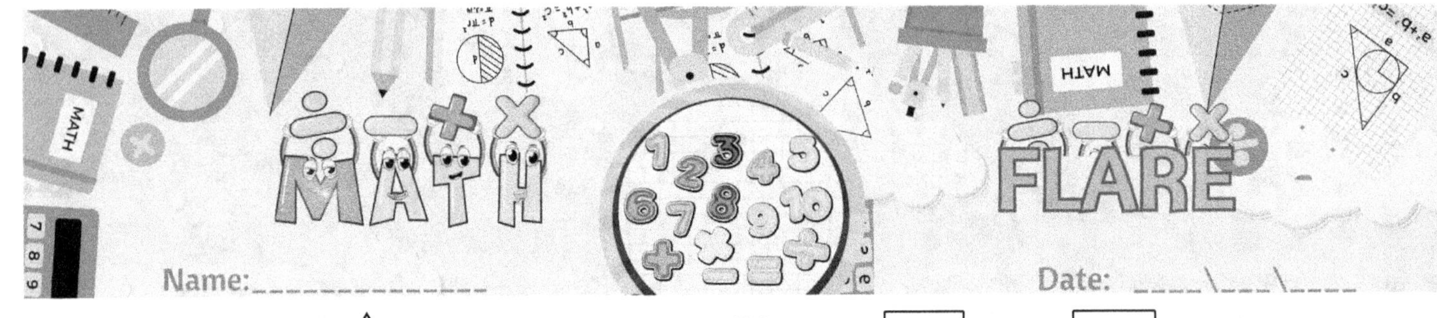

29.

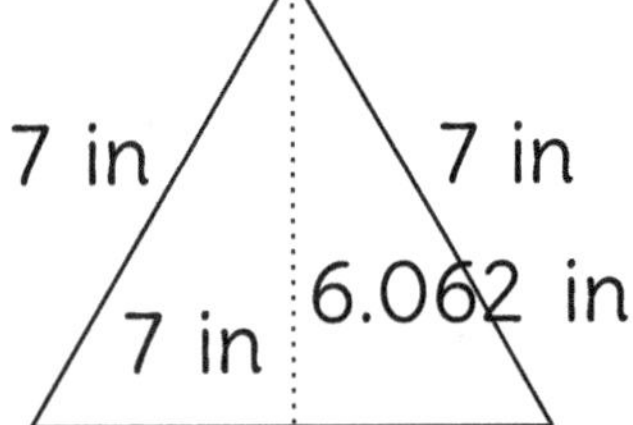

30.

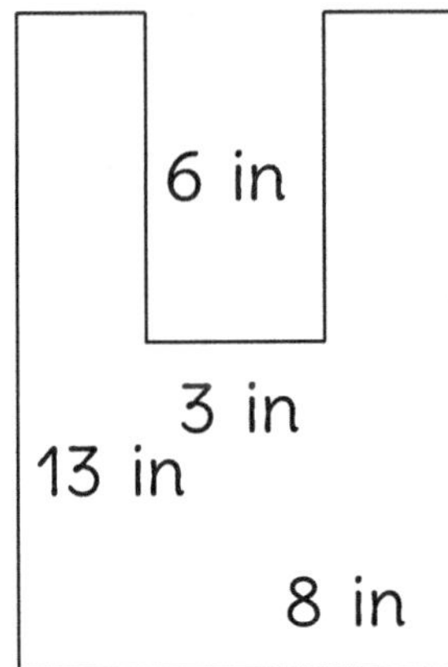

31.

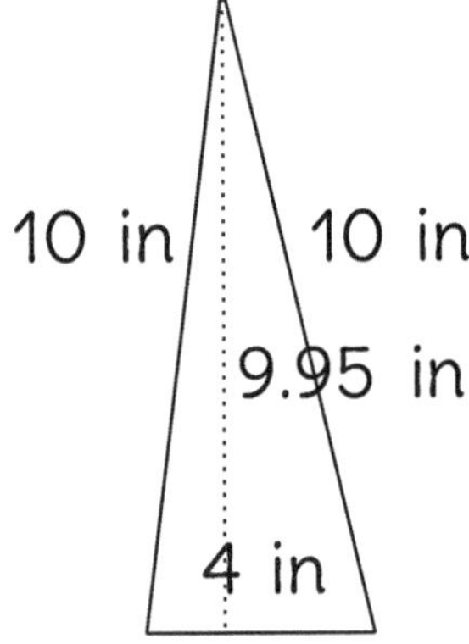

32.

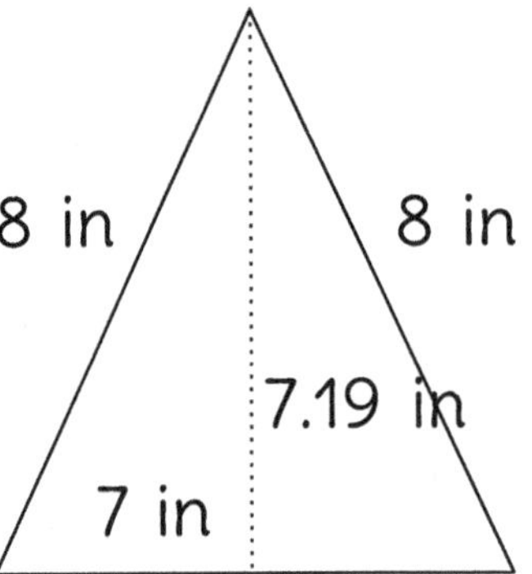

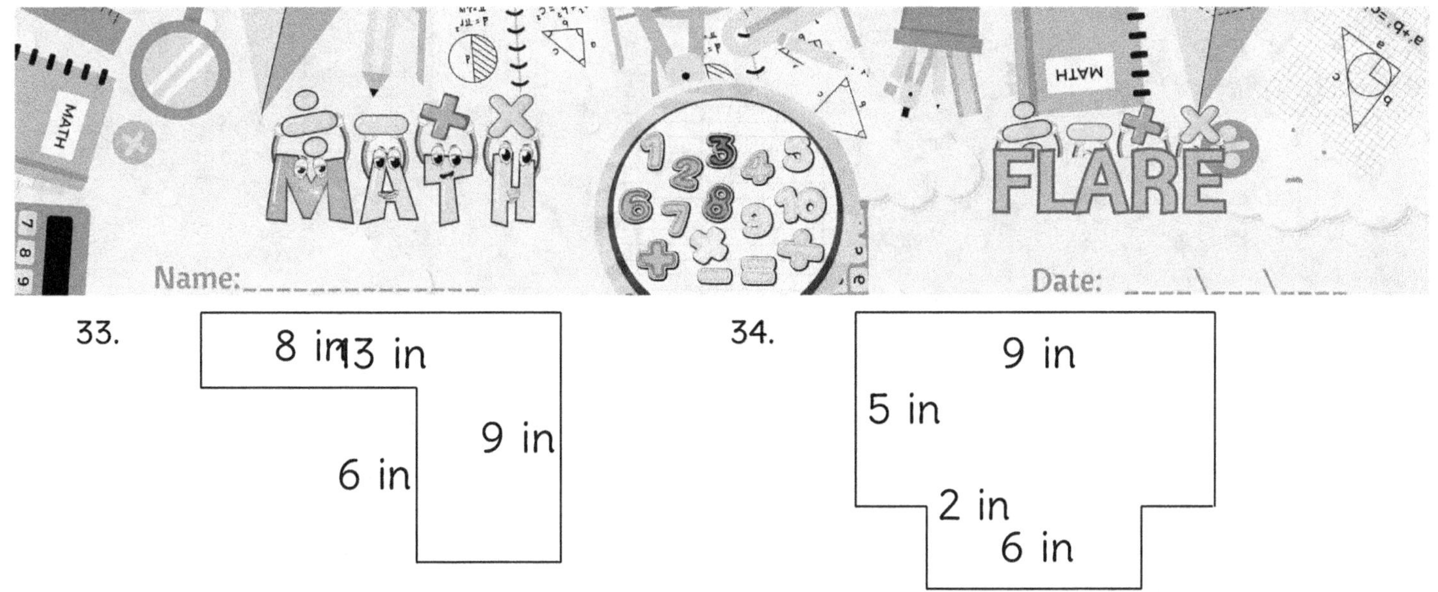

33.

34.

35.

36.
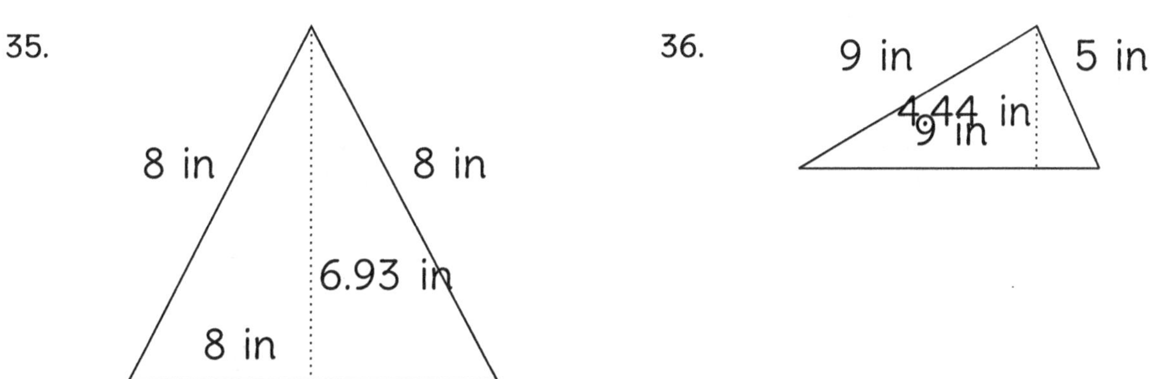

MATH
FLARE
Name:
Date:

37.

7 in
2 in
8 in
5 in

38.

6 in
7 in
6 in

39.

5 in
9 in
5 in
8 in

40.

7 in
7 in
6.062 in
7 in

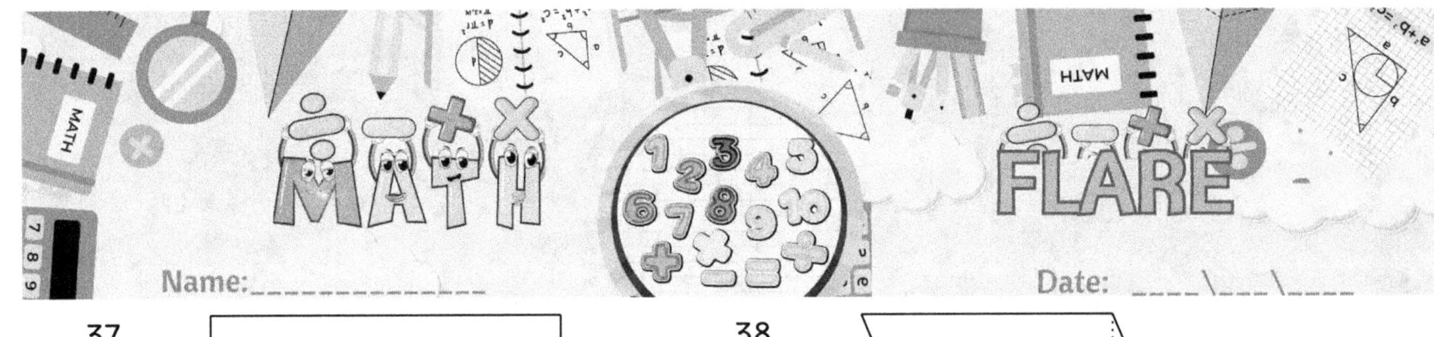

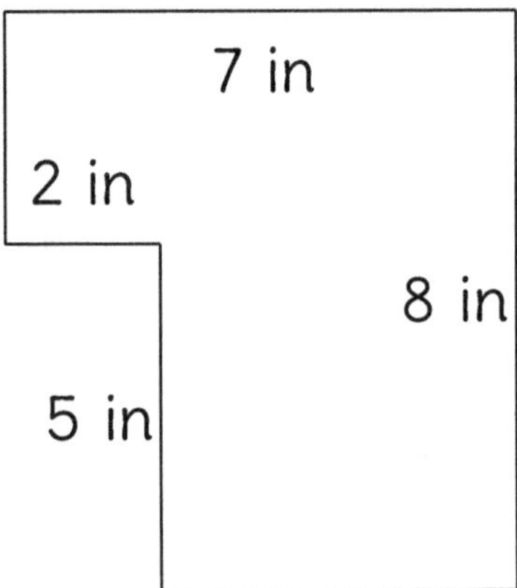

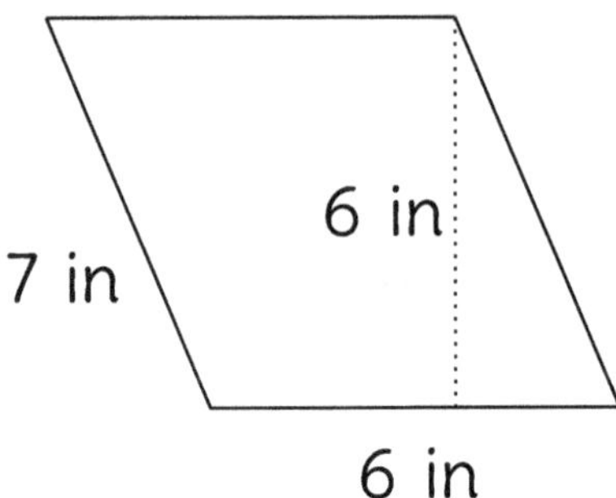

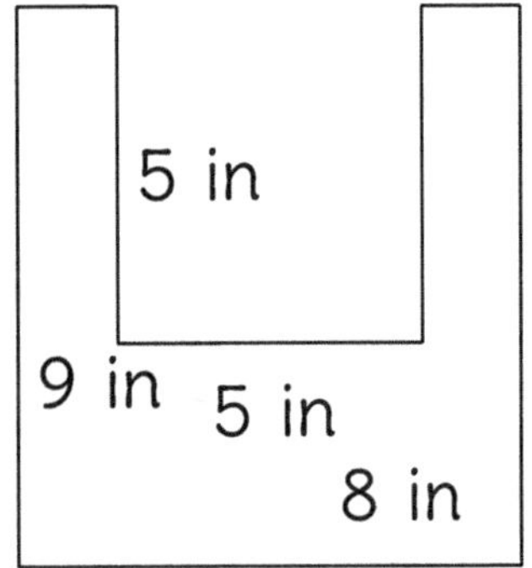

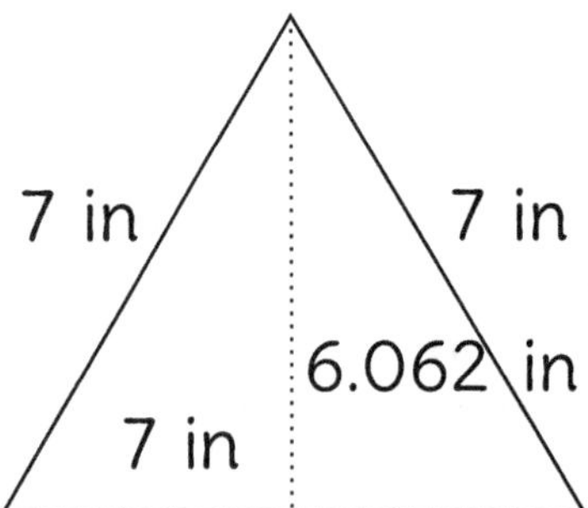

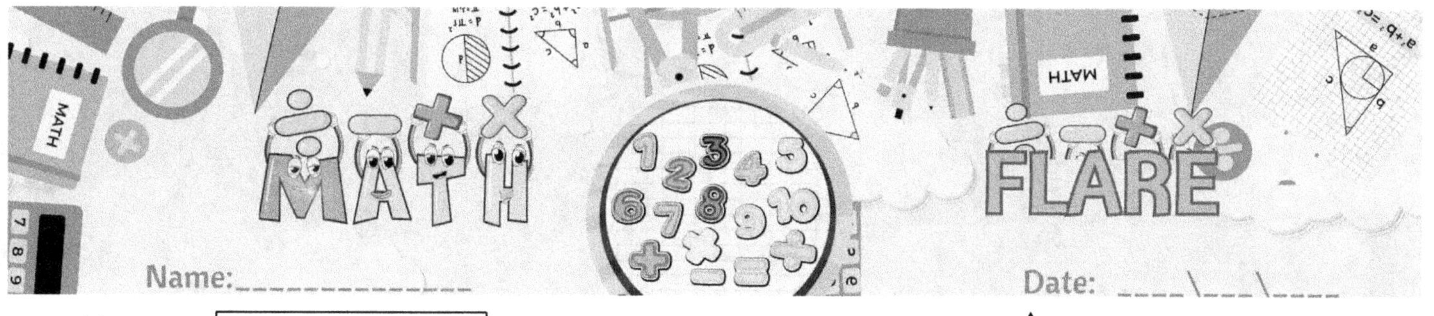

41.

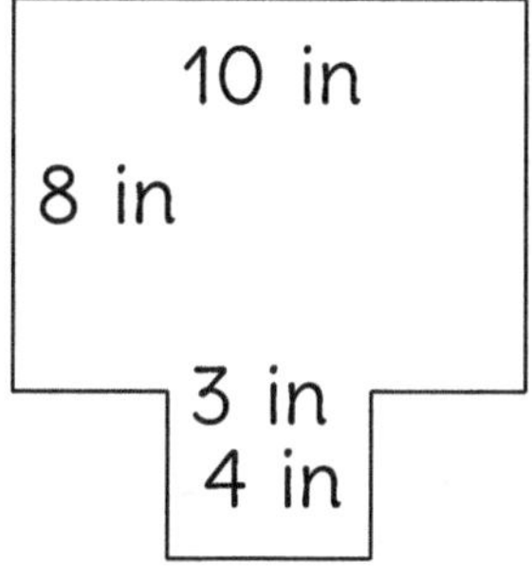

42.

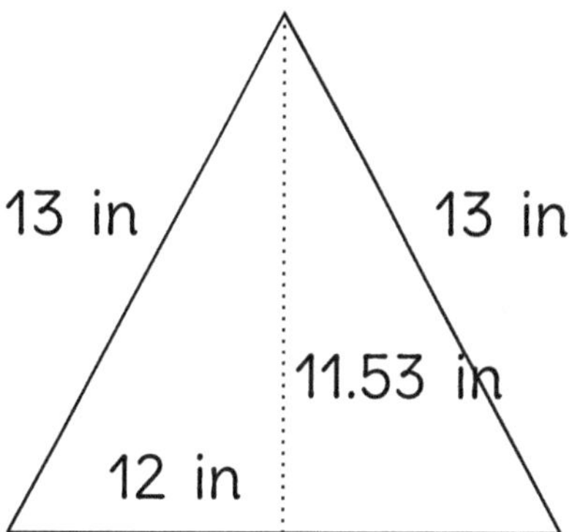

43.

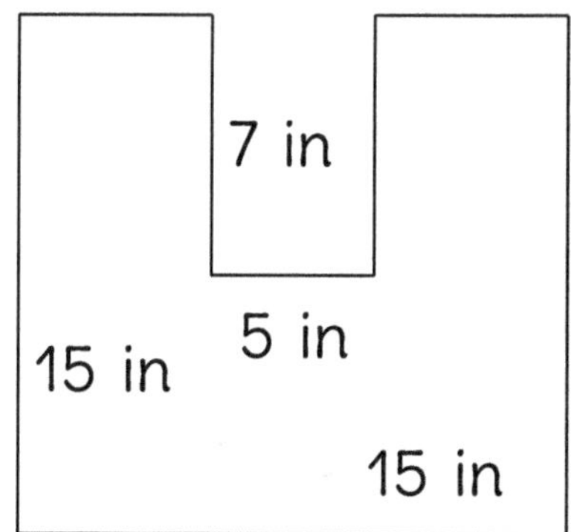

44.

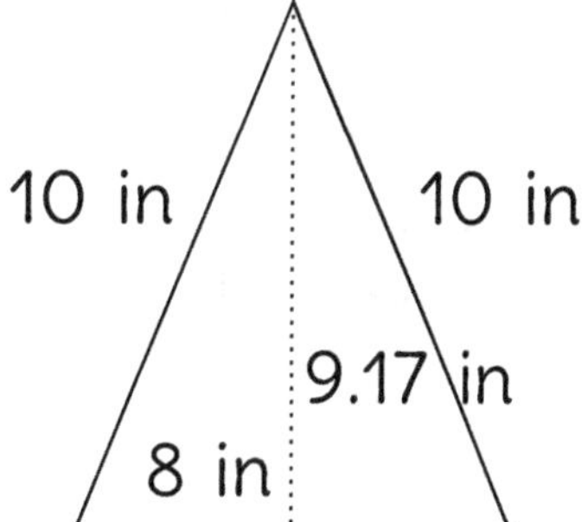

MATH
FLARE
Name:
Date:

45.

6 in
7 in
4 in

46.

7 in
7 in
7 in

47.

7 in
9 in
4 in
9 in

48.

9 in
9 in
7 in

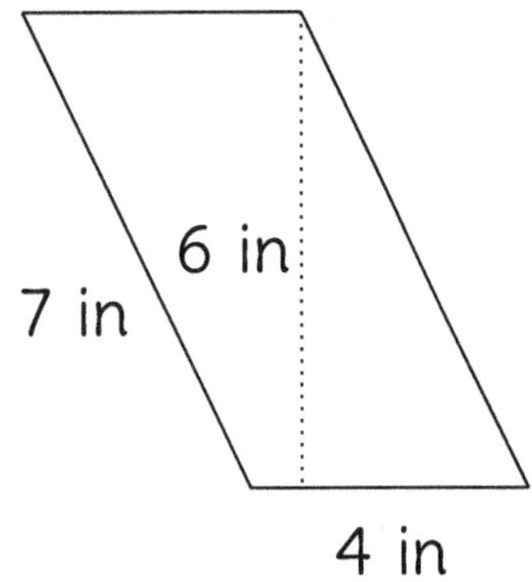

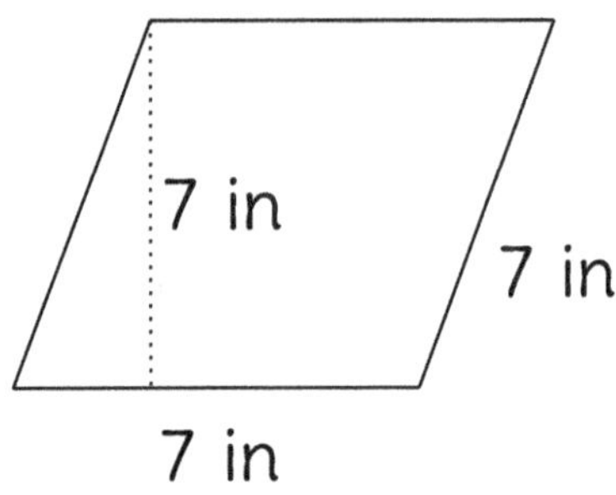

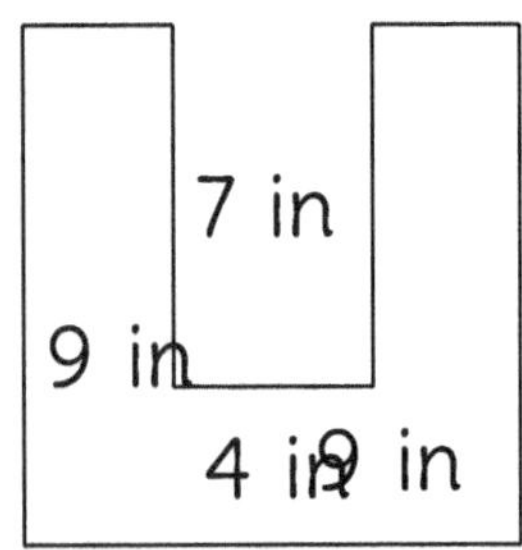

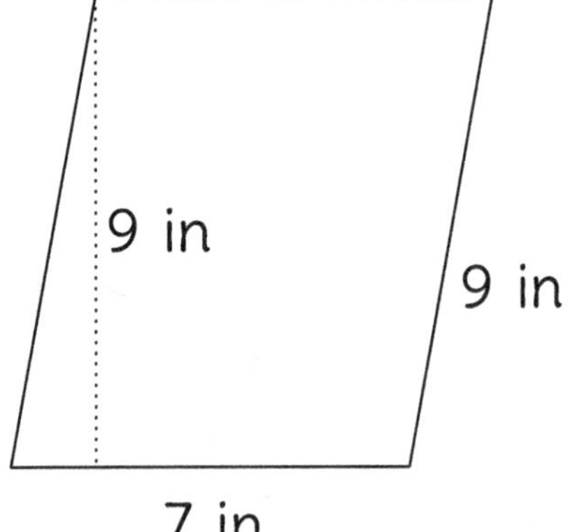

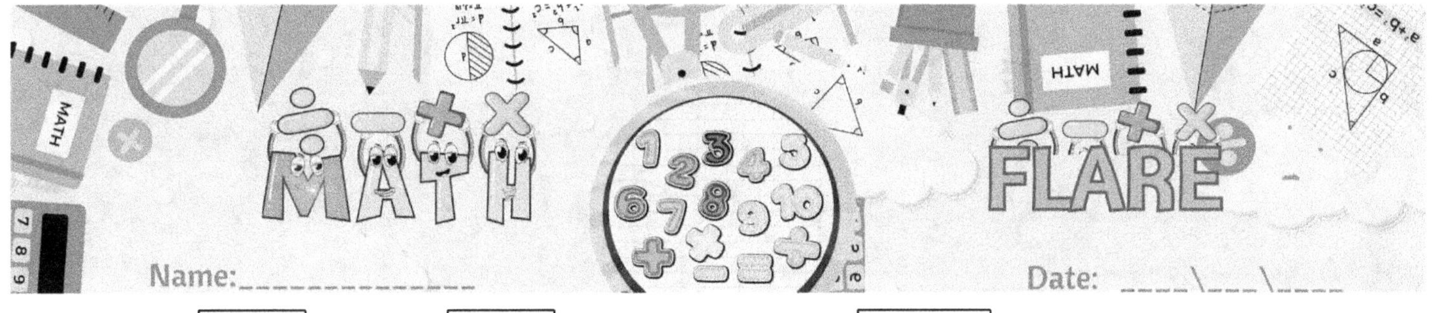

49.

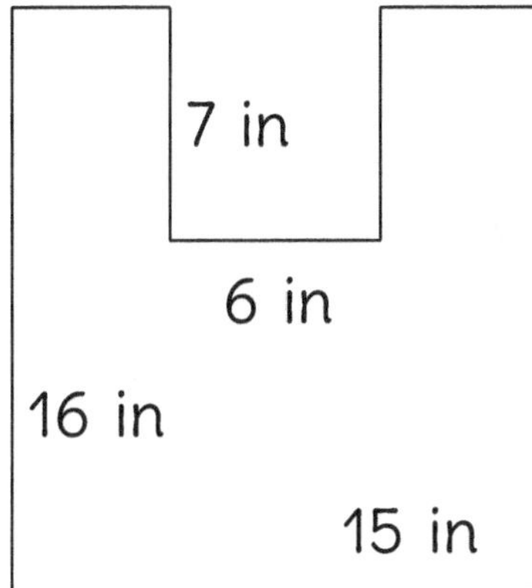

50.

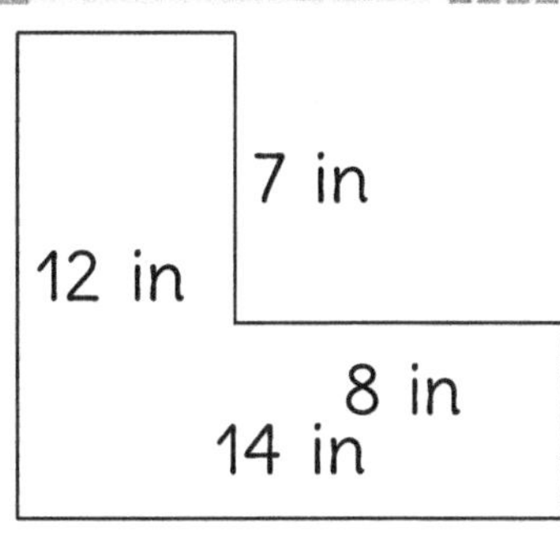

51.

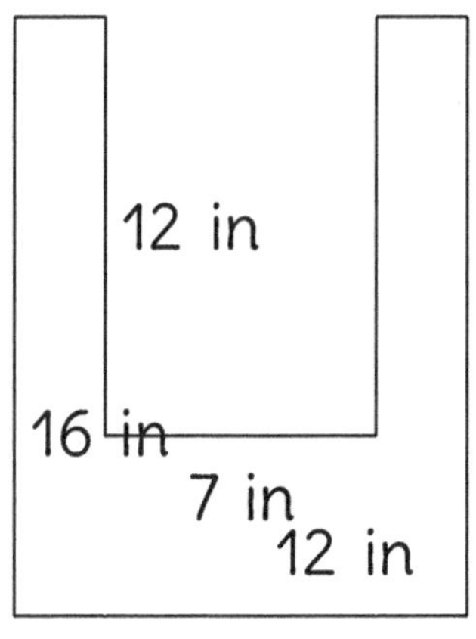

52.

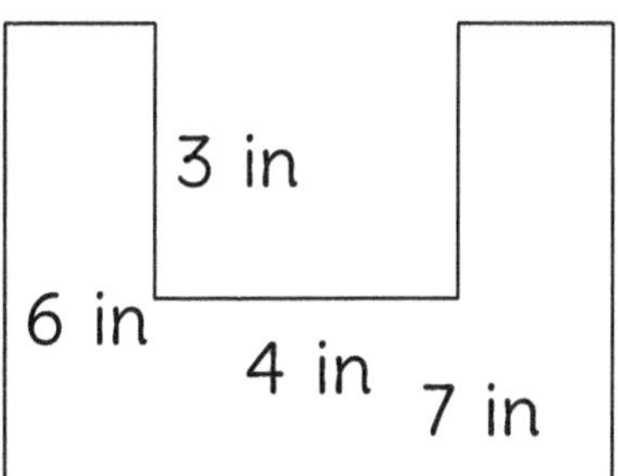

MATH
FLARE
MATH
Name:
Date:

53.

18 in
11 in
12 in
12 in
11 in

54.

7 in
7 in
6.54 in
5 in

55.

9 in
11 in
7 in

56.

12 in
7 in
3 in
3 in

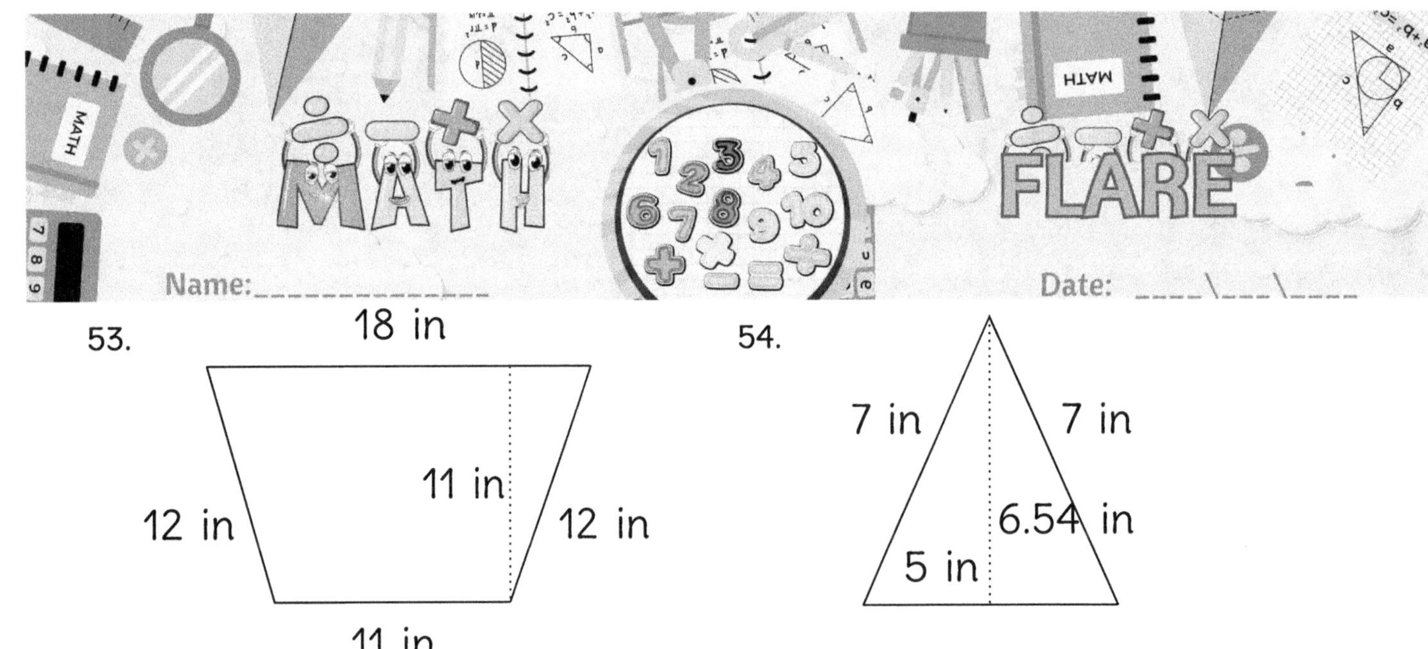

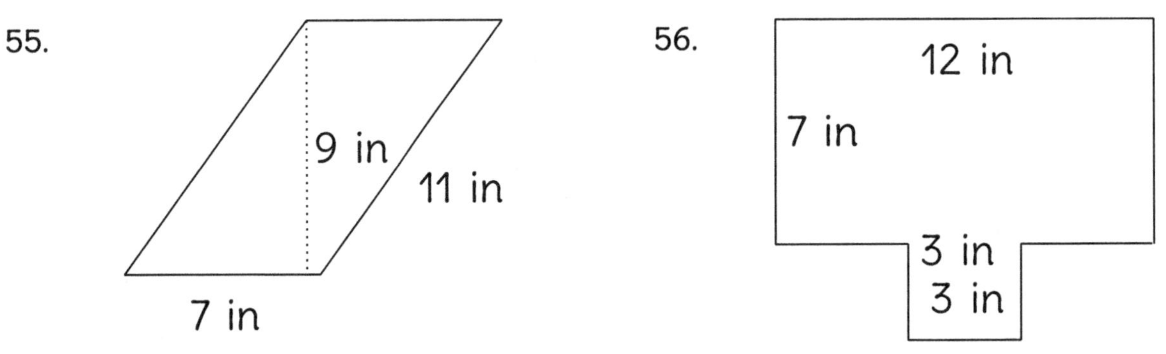

MATH
FLARE
Name:________________
Date: ____________

57.

8 in
12 in
14 in
9 in

58.

8 in
16 in
5 in
15 in

59.

12 in
10 in
11 in
10 in
4 in

60.

9 in
7 in
5 in
4 in

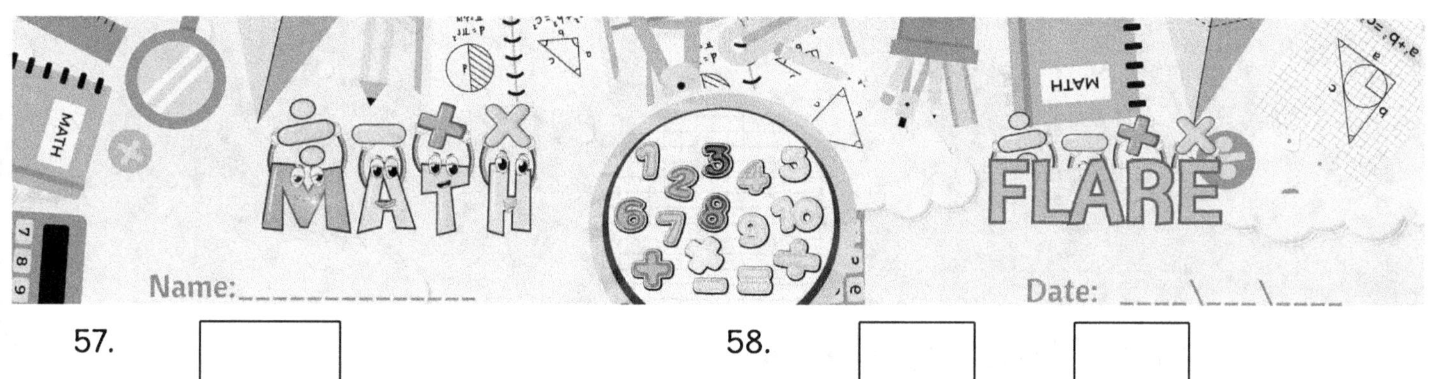

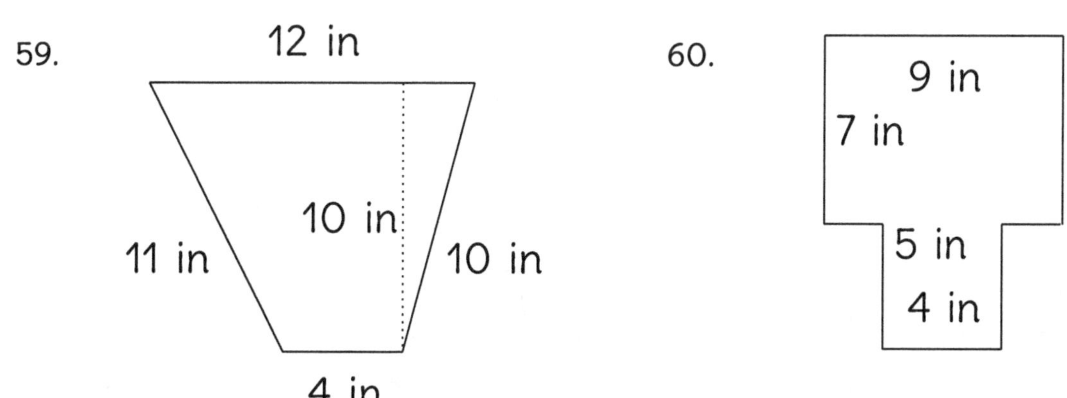

Volume and Surface Area

1.

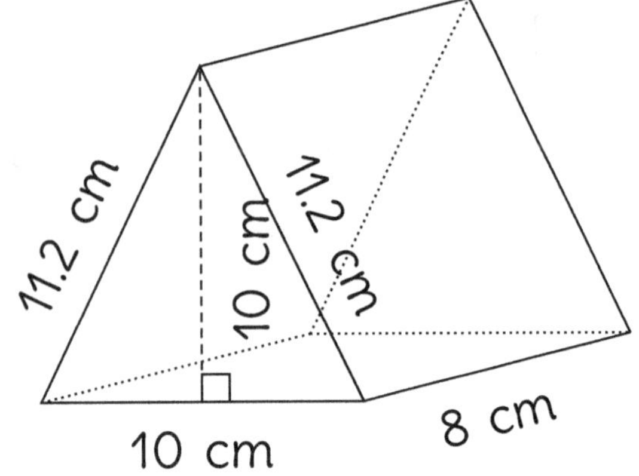

2.

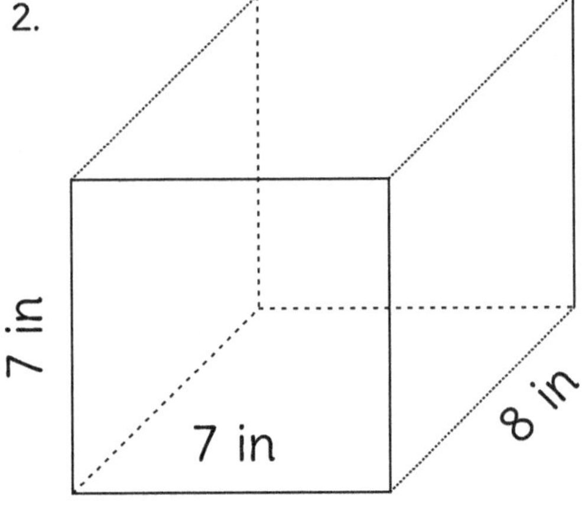

3.

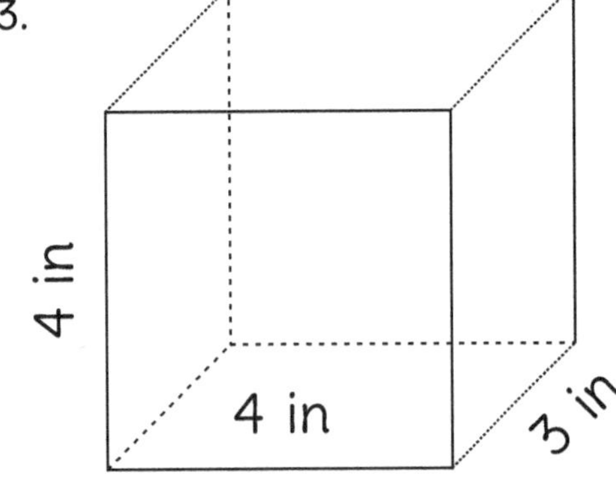

4.

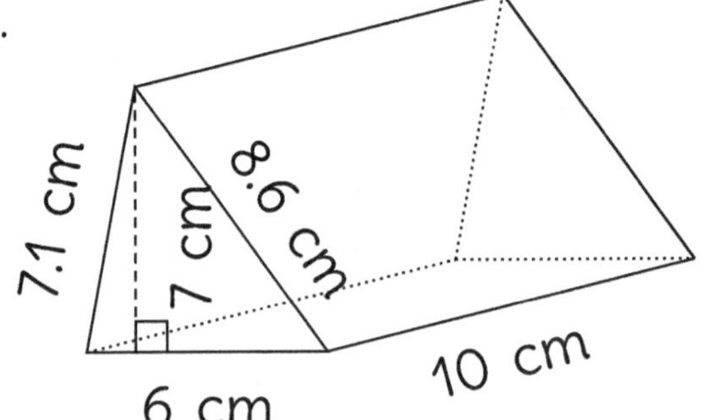

MATH
FLARE
Name:
Date:

5.

2 cm
3 cm
3 cm

6.

8.2 cm
8 cm
9.4 cm
7 cm
9 cm

7.

7 cm
5 cm

8.

9.2 ft
7 ft
6 ft
11 ft

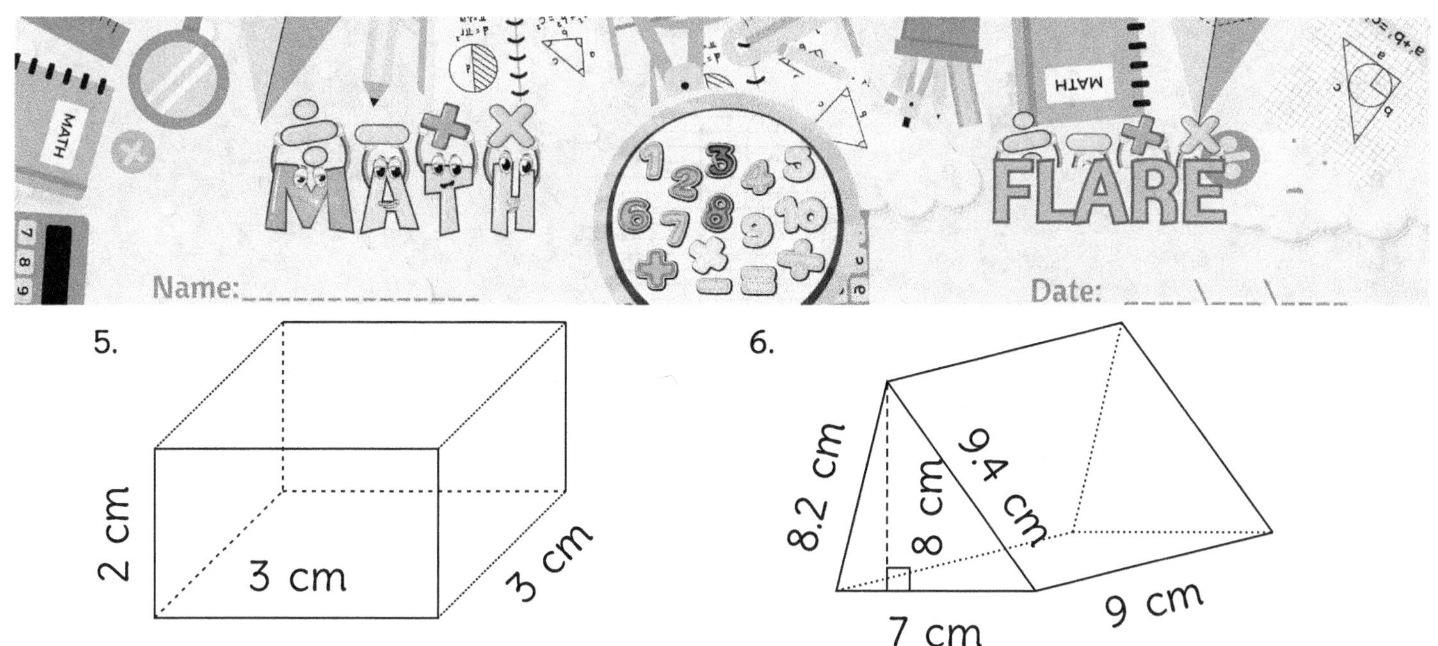

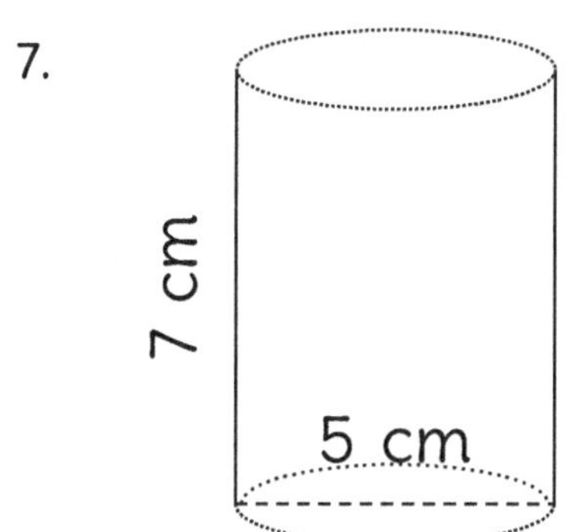

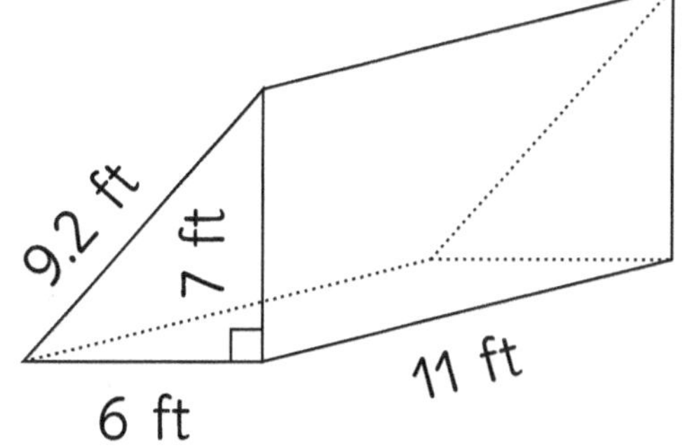

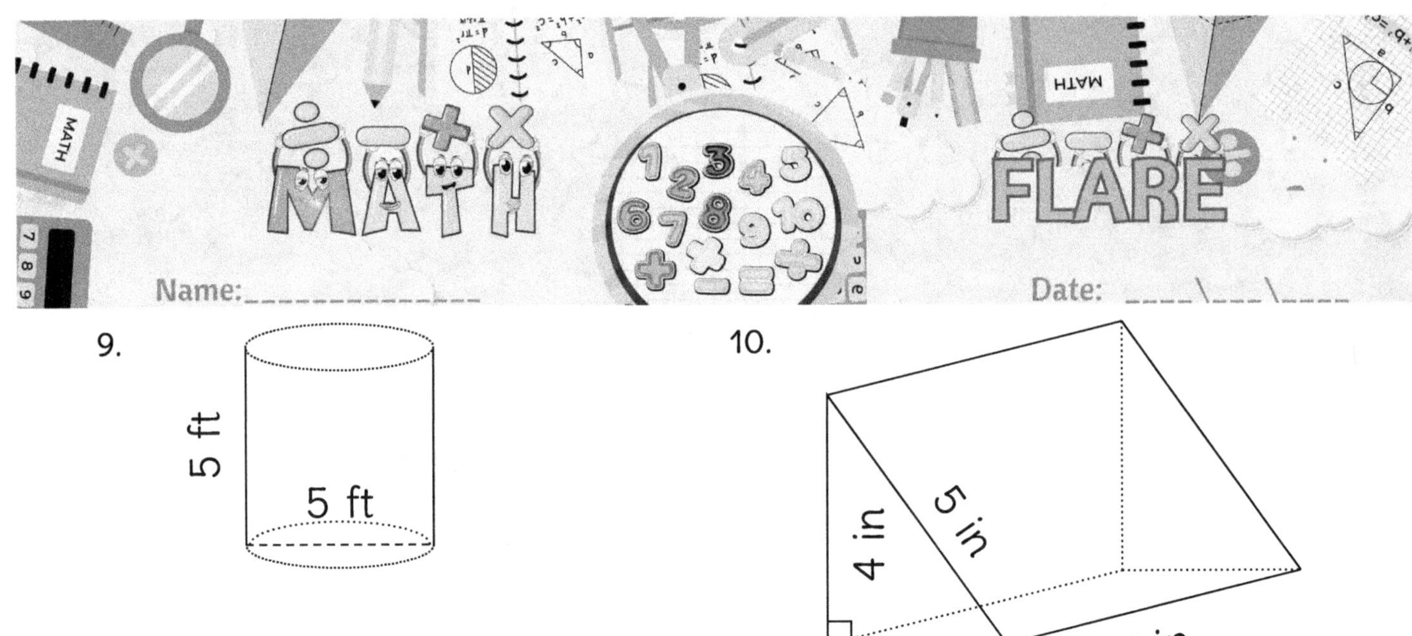

9.
5 ft
5 ft
10.
4 in
5 in
3 in
5 in

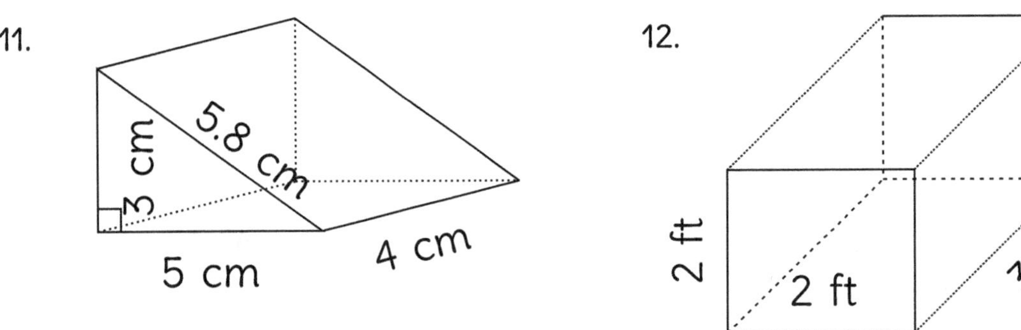

11.
3 cm
5.8 cm
5 cm
4 cm
12.
2 ft
2 ft
3 ft

MATH
FLARE
Name:________________
Date: ______________

13.

3 cm
4 cm
3 cm

14.

5 in
6 in
8 in

15.

4 in
3 in
5 in

16.

5 in
4 in
3 in
4 in

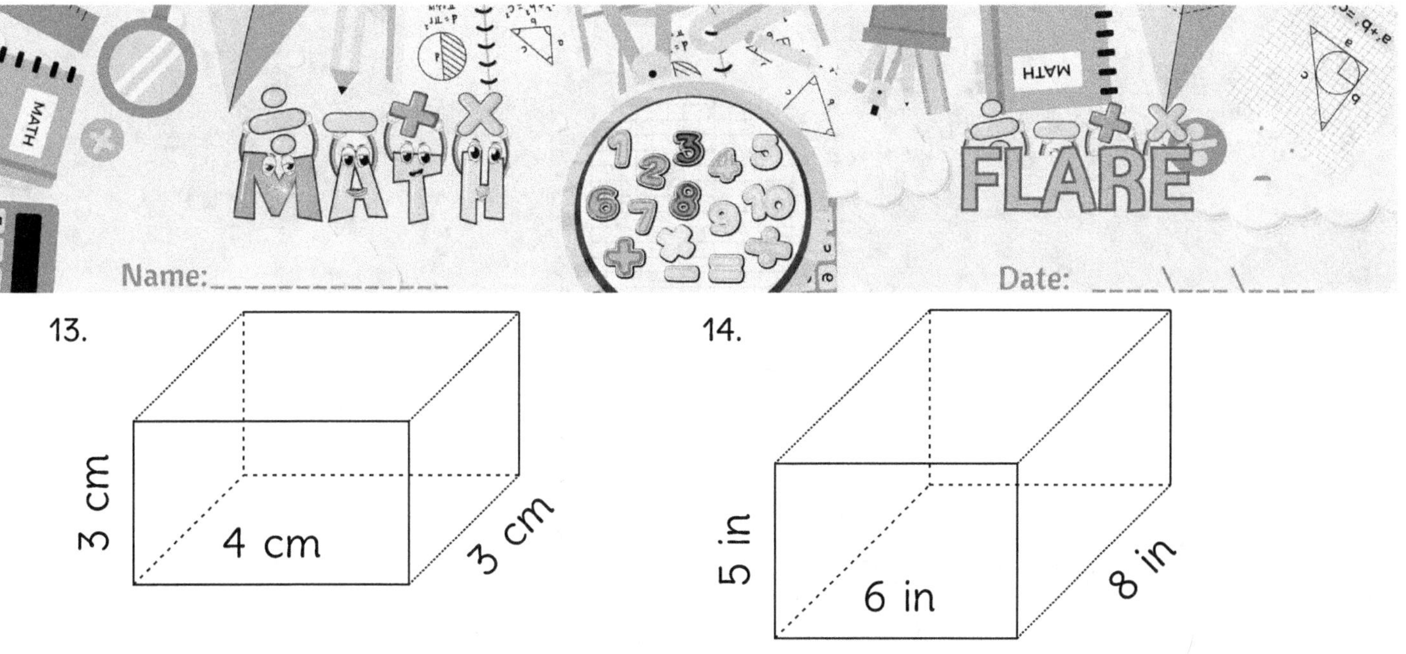

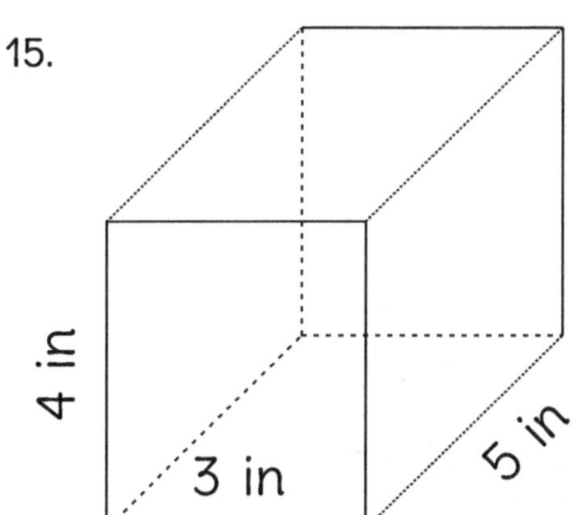

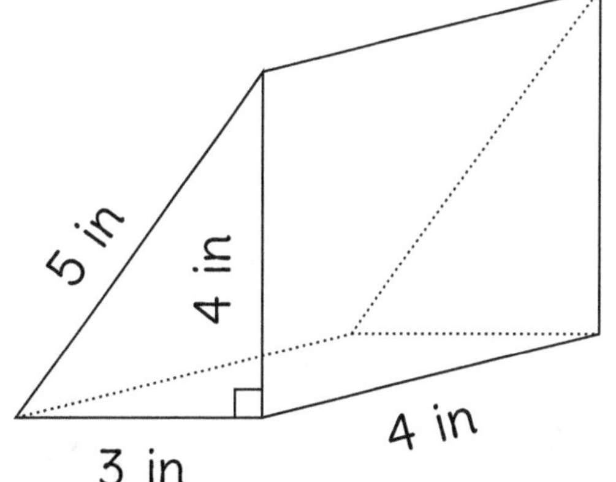

MATH
FLARE
Name:
Date:

17.

9 in
10.8 in
6 in
9 in

18.

10 ft
6 ft

19.

5.7 in
4 in
4 in
4 in

20.

5.8 ft
5 ft
5.1 ft
4 ft
4 ft

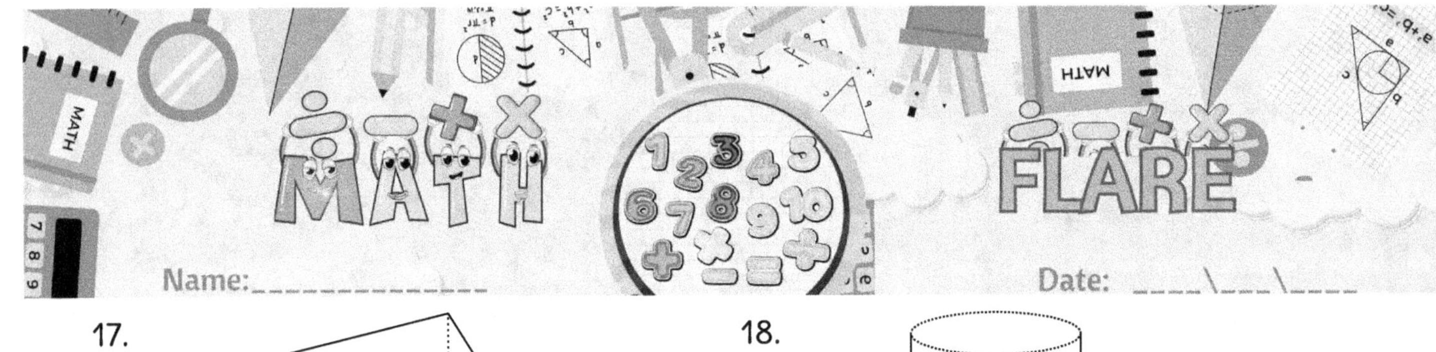

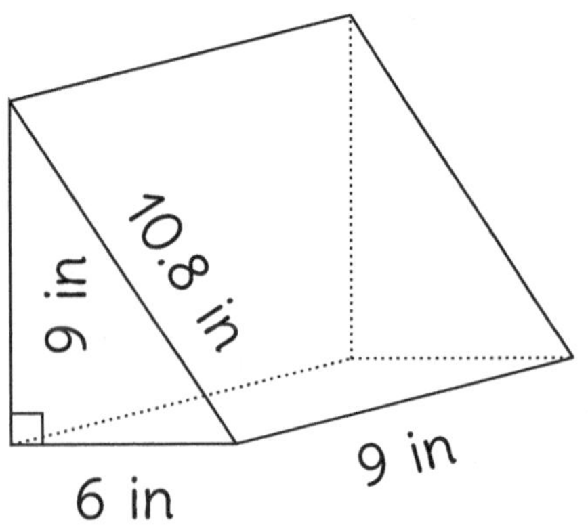

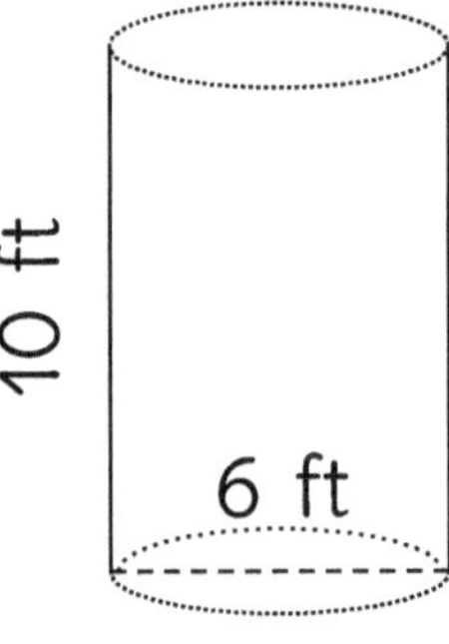

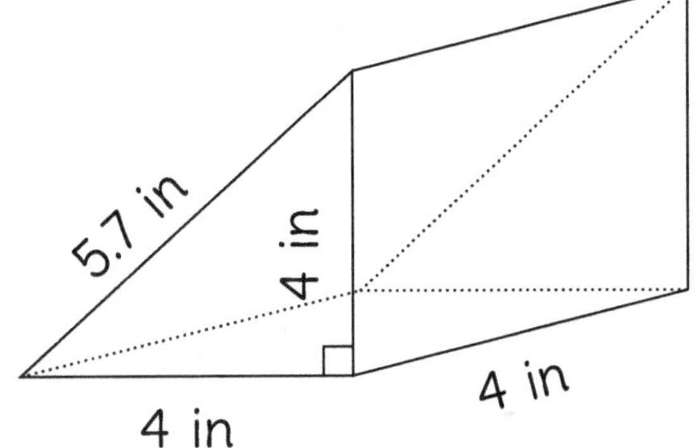

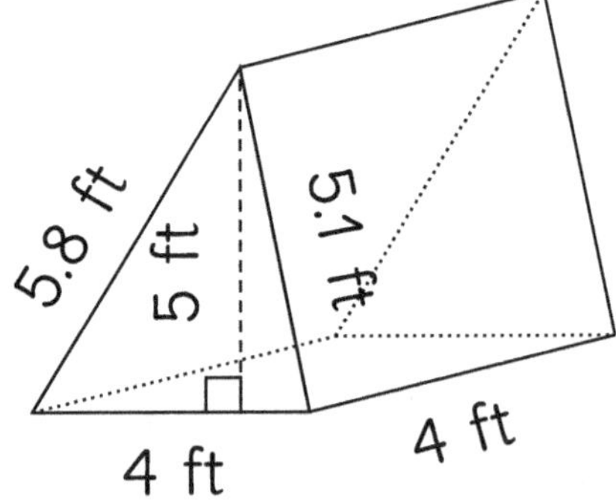

21.

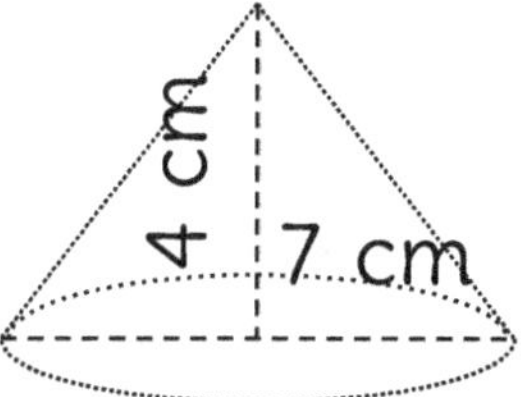

22.

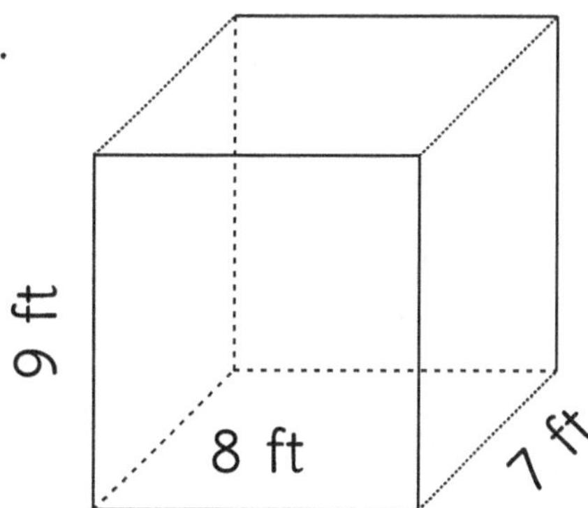

23.

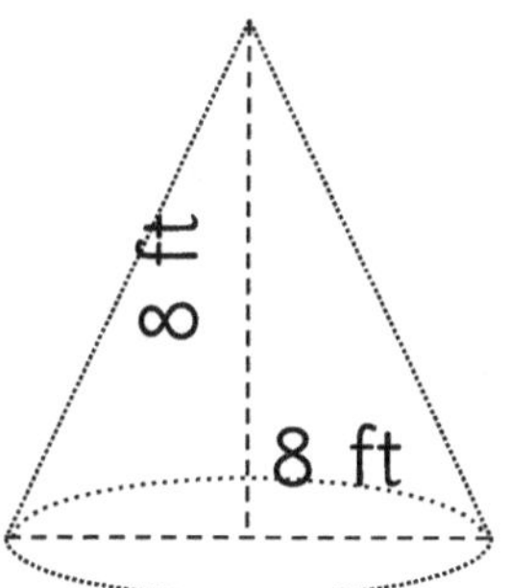

24.

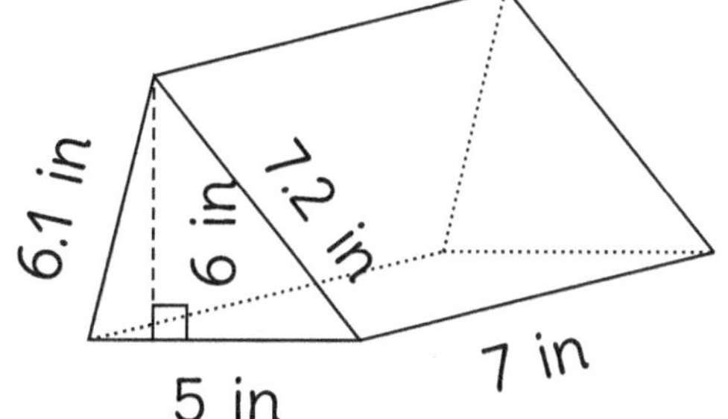

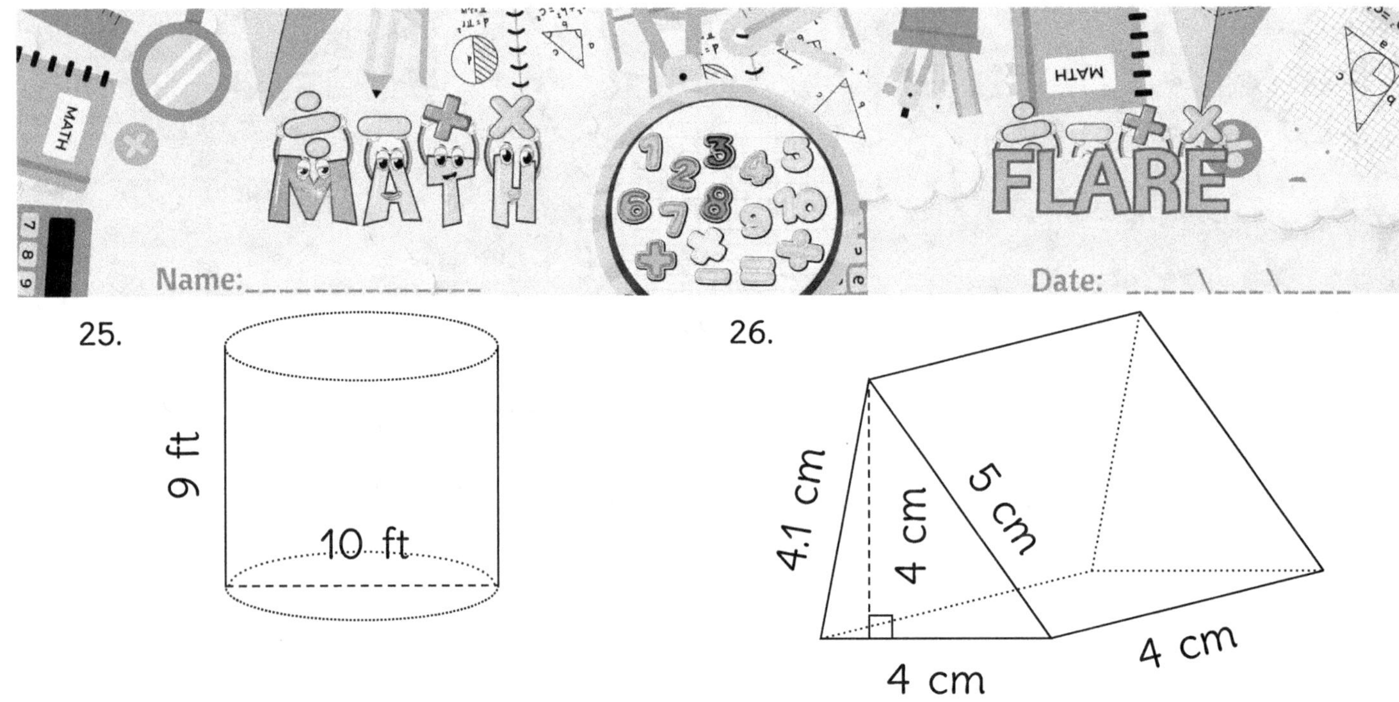

25.

26.

27.

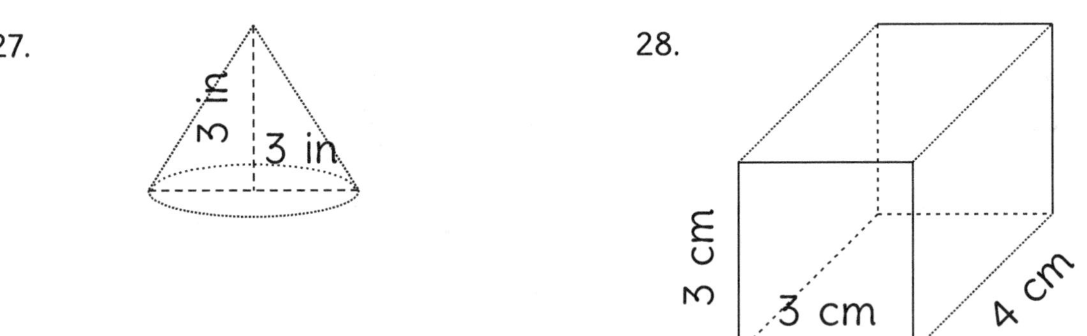

28.

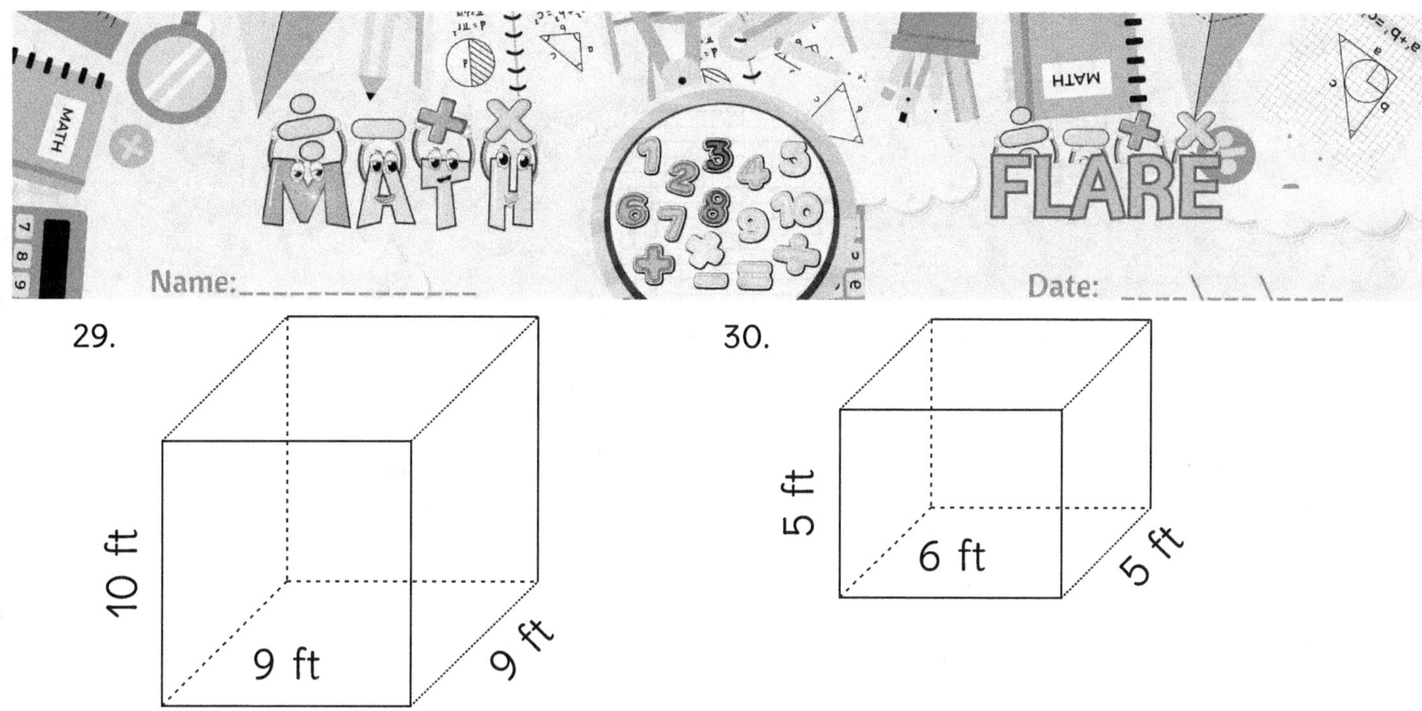

29.

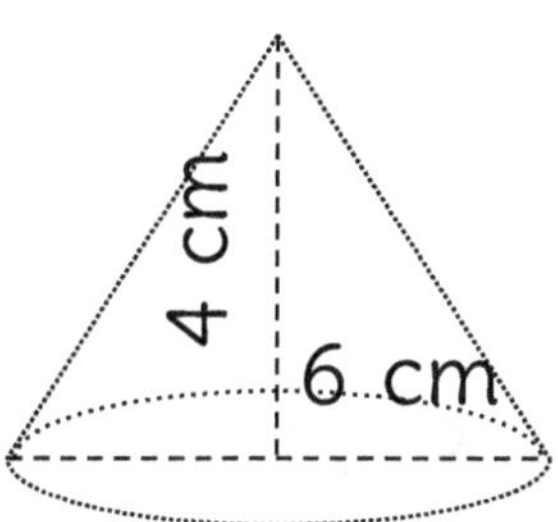

30.

31.

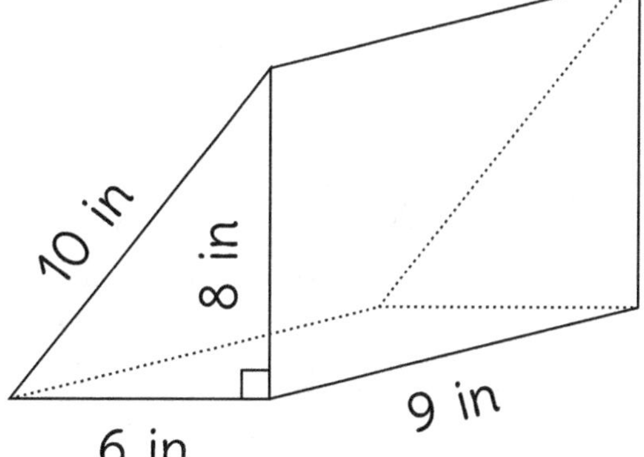

32.

33.

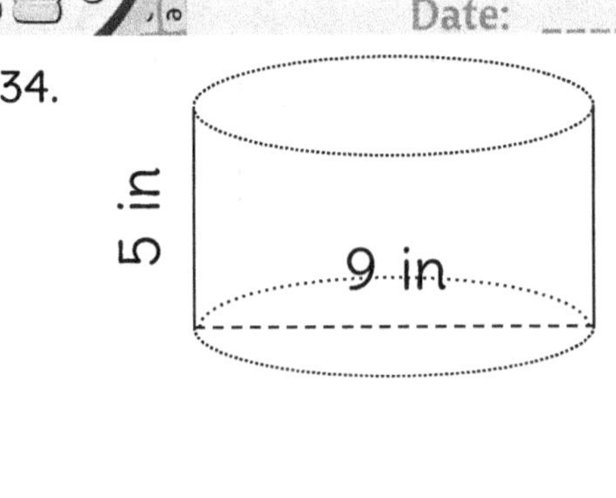

34.

35.

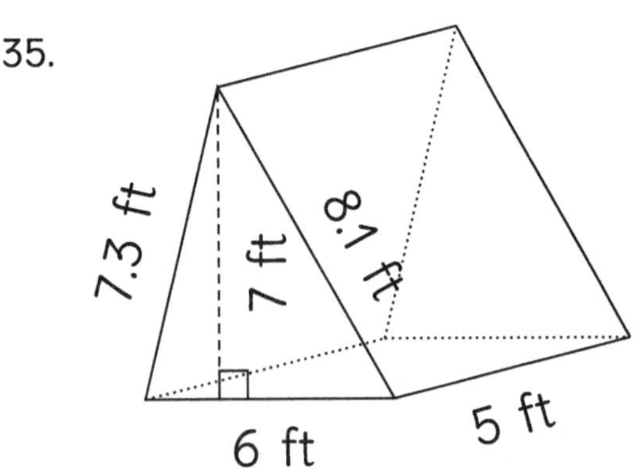

36.

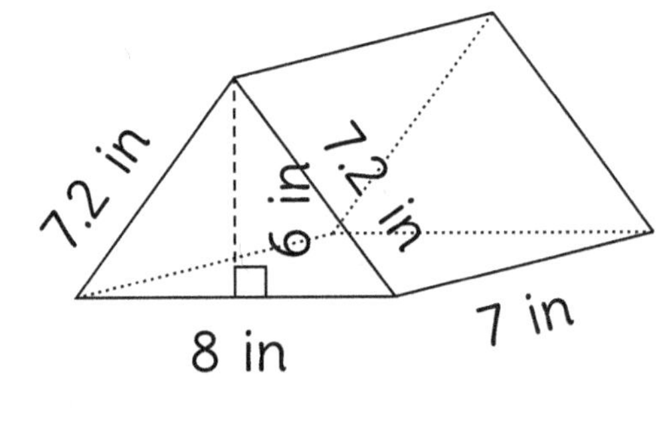

MATH
FLARE
MATH
Name:
Date:

37.

6 in
7 in

38.

7.6 in
7 in
7.6 in
6 in
8 in

39.

8.6 in
7 in
5 in
6 in

40.

7.1 ft
5 ft
7.1 ft
10 ft
7 ft

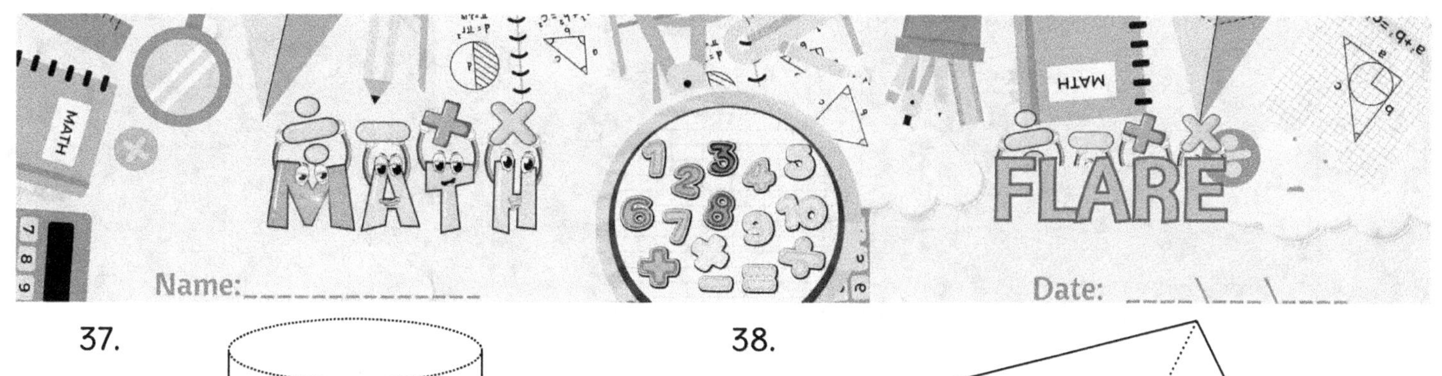

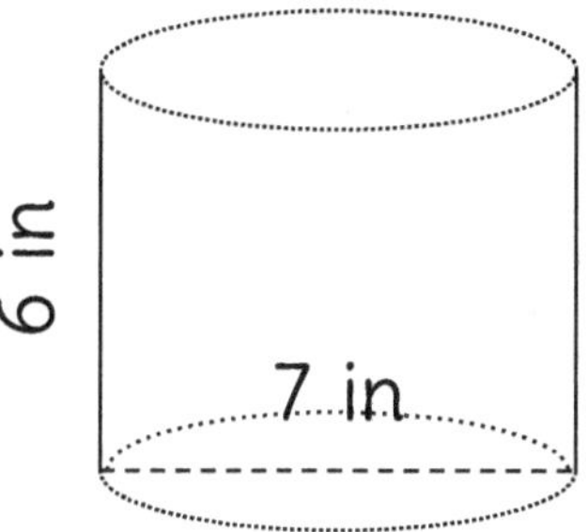

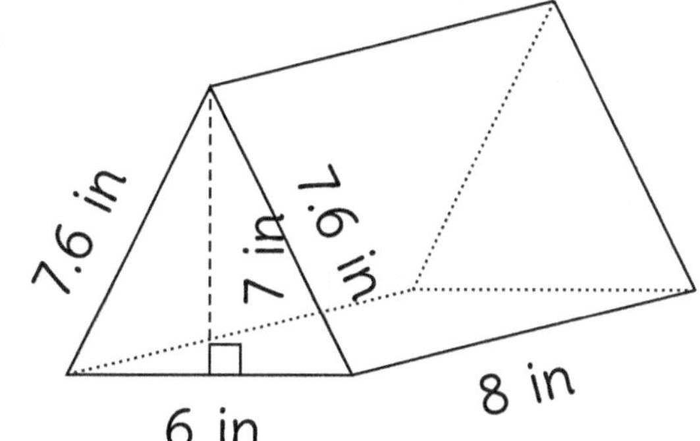

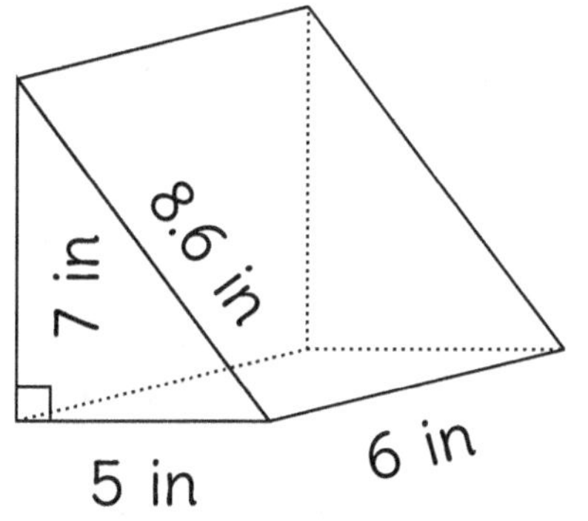

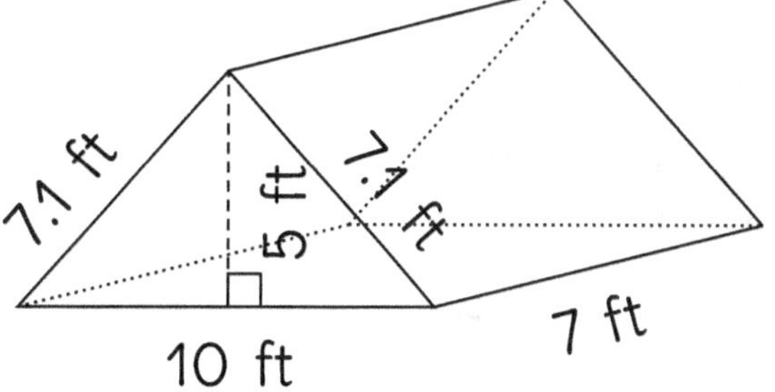

MATH
FLARE
Name: ___________________
Date: ____ \ ___ \ ____

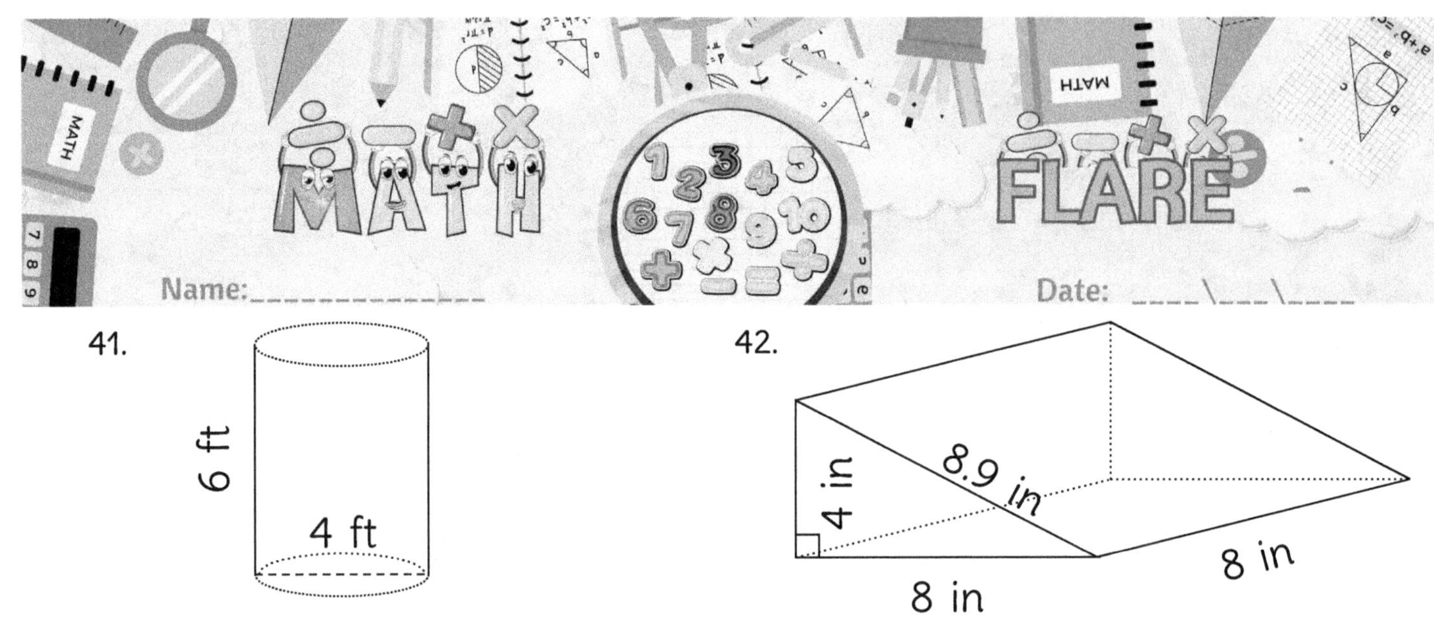

41.
6 ft
4 ft
42.
4 in
8.9 in
8 in
8 in

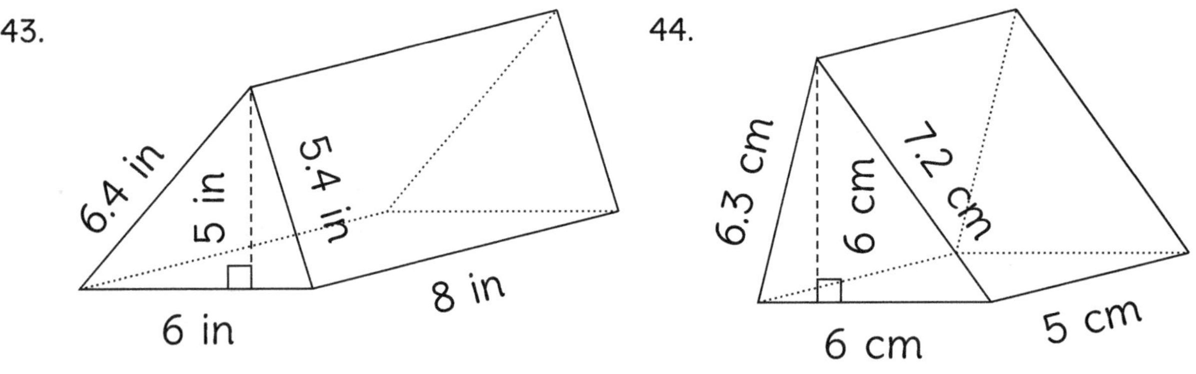

43.
6.4 in
5 in
5.4 in
6 in
8 in
44.
6.3 cm
6 cm
7.2 cm
6 cm
5 cm

MATH
FLARE
Name:
Date:

45.

8 in
5 in

46.

5 ft
6 ft
6 ft

47.

8.1 in
7 in
8.1 in
8 in
9 in

48.

4 ft
8.1 ft
7 ft
7 ft

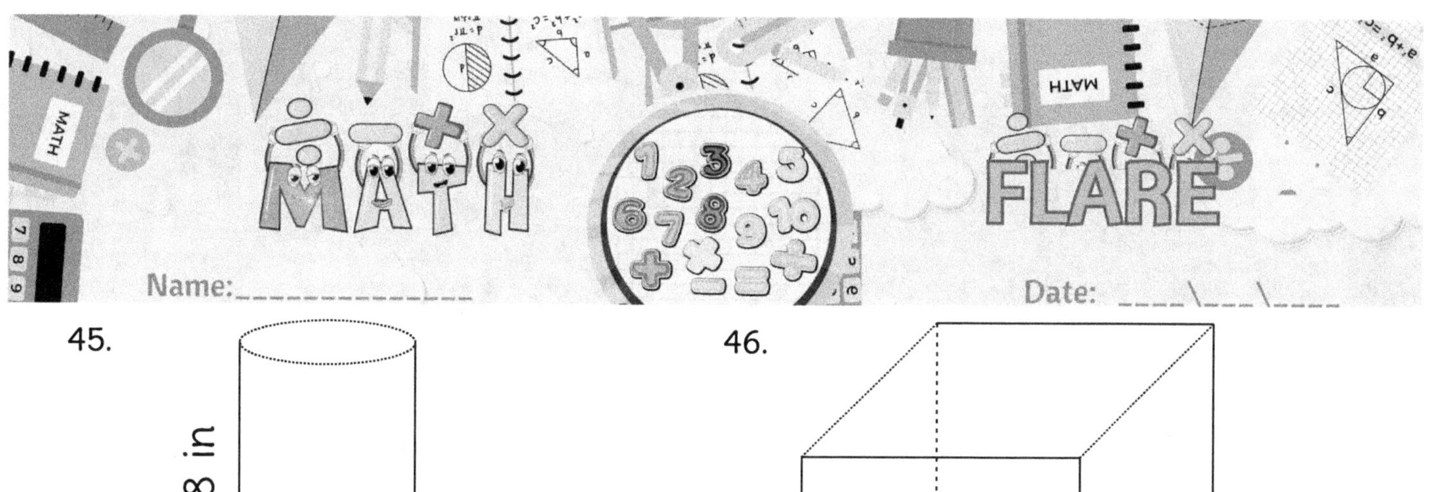

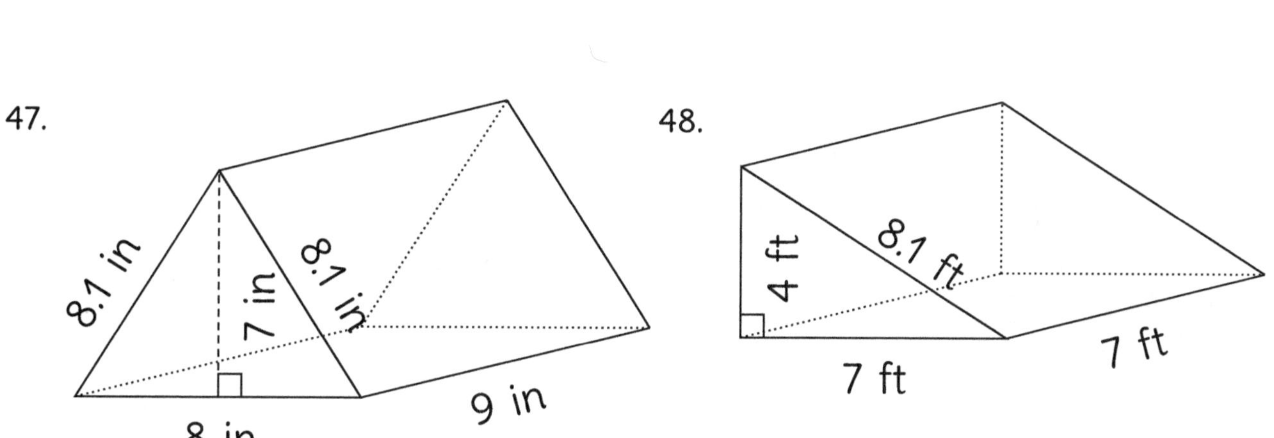

MATH
FLARE
Name:
Date:

49.

2 ft
2 ft
3 ft

50.

6 in
8 in

51.

6.4 in
4 in
5 in
6 in

52.

5 cm
7 cm

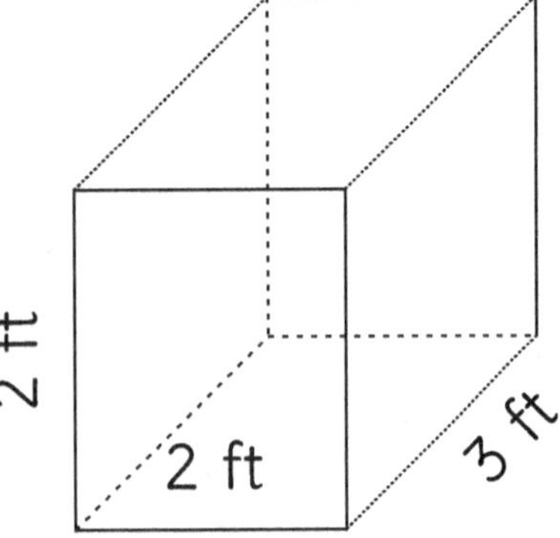

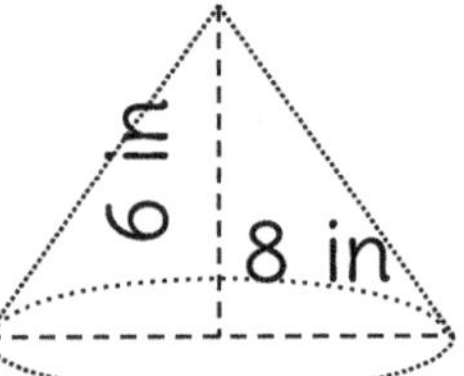

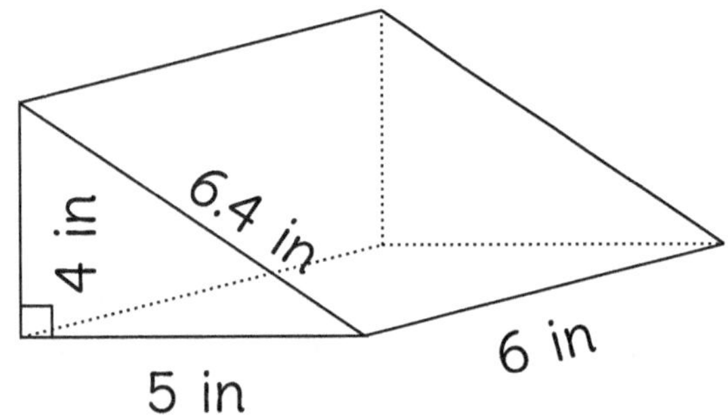

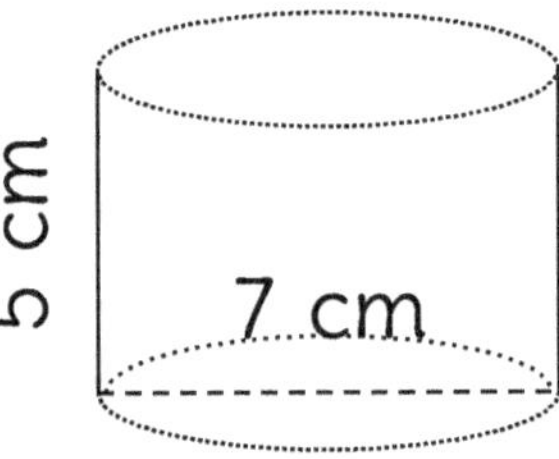

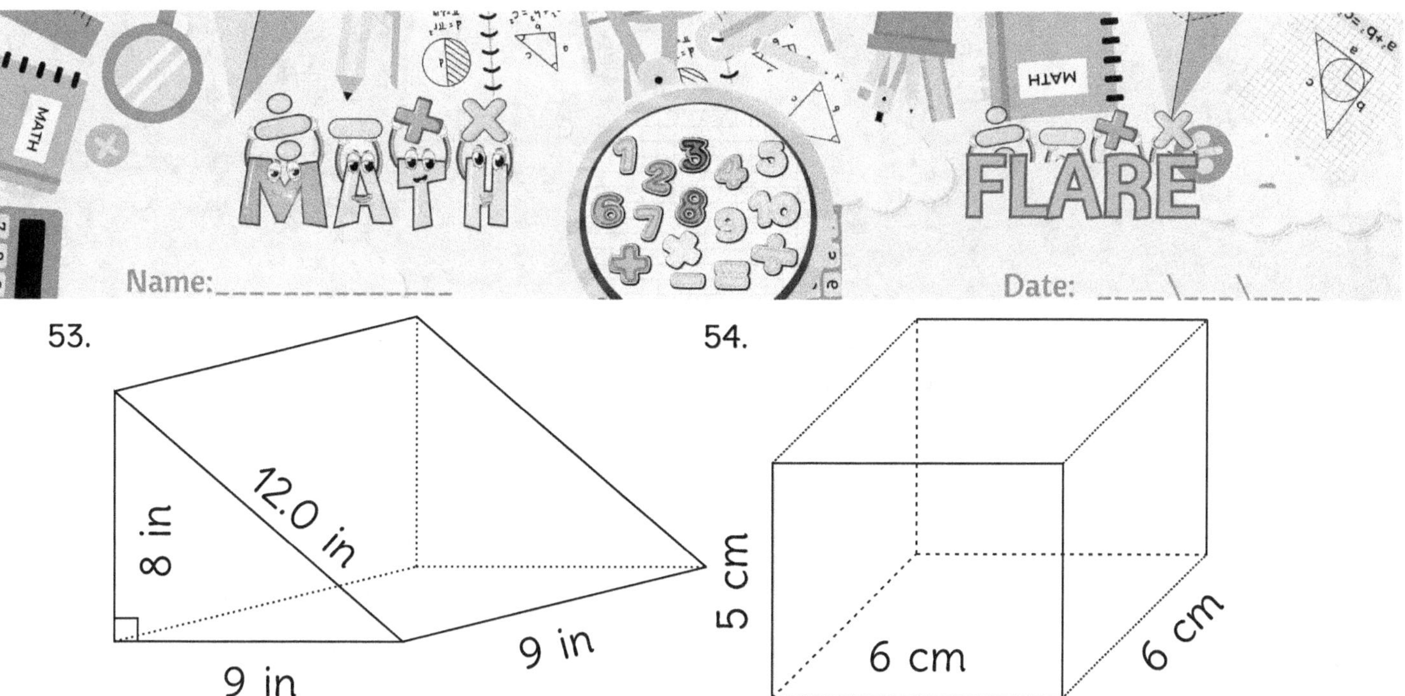

53.

54.

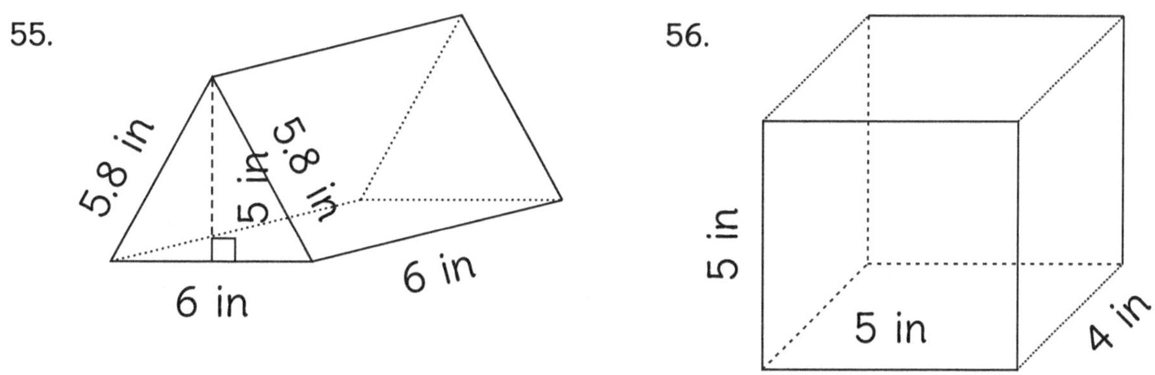

55.

56.

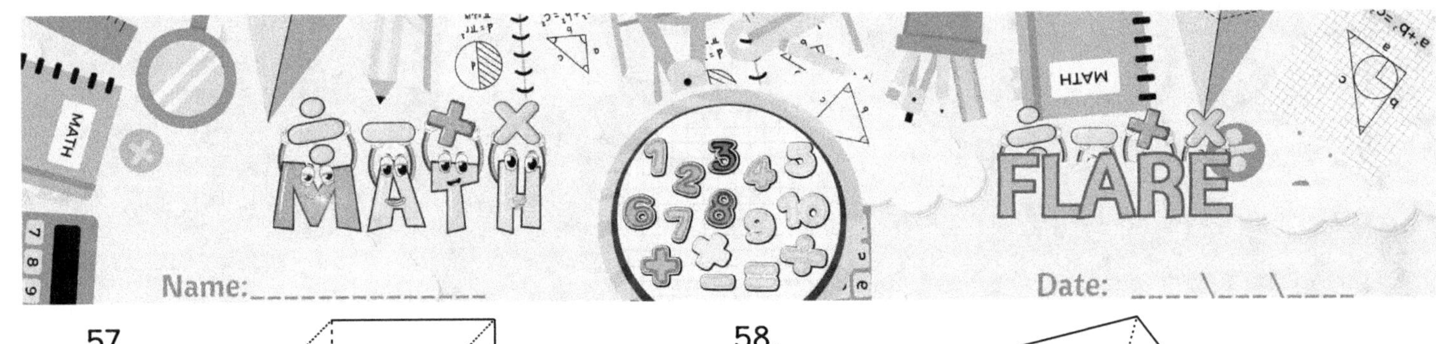

57.

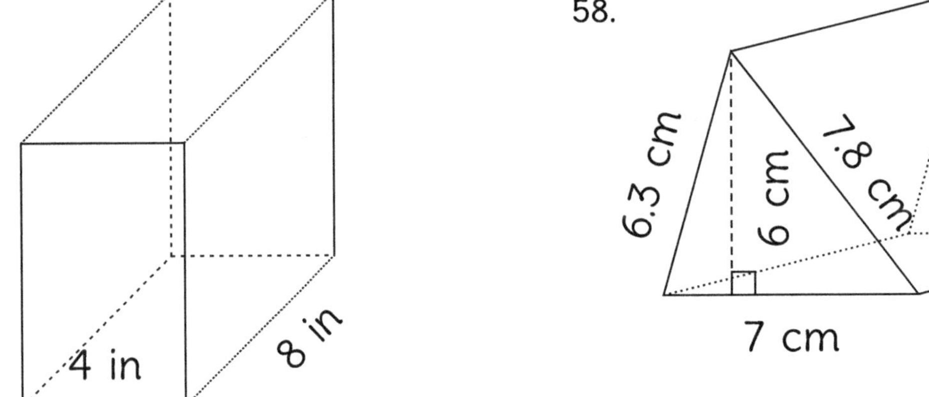

58.

59.

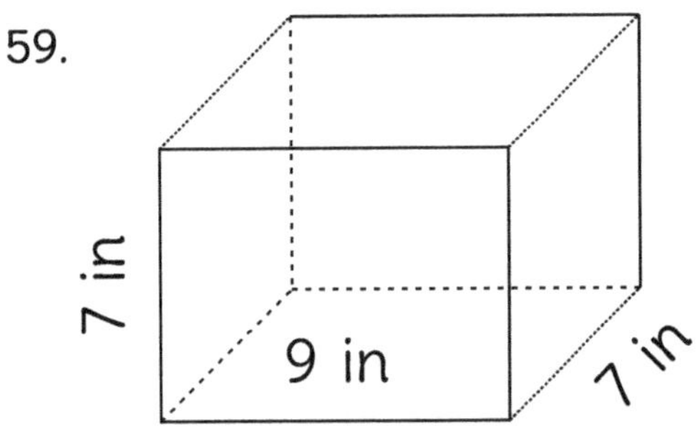

60.

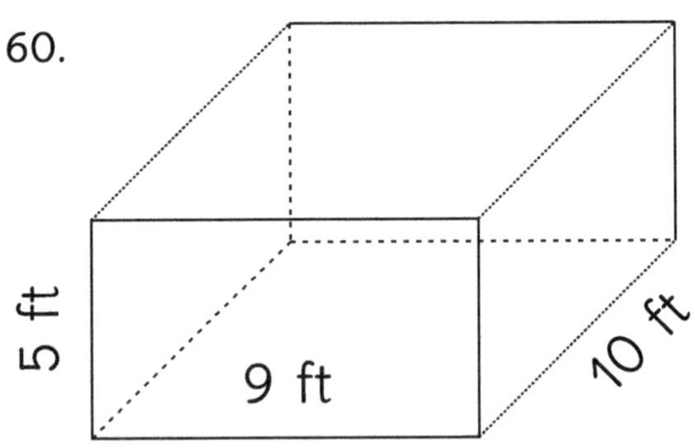

Pythagorean Theorem

1.

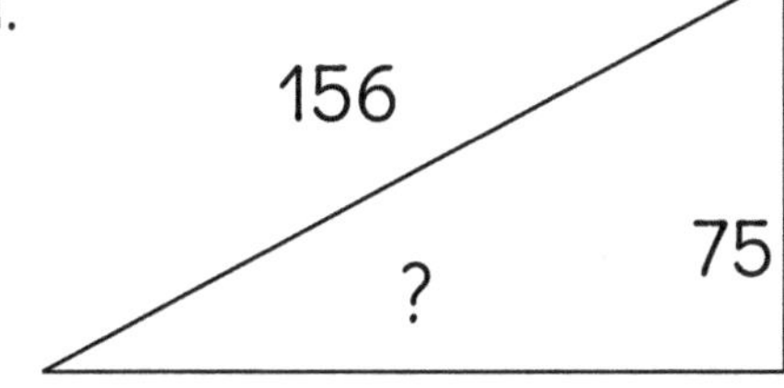

2.

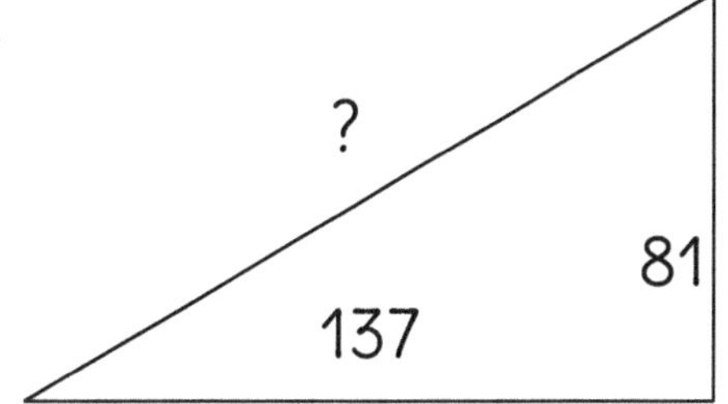

3.

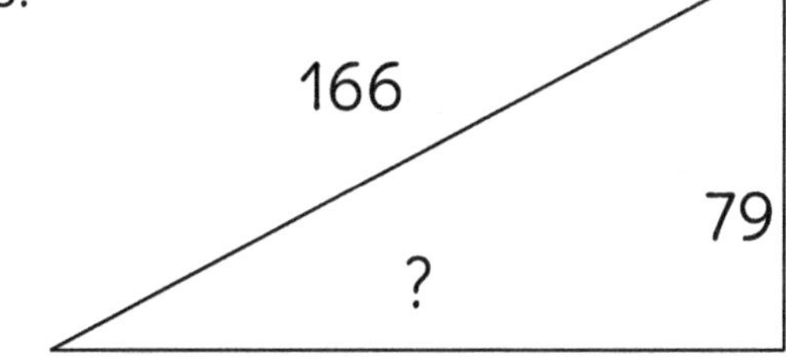

4.

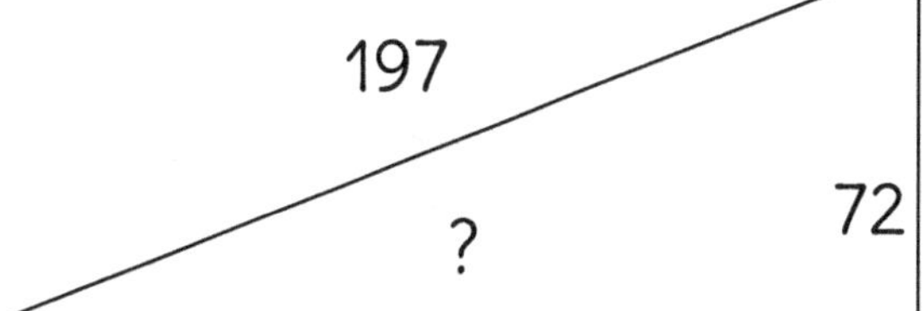

5.

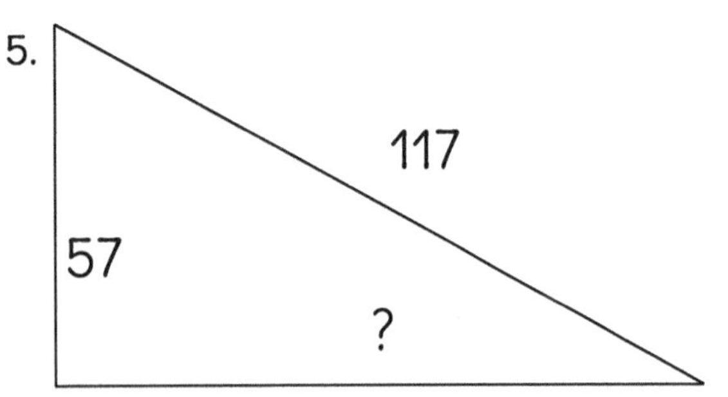

6.

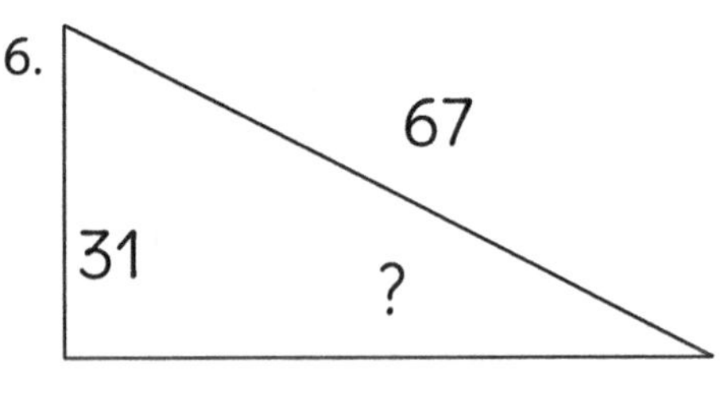

7.

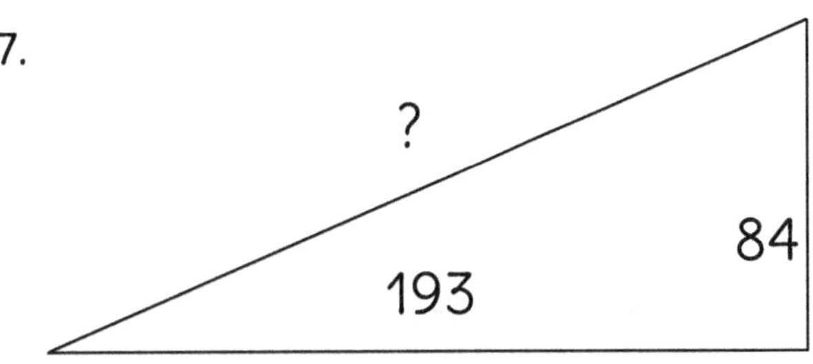

8.

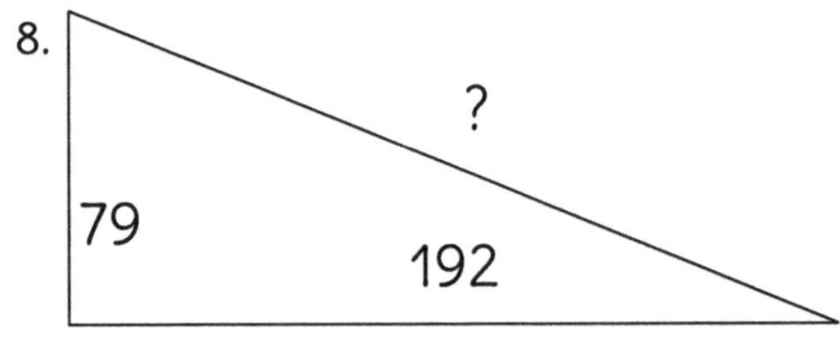

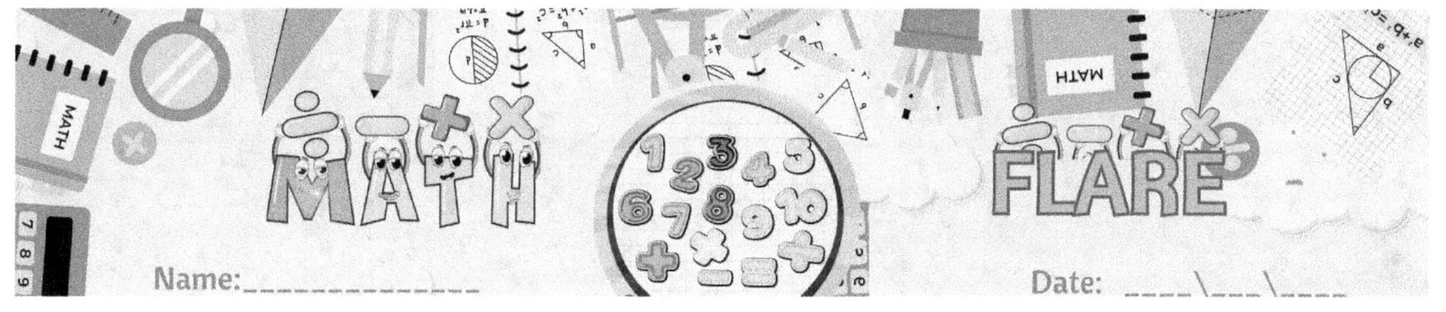

9.

64

30

?

10.

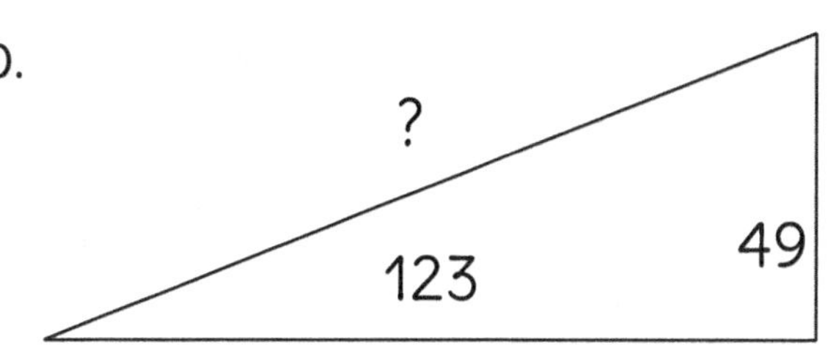

?

123

49

11.

?

85

45

12.

126

?

117

13.

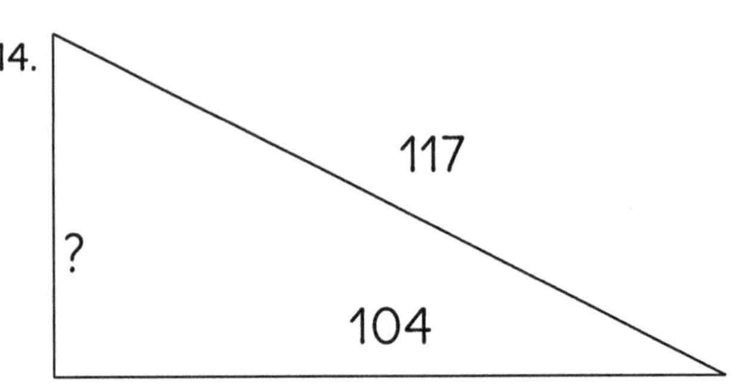

14.

15.

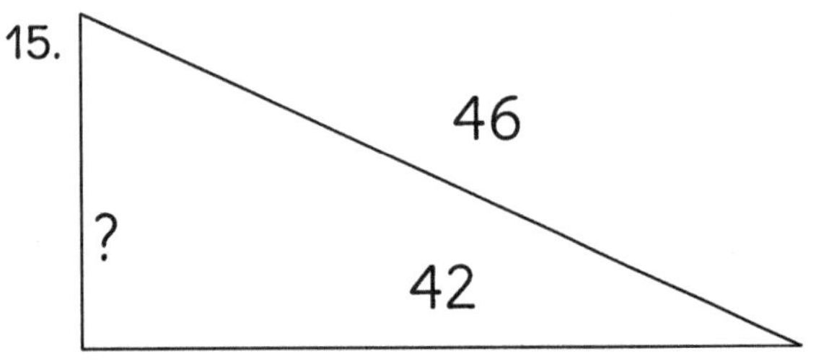

16.

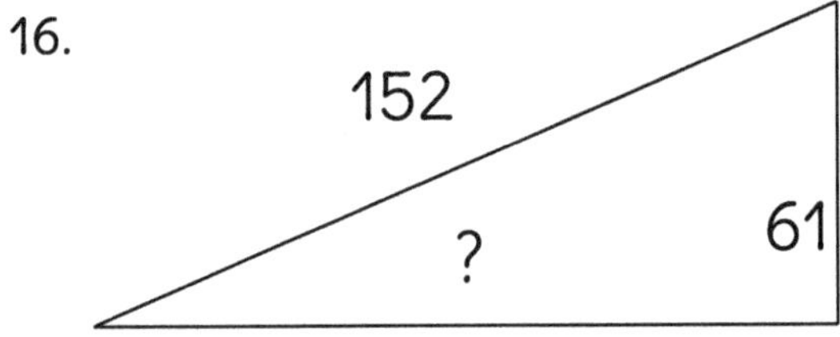

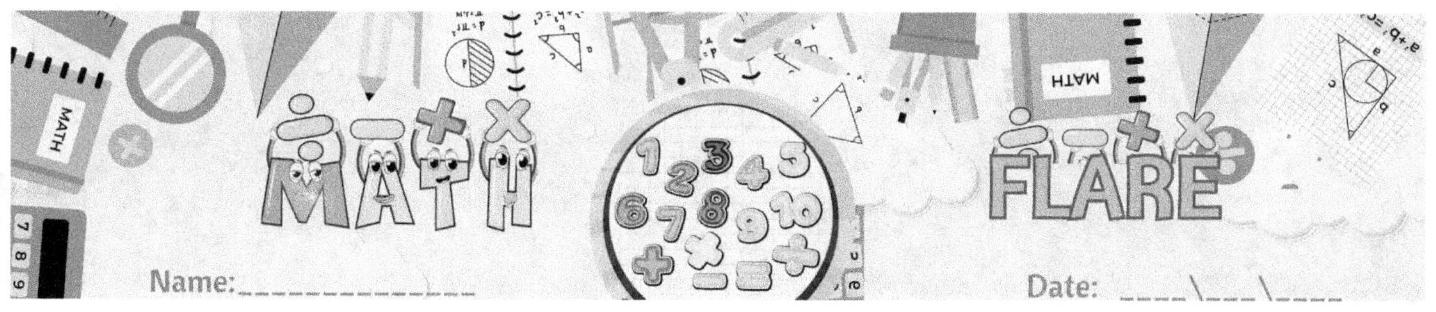

17. 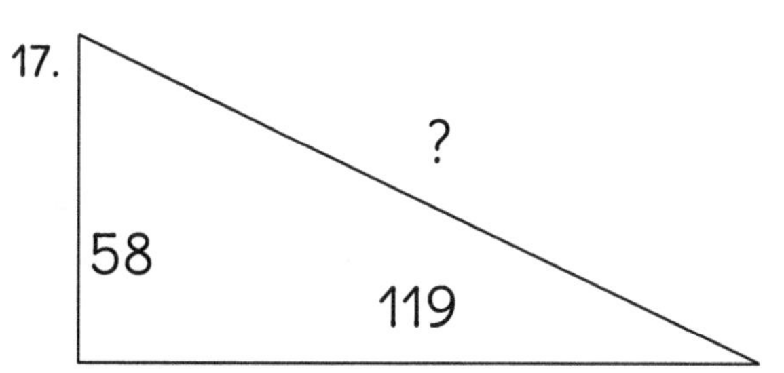

18. 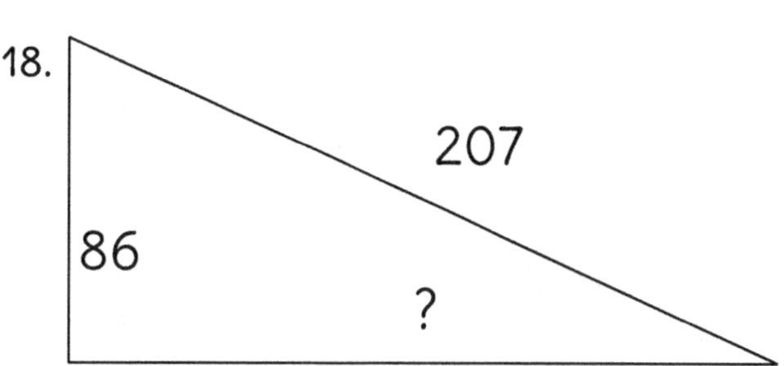

19. 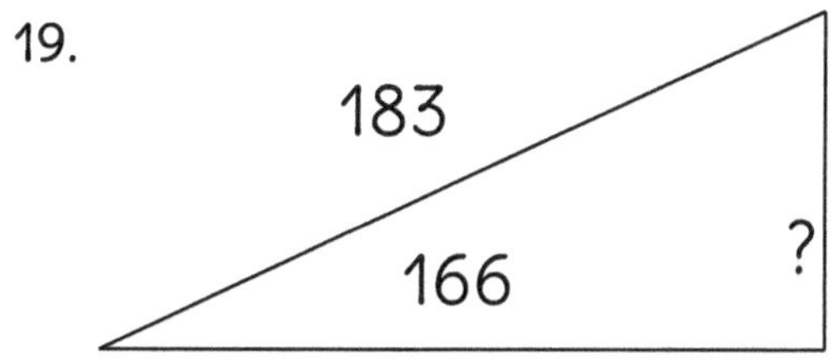

20. 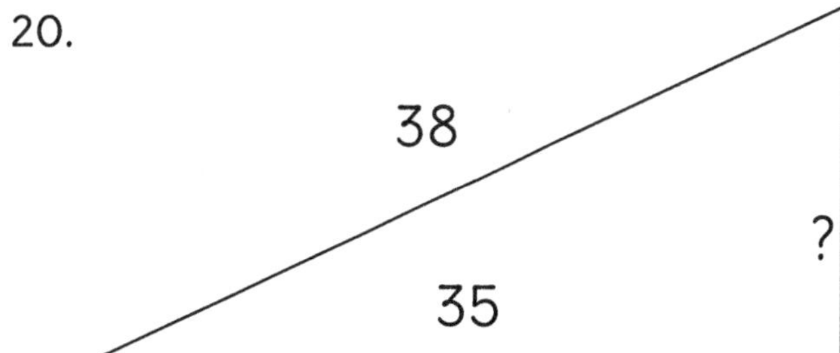

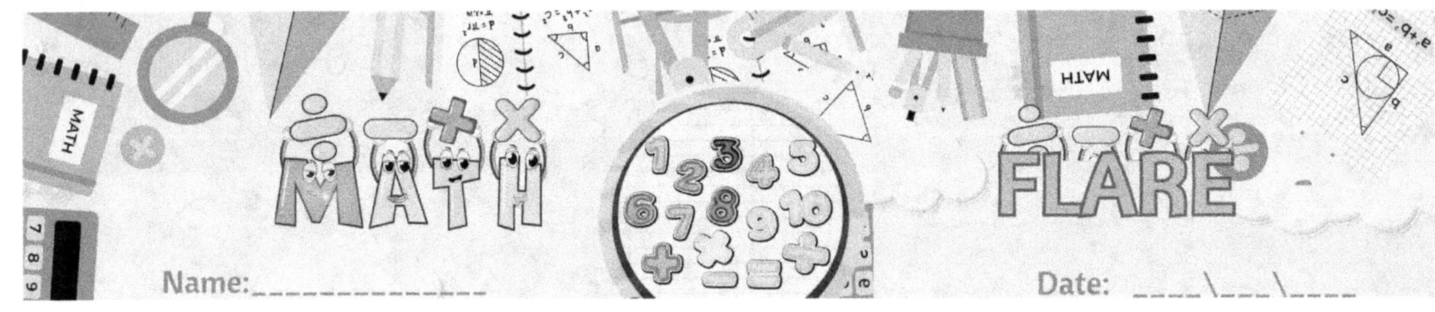

21.

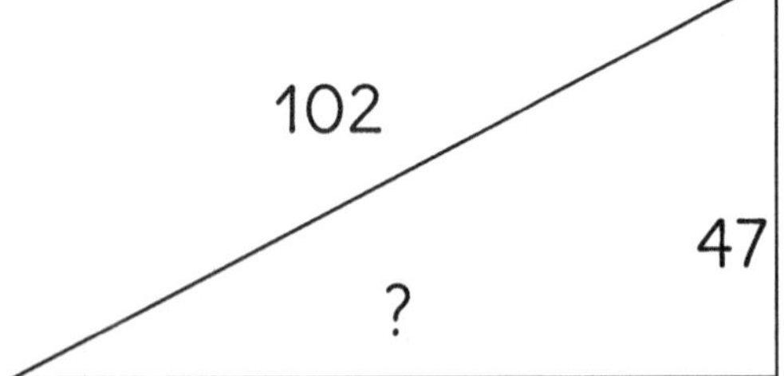

22.

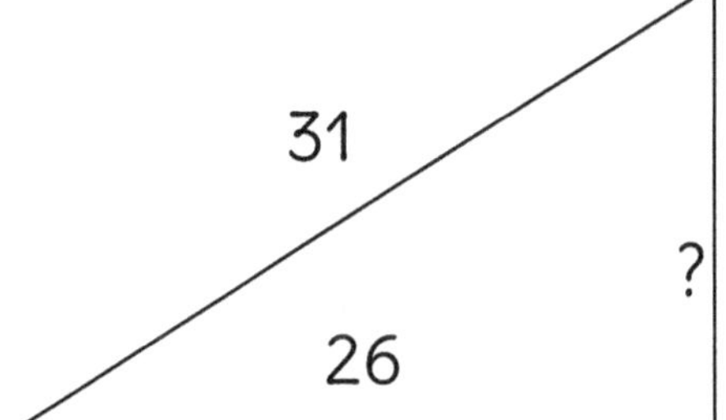

23.

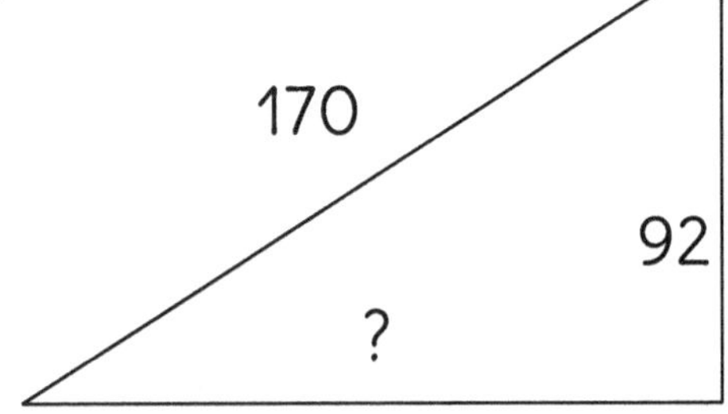

24.

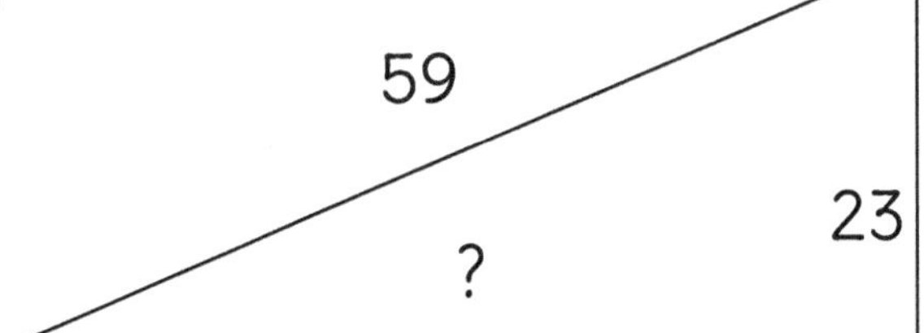

MATH
FLARE
Name:
Date:
1 2 3 4 5
6 7 8 9 10

25.

121
67
?

26.

200
?
181

27.

122
?
114

28.

152
?
62

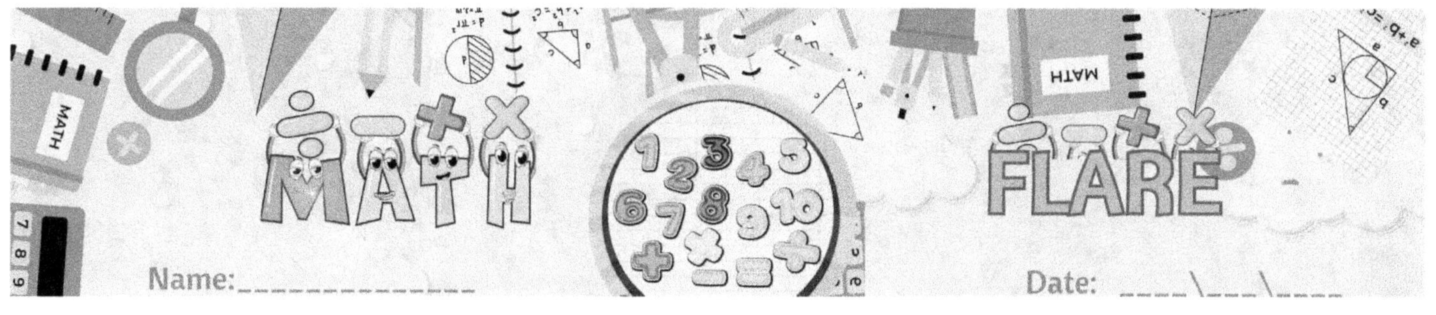

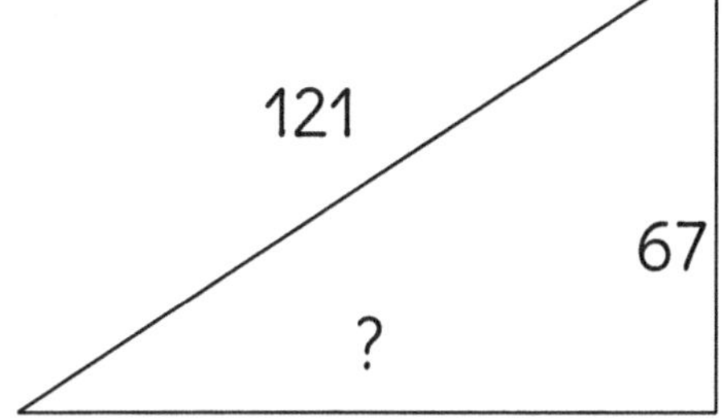

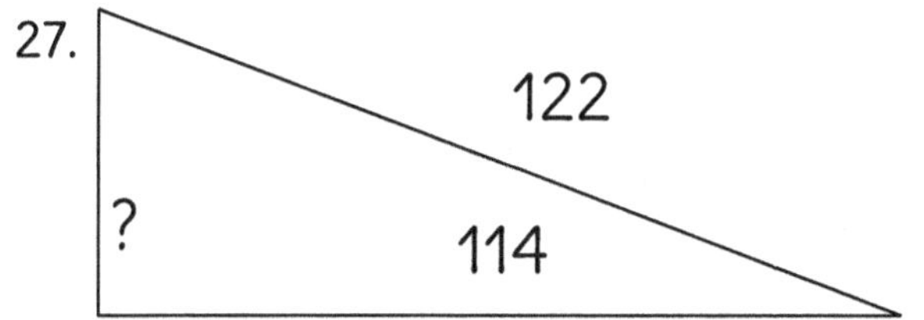

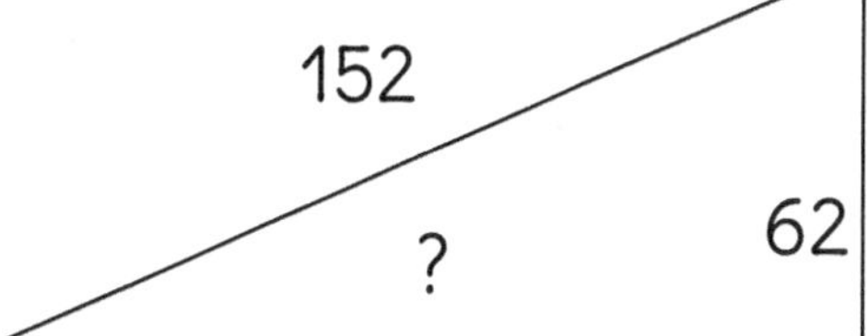

29.

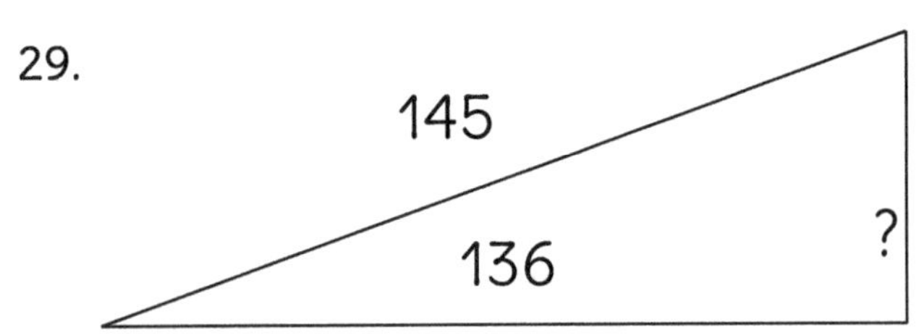

30.

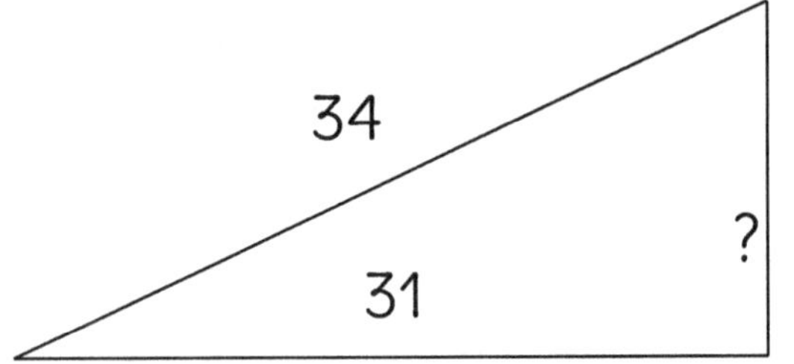

31.

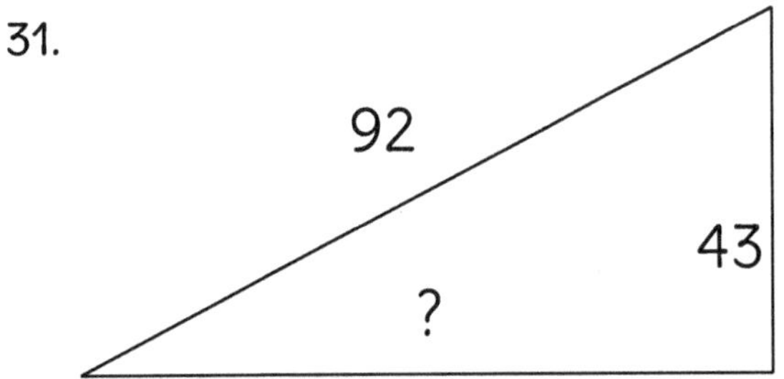

32.

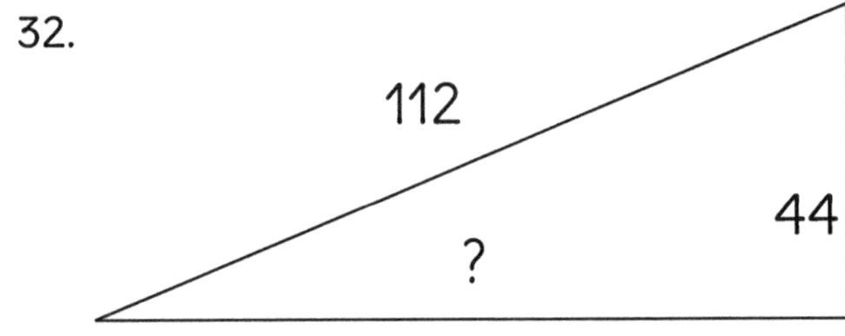

Exponents and Scientific Notations

Exponents

An exponent tells us how many times a number (called the base) is multiplied by itself. It is written as a superscript to the right of the base number. For example, in 2^3, 2 is the base and 3 is the exponent.

Rules:

1. **Product Rule**: When multiplying powers with the same base, add the exponents.

$$a^m \times a^n = a^{m+n}$$

For example:

$$2^3 = 2 \times 2 \times 2 = 8$$

$$3^2 \times 3^4 = 3^{2+4} = 3^6 = 3 \times 3 \times 3 \times 3 \times 3 \times 3 = 729$$

2. **Quotient Rule**: When dividing powers with the same base, subtract the exponents.

$$a^m \div a^n = a^{m-n}$$

For example:

$$5^3 \div 5^2 = 5^{3-2} = 5^1 = 5$$

3. **Power of a Power Rule**: When raising a power to another power, multiply the exponents.

$$(a^m)^n = a^{mn}$$

For example:

$$(2^2)^3 = 2^{2\times3} = 2^6 = 64$$

4. **Power of a Product Rule:** When raising a product to a power, distribute the power to each factor.

$$(ab)^n = a^n \times b^n$$

For example:

$$(2\times3)^2 = 2^2 \times 3^2 = 4 \times 9 = 36$$

5. **Power of a Quotient Rule:** When raising a quotient to a power, distribute the power to the numerator and denominator separately.

$$\left(\frac{a}{b}\right)^n = \frac{a^n}{b^n}$$

For example:

$$\left(\frac{4}{2}\right)^3 = \frac{4^3}{2^3} = \frac{64}{8} = 8$$

6. **Zero Exponent Rule:** Any nonzero number raised to the power of zero equals 11.

$$a^0 = 1$$

For example:

$$7^0 = 1$$

7. **Negative Exponent Rule:** A negative exponent means the reciprocal of the base raised to the positive exponent.

$$a^{-n} = \frac{1}{a^n}$$

For example:

$$2^{-3} = \frac{1}{2^3} = \frac{1}{8}$$

To evaluate expressions with exponents, we can use:

- **Repeated Multiplication**: Perform the multiplication indicated by the exponent.

- **Using the Rules of Exponents**: Apply the appropriate rule to simplify expressions involving exponents.

Scientific Notations

Scientific notation is a way to express very large or very small numbers in a concise and convenient manner. It involves writing a number as the product of a coefficient (a number between 1 and 10) and a power of 10.

This allows us to represent numbers with many zeros or decimal places more efficiently, making them easier to work with in calculations and comparisons.

$a \times 10^n$

where a is the coefficient (a number between 1 and 10) and n is the exponent, which indicates the power of 10.

For example:

Let's take the number 45,000 and express it in scientific notation.

To express 45,000 in scientific notation, we need to move the decimal point to the right until there is only one non-zero digit to its left.

1. Count the number of places we moved the decimal point. Since we moved it 4 places to the left, the exponent n will be -4.

2. The coefficient a is the number we obtain after moving the decimal point. In this case, it is 4.5.

3. Therefore, 45,000 in scientific notation is:

$$4.5 \times 10^4$$

To convert 4.5×10^4 back into standard notation, we need to multiply the coefficient 4.5 by 10 raised to the power of 4.

$$4.5 \times 10^4 = 4.5 \times (10 \times 10 \times 10 \times 10)$$

$$= 4.5 \times 10000$$

$$= 45000$$

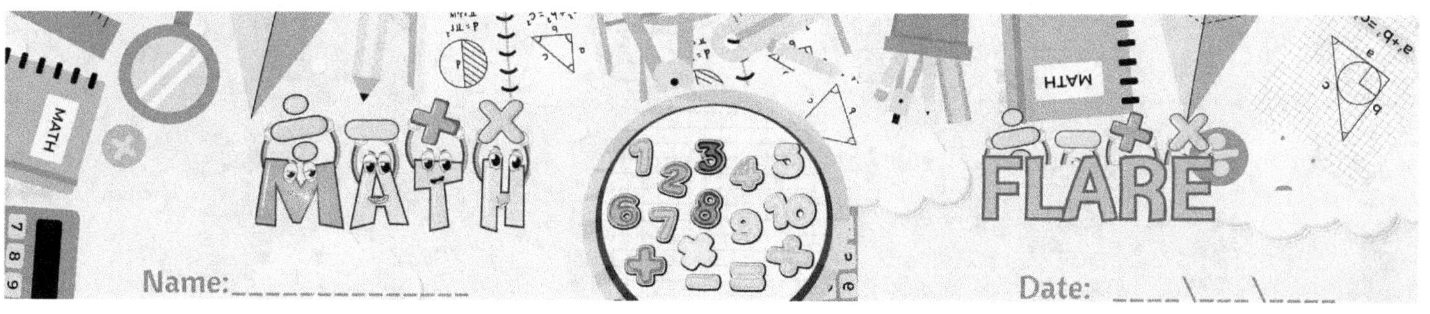

Exponents

Convert the values.

1. $19^3 =$ _______________

2. $12^4 =$ _______________

3. $6^{-2} =$ _______________

4. $13^4 =$ _______________

5. $18^{-2} =$ _______________

6. $7^{-3} =$ _______________

7. $4^{-2} =$ _______________

8. $20^2 =$ _______________

9. $19^4 =$ _______________

10. $12^3 =$ _______________

11. $4^4 =$ _______________

12. $10^{-3} =$ _______________

13. $13^3 =$ _______________

14. $8^{-2} =$ _______________

15. $19^{-3} =$ _______________

16. $16^4 =$ _______________

17. $20^{-3} =$ _______________

18. $9^2 =$ _______________

19. $10^{-2} =$ _______________

20. $7^2 =$ _______________

21. $16^3 =$ _______________

22. $17^2 =$ _______________

23. $1^{-3} =$ _______________

24. $18^4 =$ _______________

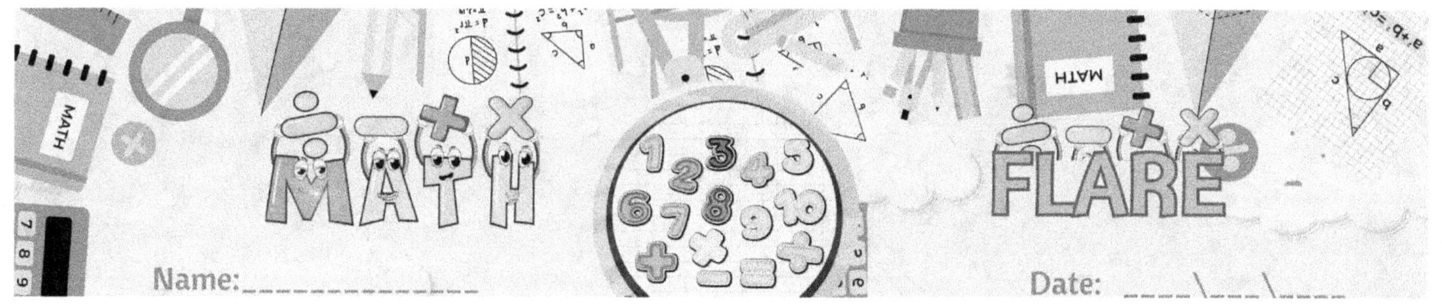

25. $17^{-2} =$

26. $2^{3} =$

27. $13^{-2} =$

28. $15^{-3} =$

29. $9^{-2} =$

30. $15^{3} =$

31. $5^{3} =$

32. $11^{-3} =$

33. $18^{2} =$

34. $1^{3} =$

35. $19^{-2} =$

36. $1^{-2} =$

37. $20^{-2} =$

38. $14^{2} =$

39. $13^{2} =$

40. $2^{-2} =$

41. $14^{3} =$

42. $3^{-3} =$

43. $6^{4} =$

44. $11^{3} =$

45. $14^{-3} =$

46. $15^{-2} =$

47. $6^{3} =$

48. $6^{2} =$

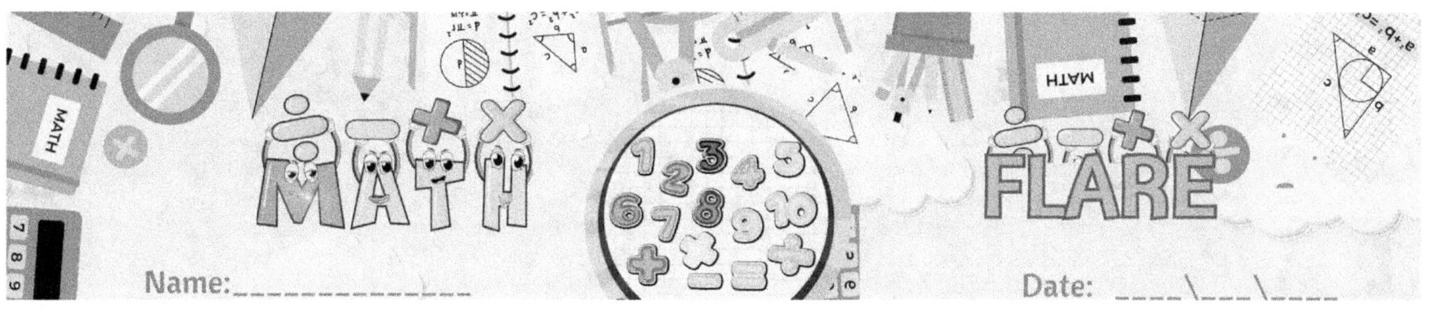

49. $9^{-3} =$ ___________

50. $7^{-2} =$ ___________

51. $4^{-3} =$ ___________

52. $14^{-2} =$ ___________

53. $5^{4} =$ ___________

54. $8^{4} =$ ___________

55. $4^{3} =$ ___________

56. $11^{2} =$ ___________

57. $1^{2} =$ ___________

58. $3^{-2} =$ ___________

59. $3^{4} =$ ___________

60. $8^{3} =$ ___________

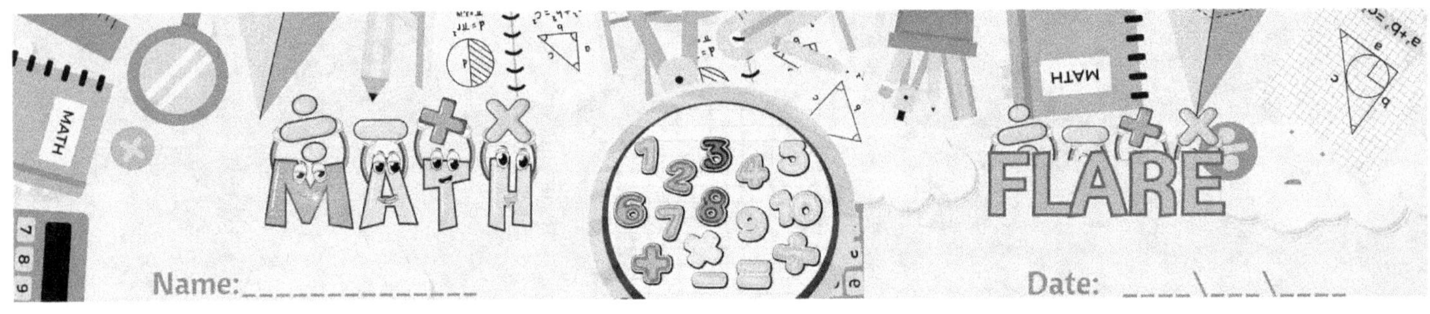

Scientific Notation

Provide the scientific notation for each value.

1. $45,000 =$ _______________

2. $6,400 =$ _______________

3. $42,000 =$ _______________

4. $7.1 \times 10^{3} =$ _______________

5. $740,000 =$ _______________

6. $3.8 \times 10^{2} =$ _______________

7. $4.43 \times 10^{6} =$ _______________

8. $1.9 \times 10^{2} =$ _______________

9. $4.8 \times 10^{4} =$ _______________

10. $9.5 \times 10^{5} =$ _______________

11. $8.3 \times 10^{2} =$ _______________

12. $85 =$ _______________

13. $56,000 =$ _______________

14. $1.93 \times 10^{6} =$ _______________

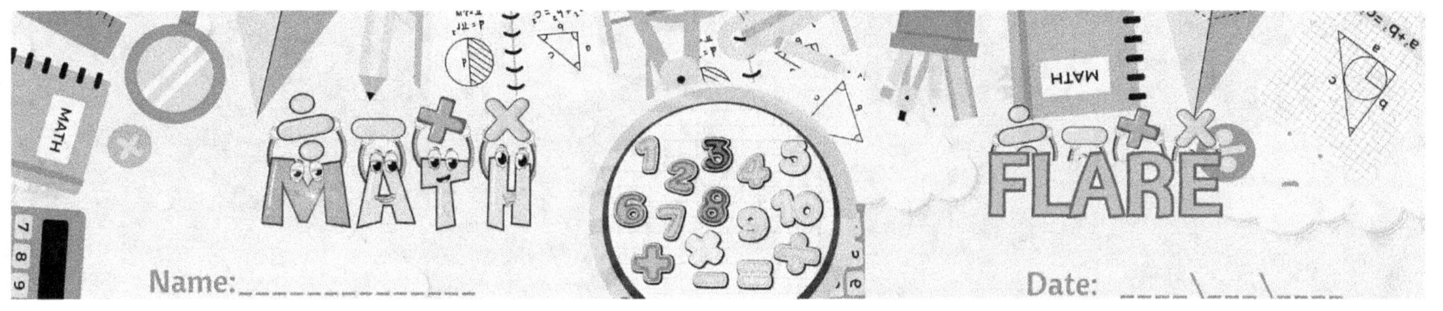

15. $55 =$ _______________

16. $455,000 =$ _______________

17. $88 =$ _______________

18. $9.5 \times 10^2 =$ _______________

19. $3.9 \times 10^5 =$ _______________

20. $910,000 =$ _______________

21. $8.3 \times 10^5 =$ _______________

22. $280 =$ _______________

23. $7 \times 10^3 =$ _______________

24. $6,163,000 =$ _______________

25. $94 =$ _______________

26. $2.45 \times 10^6 =$ _______________

27. $8,600 =$ _______________

28. $640,000 =$ _______________

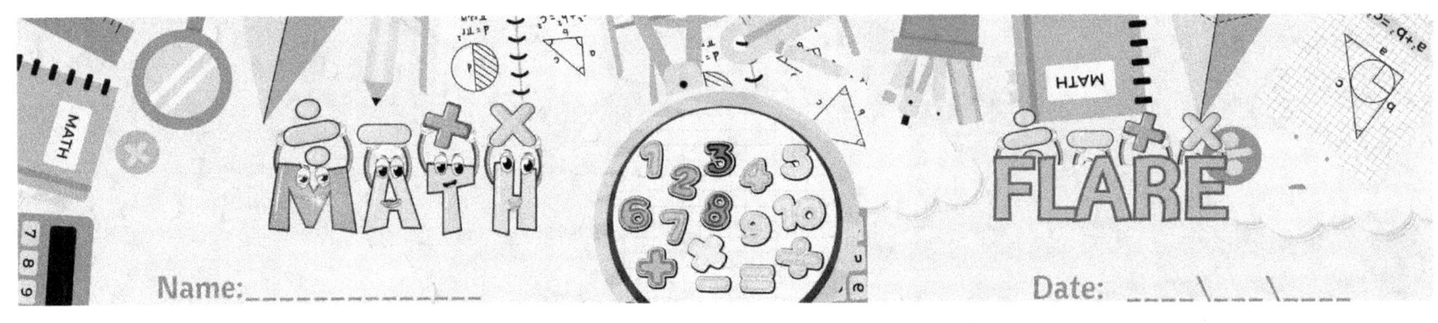

29. $47 =$ _______________

30. $9.5 \times 10^1 =$ _______________

31. $3.2 \times 10^5 =$ _______________

32. $930 =$ _______________

33. $3.5 \times 10^1 =$ _______________

34. $3,200,000 =$ _______________

35. $2.1 \times 10^1 =$ _______________

36. $7.7 \times 10^2 =$ _______________

37. $380,000 =$ _______________

38. $16 =$ _______________

39. $1.1 \times 10^3 =$ _______________

40. $4.6 \times 10^6 =$ _______________

41. $8.7 \times 10^3 =$ _______________

42. $3.9 \times 10^2 =$ _______________

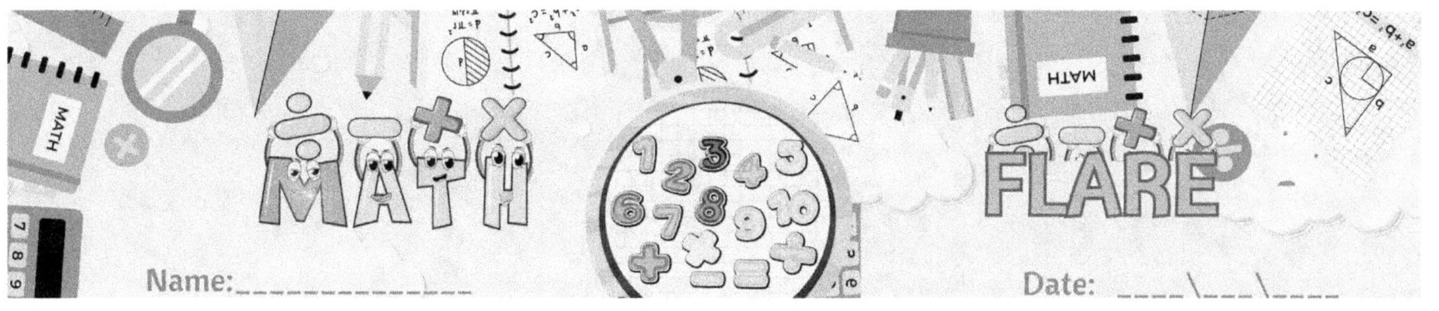

43. 7,900,000 = ______________

44. 3.5×10^2 = ______________

45. 7.2×10^2 = ______________

46. 218,000 = ______________

47. 8.344×10^6 = ______________

48. 4,000 = ______________

49. 64,000 = ______________

50. 8.6×10^1 = ______________

51. 1.8×10^1 = ______________

52. 6,600 = ______________

53. 896,000 = ______________

54. 3.1×10^2 = ______________

55. 4.3×10^6 = ______________

56. 6,154,000 = ______________

ANSWERS

Page 1: Solving One-Step Equations

1. 1	2. 4	3. 2	4. 2	5. 8	6. 8	7. 4	8. 5	9. 6
10. 10	11. 5	12. 2	13. 4	14. 3	15. 2	16. 9	17. 9	18. 3
19. 4	20. 5	21. 6	22. 10	23. 2	24. 10	25. 9	26. 9	27. 10
28. 10	29. 5	30. 10	31. 1	32. 8	33. 6	34. 10	35. 9	36. 2
37. 9	38. 8	39. 4	40. 1	41. 4	42. 5	43. 4	44. 8	45. 7
46. 9	47. 10	48. 6	49. 1	50. 9	51. 10	52. 7	53. 6	54. 7
55. 3	56. 7							

Page 8: Solving Two-Step Equations

1. 10	2. 4	3. 10	4. 2	5. 6	6. 3	7. 10	8. 10	9. 5
10. 9	11. 4	12. 8	13. 2	14. 1	15. 9	16. 9	17. 6	18. 8
19. 10	20. 2	21. 6	22. 6	23. 6	24. 8	25. 10	26. 1	27. 1
28. 7	29. 8	30. 8	31. 9	32. 8	33. 1	34. 3	35. 10	36. 7
37. 10	38. 3	39. 3	40. 9	41. 9	42. 9	43. 10	44. 10	45. 3
46. 1	47. 2	48. 8	49. 6	50. 10	51. 10	52. 10	53. 8	54. 6
55. 6	56. 8							

Page 15: Solving Multi-Step Equations

1. 2	2. 3
3. 5	4. 3
5. 6	6. 7

7. 9

8. 1

9. 9

10. 6

11. 10

12. 1

13. 8

14. 7

15. 9

16. 3

17. 10

18. 3

19. 4

20. 3

21. 6

22. 8

23. 5

24. 10

25. 3

26. 4

27. 3

28. 10 or -199 or -198 or -197 or...

29. 7

30. 2

31. 6

32. 1

33. 4

34. 1 or -199 or -198 or -197 or...

35. 1

36. 1

37. 3

38. 9

39. 5

40. 8

41. 3

42. 8

43. 5

44. 8

45. 7

46. 1

47. 5

48. 9

49. 3

50. 4

51. 9 or -199 or -198 or -197 or...

52. 9

53. 3

54. 4 or -199 or -198 or -197 or...

55. 6

56. 2

Page 22: Equations: (One Side)

1. x = -1
2. x = 8
3. k = -4
4. m = 4
5. x = -3
6. k = -1
7. m = 17
8. m = 1
9. x = 2
10. y = 5
11. x = 20
12. m = 18
13. m = -10
14. k = 8
15. x = 171
16. z = 17
17. y = -6
18. k = 9
19. k = 17
20. k = -9
21. m = 0
22. m = 17
23. m = 7
24. z = 0
25. k = -15
26. m = 0
27. x = -4
28. k = 19
29. y = -4
30. z = 3
31. m = 15
32. k = 15
33. y = -8
34. m = 18
35. z = 5
36. z = -3
37. y = -10
38. m = 4
39. z = 17
40. k = 10
41. z = -6
42. k = -1
43. k = -63
44. x = 0
45. y = -7
46. m = 12
47. m = 8
48. x = 20
49. x = 15
50. x = 8
51. z = 132
52. z = 9
53. k = 7
54. z = -99
55. k = 5
56. m = 19

Page 29: Equations (Two Sides)

1. b = -9
2. m = -4
3. b = -2
4. x = 4
5. x = -8
6. m = 5
7. x = 4
8. m = -4
9. a = -8
10. a = 1
11. a = 9
12. a = 9
13. m = 1
14. z = -1
15. x = 10

16. m = 10   17. y = 9   18. m = -2   19. s = -5   20. b = -2

21. k = 4   22. y = 10   23. m = -3   24. k = 9   25. m = 5

26. b = 1   27. s = 5   28. z = -7   29. s = 1   30. m = 10

31. a = 3   32. b = -2   33. s = 1   34. z = -3   35. m = -6

36. k = 3   37. m = 6   38. b = 3   39. z = 2   40. z = 5

41. s = -8   42. x = 8   43. z = 1   44. a = 6   45. z = -3

46. b = -8   47. m = -9   48. s = 3   49. m = 5   50. z = 4

51. z = 1   52. k = 7   53. z = 4   54. s = -7   55. b = 7

56. m = 1

Page 36: Simplify Expressions

1. 12k + 15   2. 35k - 2   3. 11x + 12   4. 48m + 145

5. -11x + 17   6. 2k   7. 4x + 1   8. 7m + 14

9. 4y + 35   10. 12m + 30   11. 4k - 24   12. -30x + 15

13. -25m - 17   14. -13z   15. 9k - 3   16. -3k - 12

17. 15k + 3   18. -10m + 10   19. -14z - 17   20. -25x - 13

21. -3z - 13   22. -5x - 9   23. 8y + 4   24. -18z + 1

25. 98k + 64   26. 3y   27. 16z + 39   28. 13m + 11

29. 14k   30. 11k + 17   31. 29z - 2   32. 16y + 1

33. 30m + 15   34. -10x   35. -16m - 8   36. -140z + 136

37. -13x - 2   38. 216k - 278   39. 13m + 17   40. 15k + 29

41. -18y   42. 23k   43. 6y + 20   44. 98y + 33

45. -17k - 24   46. 28y + 24   47. 21m + 16   48. 9k - 19

49. -m + 18   50. -143m + 35   51. 20y - 6   52. 10x - 28

53. 15x + 18   54. -4y + 1   55. 19m + 15   56. -18y + 5

57. 12m + 23   58. 6y   59. -91k + 74   60. 13y - 11

Page 48: Evaluating Equations

1. 14   2. -1   3. 15   4. 8   5. 16   6. 32   7. 10   8. 10   9. 7

10. -2

Page 49: Evaluating Equations

1. 80   2. -4   3. 15   4. 90   5. 9   6. 12   7. 60   8. 3   9. 25

10. 36

Page 50: Evaluating Equations

1. 53   2. 1   3. 2   4. 8   5. 234   6. 11   7. 9   8. 52

9. 50   10. 45

Page 51: Evaluating Equations

1. 1   2. 60   3. 24   4. 20   5. 29   6. 2   7. 36   8. 27   9. 10

10. 36

Page 52: Evaluating Equations

1. 28   2. 31   3. 56   4. 6   5. 2   6. 1   7. 3   8. 6

9. 34   10. -45

Page 53: Evaluating Equations

1. 38   2. 7   3. 24   4. 10   5. 1   6. 14   7. -51   8. 40   9. 33

10. 1

Page 54:   Evaluating Equations

1. 1   2. 1   3. 12   4. 1.4   5. 9   6. 10   7. 0.4   8. 72   9. 60

10. 1

Page 55:   Evaluating Equations

1. 4   2. 14   3. 1   4. 38   5. 34   6. 1   7. -5   8. 27   9. 4

10. 10

Page 56:   Evaluating Equations

1. 3   2. -2   3. 13   4. 7   5. 4   6. 9   7. 4   8. 18   9. 11   10. 8

Page 57:   Evaluating Equations

1. 5   2. 1   3. 0   4. 35   5. -2   6. 1   7. 14   8. 11   9. 6

10. 10

Page 58:   Evaluating Equations

1. -7   2. 1   3. 1   4. 6   5. 16   6. 39   7. 32   8. 20   9. 36   10. 1

Page 59:   Evaluating Equations

1. 9   2. 15   3. 15   4. 82   5. 45   6. 16   7. 14   8. 10   9. 31   10. 2

Page 60:   Evaluating Equations

1. 14   2. -1   3. 15   4. 8   5. 16   6. 32   7. 10   8. 10   9. 7

10. -2

Page 61:   Verbal Algebra Expressions

1. 11   2. 18   3. 0   4. 7

5. 7, 68   6. 7, 4   7. 6, 8, 10   8. 6

9. 5, 6   10. 1   11. 11   12. 10, 7

Page 61: Verbal Algebra Expressions

1. 11	2. 18	3. 0	4. 7
5. 7, 68	6. 7, 4	7. 6, 8, 10	8. 6
9. 5, 6	10. 1	11. 11	12. 10, 7
13. 18	14. 5, 12, 45	15. 24	16. 16
17. 7, 55	18. 2	19. 1	20. 7
21. 4	22. 12	23. 8	24. 2
25. 3	26. 35, 7	27. 3, 5	28. 11
29. 7	30. 4	31. 2	32. 7
33. 5	34. 8, 56	35. 2	36. 3
37. 6, 8, 10, 12	38. 2, 1	39. 5, 6, 7	40. 16, 6
41. 7, 28	42. 12, 7		

Page 71: Standard Linear Equations

1. -4	13. 10	25. -2	37. 5
2. -6	14. -7	26. -7	38. 6
3. 6	15. 3	27. 0	39. -5
4. 10	16. -1	28. 1	40. -8
5. 1	17. 2	29. 4	41. 4
6. 10	18. 3	30. -2	42. 6
7. -5	19. -6	31. 8	43. 1
8. 8	20. -2	32. -8	44. 0
9. -3	21. -1	33. -8	45. 2
10. 4	22. -3	34. -1	46. 7
11. 3	23. 7	35. -4	47. -2
12. -9	24. -9	36. -2	48. -7

Page 77: Graphing Linear Equations

1. $y = \frac{-7}{4}x - 4$

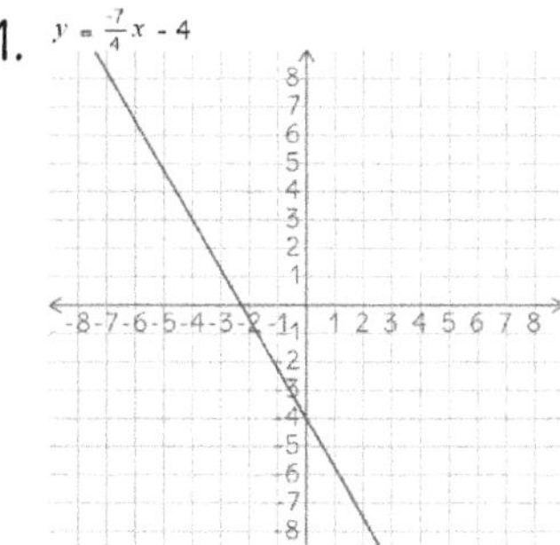

2. $y = \frac{-5}{2}x + 3$

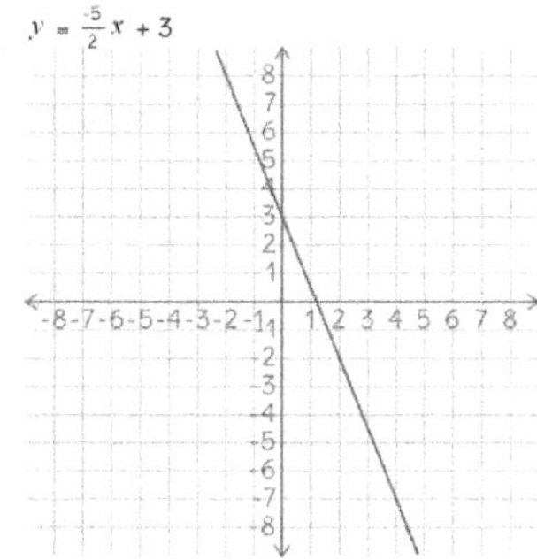

3. $y = \frac{-3}{4}x - 4$

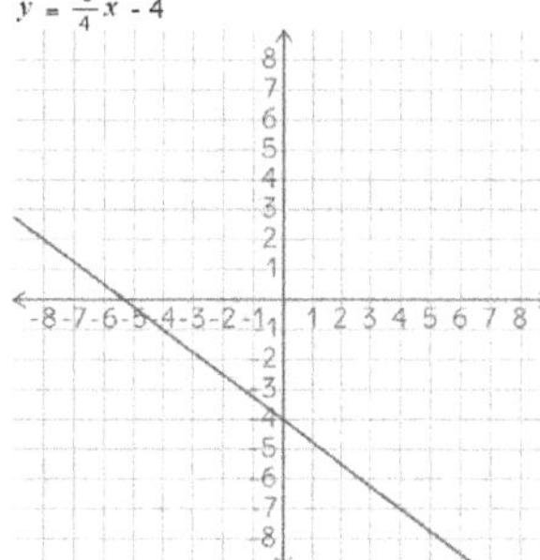

4. $y = \frac{-5}{4}x + 6$

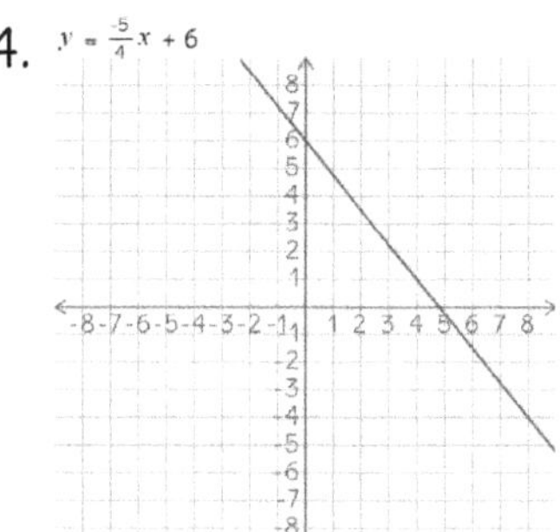

5. $y = \frac{5}{4}x - 5$

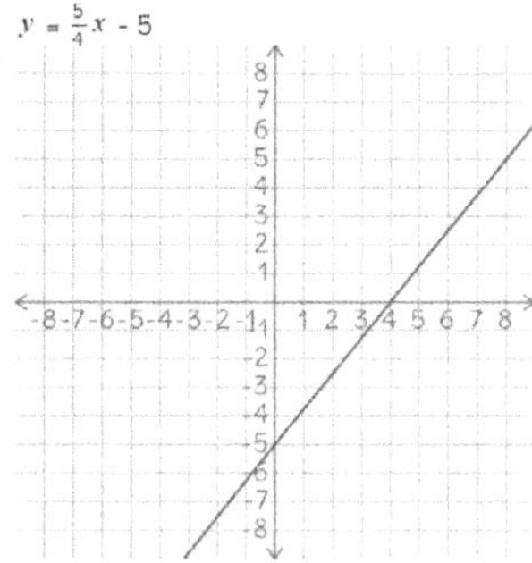

6. $y = x + 7$

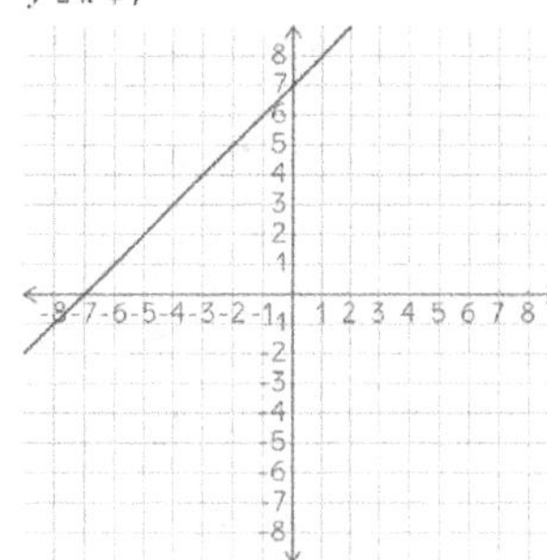

7. $y = \frac{-5}{2}x + 2$

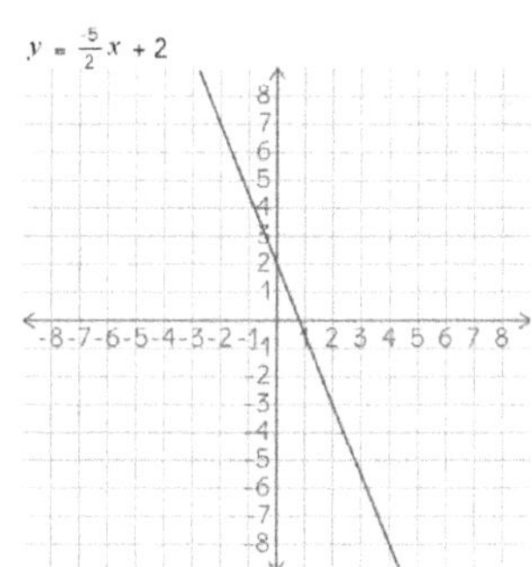

8. $y = \frac{3}{2}x + 7$

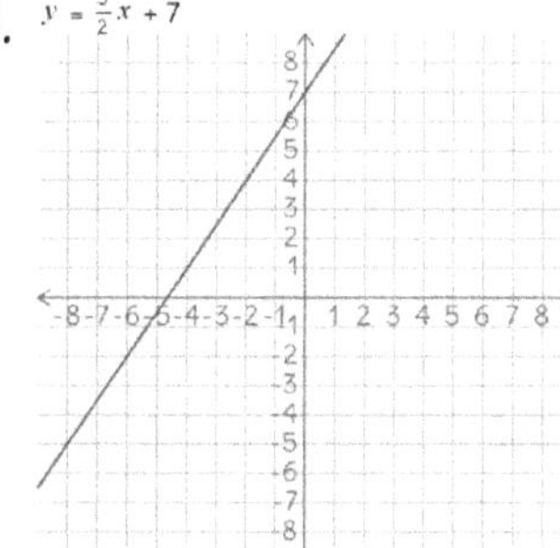

9. $y = \frac{7}{4}x - 8$

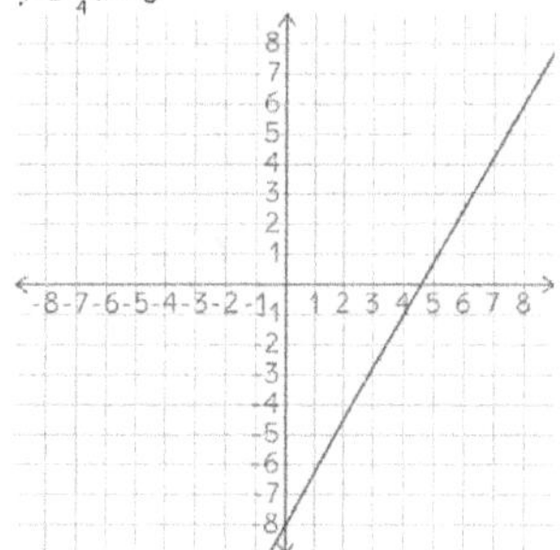

10. $y = \frac{5}{4}x - 4$

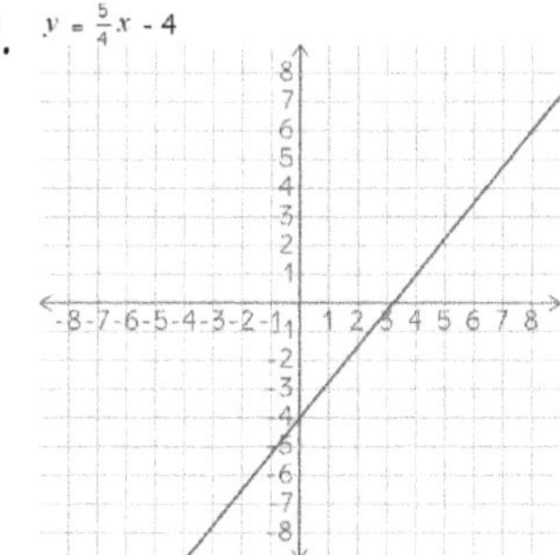

Page 87: System of Equations

1. 1. x = 0.44, y = -0.11
2. 2. x = 0.2, y = 0.7
3. 3. x = 1.15, y = 0.23
4. 4. x = 13.0, y = -6.0
5. 5. x = -0.24, y = 1.68
6. 6. x = 0.45, y = 1.52
7. 7. x = -0.3, y = 0.96
8. 8. x = 2.67, y = -4.0
9. 9. x = 13.5, y = -6.5
10. 10. x = 0.5, y = 1.0
11. 11. x = 1.33, y = 0.0
12. 12. x = 0.75, y = 0.5
13. 13. x = 0.21, y = -0.07
14. 14. x = 2.59, y = 1.24
15. 15. x = 1.57, y = -0.86
16. 16. x = -0.16, y = 0.8
17. 17. x = -0.71, y = 2.57
18. 18. x = -1.0, y = 1.4
19. 19. x = 0.33, y = 1.17
20. 20. x = 0.17, y = 1.07
21. 21. x = 0.75, y = -0.75
22. 22. x = 0.9, y = -0.59
23. 23. x = 0.35, y = 0.74
24. 24. x = 13.0, y = -5.0
25. 25. x = 5.8, y = -8.0
26. 26. x = 0.28, y = 0.5
27. 27. x = -0.36, y = 1.64
28. 28. x = 1.09, y = -0.58
29. 29. x = -1.38, y = 1.5
30. 30. x = 15.0, y = -49.0

Page 97: Quadratic Equations

1. 3.081, -0.081	21. -1.318, 1.518	41. -1, 1
2. 1.8, -1	22. -3.6, 3	42. -2, 2.2
3. 4, -5.5	23. -1.333, 3	43. -1, 1.5
4. -1.471, 1.36	24. -3.089, 0.755	44. -1, 4
5. 4, -4	25. -3, 7	45. -7, 7
6. 2.387, 0.279	26. 14, -3	46. 5, -5
7. -0.719, -2.781	27. 0.127, 0.873	47. 12, -2
8. -2.576, 4.076	28. 0.703, -2.37	48. 2, -4
9. -1.833, 3	29. 1, -3	49. 0.5, -2
10. No real solution.	30. -1, -2	50. 4.75, -2
11. 2, 1	31. -1, 1	51. 2.061, -0.347
12. -1.408, 3.408	32. -7, 5	52. -2.128, 1.128
13. 7, -4	33. 3, -1.667	53. -2, 2
14. 0.171, -1.171	34. -2, 0.5	54. -5, 5
15. -1, -5	35. -0.24, 0.462	55. 4, -4
16. -3, 3	36. No real solution.	56. 2.708, -1.108
17. -4.25, 5	37. -2.065, 1.065	57. 2.536, 9.464
18. -5, 5	38. No real solution.	58. 2, -4
19. 3.708, -1.708	39. -0.918, 2.043	59. No real solution.
20. 0.268, -0.934	40. 1.225, -1.225	60. -1.831, 0.956

Page 105: Polynomials: Addition and Subtraction

1. $7x^3 + 12$
2. $b^4 - 13b$
3. $3k^3 - 9k^2$
4. $9p - 4$
5. $-7b^3 - b^2 + 5$
6. $3x^3 + 2x^2$
7. $9x^3 - x^2$
8. $7k^3 - 4k^2$
9. $13b^4 + 11b^3$
10. $7n^3 + 7n$
11. $p^4 + 15p^3$
12. $7x^4 + 3x^2 + 2$
13. $-8p^4 + 13p^3$
14. $2x^3 + 11x$
15. $-5k^3$
16. $13v^3 - 2v^2$
17. $-11v^4 + 4$
18. $10p^2 + 10$
19. $-9r^2 - r$
20. $-14a^4 + 4a^3$
21. $x - 13$
22. $-3x^3 + 16x^2$
23. $-x^4 + 2x^3$
24. $10n$
25. $7x^4 - 7x^3$
26. $-6a^3 + 4$
27. $9x^4 + 4x^3$
28. $2x^2 + 1$
29. $-2b^4 - 2$
30. $-x^4 - 5x^2$
31. $6x^4 + 12x + 2$
32. $-n^4 + 2n - 5$
33. $4x^4 + 6x^3 + 3x^2$
34. $10r^2 - 1$
35. $-4p^4 + 3p^3 - 4p^2$
36. $11n^4 - 5n^3 + 5n^2$
37. $-13n^4 + 4n + 10$
38. $-5r^4 - 3r^2 + 15r$
39. $-p^3 - 9p + 14$
40. $6b^3 + 5b^2 + b$
41. $2x^3 + 6x^2 + 2$
42. $3x^3 + 4x - 1$
43. $4b^4 - 7b^3 + 11$
44. $3n^4 + 11n - 5$
45. $-7b^4 - 2b^2 + 7$
46. $3r^3 - 4r^2 + 5r$
47. $5n^3 + 3n^2 - 4n$
48. $12m^3 + 3m^2$
49. $7a + 3$
50. $7n^4 + 2n - 3$
51. $13v^4 - 8v^3 + 7$
52. $-7n^3 + 10n + 1$
53. $5m^3 - 2$
54. $x^3 - 14x^2 + 2$
55. $13r^4 + 3r^3 + 6r$
56. $11n^2 - 12n + 3$
57. $-8x^4 + 10x^3 - x^2$
58. $x^4 + 7x + 4$
59. $-6p^4 + 6$
60. $7n^3 + 6n^2 - 10n$
61. $10b^3 + 3b$
62. $-n^4 + 3n^3 + 6$
63. $3x^4 + 4x^3 + x^2 + 7$
64. $-3b^4 - b^3 + 8b$
65. $12x^4 - x^3 - 7x^2 - 1$
66. $-6b^3 - 14b^2 - 4b$
67. $13x^4 - 7x^3 + 11x$
68. $-2k^4 - 3k^3 - k + 2$
69. $7m^4 - 4m^3 - 13$
70. $-8n^4 + 11n^3$
71. $-x^4 + x^3 + 7x^2 + 7x$
72. $2x^4 + 6x - 6$
73. $x^4 + 3x^2 + 5$
74. $-3p^4 + 9p^2 - 7p$
75. $-2a^3 - 5a^2 - 4a$
76. $b^3 + 6b^2 + 3b$
77. $-3n^4 - 14n^2 + 6n$
78. $4n^4 + 4n^2 + 9$
79. $-13k^3 + k + 3$
80. $-5v^4 + 15v^3 - v$
81. $-11m^4 + 9m^3 + 11m$
82. $2n^4 - n^2 - 11n$
83. $-2b^4 + 3b^3 + 6b - 5$
84. $10x^3 - 5x - 5$
85. $3v^4 - 11v^3 - 2v^2 + 7$
86. $-5x^4 + 8x^2 - 10x + 5$
87. $8n^4 + n^3 - 3n^2 + 12n$
88. $-4n^3 - 2n^2 - 12$
89. $3n^4 + 6n^3 - 5$

Page 120: Polynomials: Multiplication

1. $6x^2 - 28xy - 48y^2$
2. $56a^2 + 4ab - 12b^2$
3. $20x^2 - xy - y^2$
4. $40m^2 - 30mn - 10n^2$
5. $7a^2 + 36ab + 32b^2$
6. $64x^2 - 8xy - 6y^2$
7. $32x^2 - 4xy - 15y^2$
8. $8m^2 - 38mn + 42n^2$
9. $3u^2 - 3v^2$
10. $21x^2 + 12xy - 9y^2$
11. $5u^2 - 25uv - 30v^2$
12. $12m^2 + 52mn + 16n^2$
13. $28x^2 - 7xy - 21y^2$
14. $35a^2 - 7ab - 42b^2$
15. $32x^2 + 28xy - 49y^2$
16. $8a^2 + 12ab - 56b^2$
17. $10x^2 + 17xy - 20y^2$
18. $16m^2 - 18mn + 5n^2$
19. $14x^2 + 41xy - 28y^2$
20. $48x^2 - 60xy + 12y^2$
21. $14x^2 + 34xy + 12y^2$
22. $2x^2 + 19xy + 42y^2$
23. $64a^2 - 112ab + 49b^2$
24. $14x^2 - 32xy - 30y^2$
25. $3u^2 - 26uv + 48v^2$
26. $x^2 + xy - 42y^2$
27. $28x^2 - 3xy - 40y^2$
28. $15m^2 - 2mn - 24n^2$
29. $24m^2 - 6mn - 3n^2$
30. $6a^2 - 16ab + 10b^2$
31. $8u^3 + 14u^2v - 58uv^2 - 48v^3$
32. $14m^3 + 36m^2n - 39mn^2 + 9n^3$
33. $6x^3 + 13x^2y - 29xy^2 - 42y^3$
34. $2x^3 - 10x^2y - 15xy^2 + 18y^3$
35. $5m^3 - 17m^2n + 19mn^2 - 7n^3$
36. $24x^3 + 28x^2y - 26xy^2 - 5y^3$
37. $16x^3 - 48x^2y + 31xy^2 + 7y^3$
38. $14x^3 - 34x^2y - 23xy^2 + 15y^3$
39. $20x^3 + 25x^2y - 15xy^2 - 5y^3$
40. $30x^3 + 28x^2y + 2xy^2 + 24y^3$
41. $18x^3 + 36x^2y - 20xy^2 - 24y^3$
42. $15x^3 + 49x^2y + 80xy^2 + 64y^3$
43. $3u^3 - 10u^2v - 3uv^2 + 18v^3$
44. $4a^3 - 22a^2b + 4ab^2 + 30b^3$
45. $32x^3 - 92x^2y + 64xy^2 - 7y^3$
46. $14x^3 + 16x^2y - 36xy^2 - 24y^3$
47. $8x^3 - 38x^2y + 19xy^2 + 20y^3$
48. $14m^3 - 32m^2n - 36mn^2 + 18n^3$
49. $24x^3 - 12xy^2 + 12y^3$
50. $9a^3 - 12a^2b - 9ab^2 - 28b^3$
51. $6x^3 - 7x^2y + 8xy^2 - 7y^3$
52. $35a^3 - 16a^2b - 13ab^2 + 6b^3$
53. $64x^3 + 56x^2y + 22xy^2 + 12y^3$
54. $4x^3 + 24x^2y + 38xy^2 + 24y^3$
55. $6m^3 - 38m^2n + 38mn^2 + 42n^3$
56. $6x^3 - 27x^2y + 17xy^2 - 20y^3$
57. $7a^3 - 7a^2b - 22ab^2 + 16b^3$
58. $12x^3 - 34x^2y + 48xy^2 - 36y^3$
59. $35x^3 - 41x^2y - 13xy^2 + 15y^3$
60. $21u^3 - 10u^2v - 9uv^2 - 8v^3$
61. $2m^4 - 18m^3n + 33m^2n^2 + 15mn^3 - 25n^4$
62. $2u^4 + 14u^3v + 25u^2v^2 + 2uv^3 - v^4$
63. $32u^4 + 12u^3v - 9u^2v^2 + 15uv^3 - 10v^4$
64. $2x^4 - 9x^3y + 16x^2y^2 - 16xy^3 - 8y^4$
65. $4x^4 - 24x^3y + 19x^2y^2 + 54xy^3 + 7y^4$
66. $30x^4 - 53x^3y - 5x^2y^2 - 48xy^3 - 56y^4$
67. $21a^4 + 14a^3b + 57a^2b^2 + 44ab^3 + 35b^4$
68. $8u^4 + 2u^3v + 23u^2v^2 + 25uv^3 + 56v^4$
69. $6a^4 - a^3b + 2a^2b^2 - 19ab^3 - 42b^4$
70. $56x^4 - 74x^3y + 50x^2y^2 - 12xy^3 - 12y^4$
71. $14m^4 - m^3n + 17m^2n^2 - 27mn^3 - 35n^4$
72. $2x^4 + 18x^3y + 17x^2y^2 + 36xy^3 - 10y^4$
73. $35x^4 + 91x^3y + 54x^2y^2 - 20xy^3 - 24y^4$
74. $21x^4 - 47x^3y - 55x^2y^2 - 4xy^3 + 4y^4$
75. $30m^4 - 4m^3n + 31m^2n^2 + 24mn^3 + 7n^4$
76. $42a^4 - 26a^3b + 24a^2b^2 - 8ab^3 - 32b^4$

77. $24x^4 - 10x^3y + 41x^2y^2 + 14xy^3 - 6y^4$
78. $28x^4 + 14x^3y - 58x^2y^2 - 20xy^3 + 16y^4$
79. $24a^4 + 10a^3b + a^2b^2 - 11ab^3 - 5b^4$
80. $64m^4 - 96m^3n + 3m^2n^2 + 12mn^3 - 32n^4$
81. $x^4 + 11x^3y + 33x^2y^2 + 22xy^3 - 28y^4$
82. $3x^4 - 4x^3y - 9x^2y^2 + 8xy^3 - y^4$
83. $16x^4 + 8x^3y + 4x^2y^2 + 30xy^3 - 18y^4$
84. $4x^4 + 9x^2y^2 - 21xy^3 + 8y^4$
85. $25u^4 - 5u^3v - 10u^2v^2 + 62uv^3 - 48v^4$
86. $56u^4 - 32u^3v - 82u^2v^2 - 2uv^3 + 12v^4$
87. $10x^4 + 21x^3y + 43x^2y^2 + 45xy^3 + 25y^4$
88. $40x^4 - 32x^3y + 26x^2y^2 - 70xy^3 - 48y^4$
89. $30x^4 + 37x^3y - 44x^2y^2 - 33xy^3 + 10y^4$
90. $42x^4 - 26x^3y - 13x^2y^2 + 4xy^3 - 15y^4$

Page 135: Area and Perimeter

1. P=40 A=51
2. P=52 A=132
3. P=24 A=27.71
4. P=28 A=33
5. P=42 A=68
6. P=50 A=114
7. P=35 A=66
8. P=39 A=73.18
9. P=58 A=118
10. P=40 A=56.84
11. P=22 A=28
12. P=60 A=149
13. P=42 A=98
14. P=39 A=82
15. P=26 A=36

16. P=48 A=111   17. P=46 A=96   18. P=22 A=24

19. P=52 A=150   20. P=34 A=66   21. P=54 A=79

22. P=64 A=180   23. P=54 A=140.29   24. P=26 A=30

25. P=26 A=34   26. P=40 A=65   27. P=42 A=84.87

28. P=24 A=27.71   29. P=21 A=21.22   30. P=54 A=86

31. P=24 A=19.9   32. P=23 A=25.16   33. P=44 A=69

34. P=32 A=57   35. P=24 A=27.72   36. P=23 A=19.98

37. P=30 A=46   38. P=26 A=36   39. P=44 A=47

40. P=21 A=21.22   41. P=42 A=92   42. P=38 A=69.18

43. P=74 A=190   44. P=28 A=36.68   45. P=22 A=24

46. P=28 A=49   47. P=50 A=53   48. P=32 A=63

49. P=76 A=198   50. P=52 A=112   51. P=80 A=108

52. P=32 A=30   53. P=53 A=160   54. P=19 A=16.35

55. P=36 A=63   56. P=44 A=93   57. P=52 A=96

58. P=78 A=200   59. P=37 A=80   60. P=42 A=83

Page 150: Volume and Surface Area

1. V=400 cm^3 cm^3 SA=359.2 cm^2 cm^2

2. V=392 in^3 in^3 SA=322 in^2 in^2

3. V=48 in^3 in^3 SA=80 in^2 in^2

4. V=210 cm^3 cm^3 SA=259.0 cm^2 cm^2

5. V=18 cm^3 cm^3 SA=42 cm^2 cm^2

6. V=252 cm³ cm³ SA=277.4 cm² cm²

7. V=137.44 cm³ cm³ SA=149 cm² cm²

8. V=231 ft³ ft³ SA=286.2 ft² ft²

9. V=98.17 ft³ ft³ SA=118 ft² ft²

10. V=30 in³ in³ SA=72 in² in²

11. V=30 cm³ cm³ SA=70.2 cm² cm²

12. V=12 ft³ ft³ SA=32 ft² ft²

13. V=36 cm³ cm³ SA=66 cm² cm²

14. V=240 in³ in³ SA=236 in² in²

15. V=60 in³ in³ SA=94 in² in²

16. V=24 in³ in³ SA=60 in² in²

17. V=243 in³ in³ SA=286.2 in² in²

18. V=282.74 ft³ ft³ SA=245 ft² ft²

19. V=32 in³ in³ SA=70.8 in² in²

20. V=40 ft³ ft³ SA=79.6 ft² ft²

21. V=51 cm³ cm³ SA=97 cm² cm²

22. V=504 ft³ ft³ SA=382 ft² ft²

23. V=134 ft³ ft³ SA=163 ft² ft²

24. V=105 in³ in³ SA=158.1 in² in²

25. V=706.86 ft³ ft³ SA=440 ft² ft²

26. V=32 cm³ cm³ SA=68.4 cm² cm²

27. V=7 in³ in³ SA=23 in² in²

28. V=36 cm³ cm³ SA=66 cm² cm²

29. V=810 ft³ ft³ SA=522 ft² ft²

30. V=150 ft³ ft³ SA=170 ft² ft²

31. V=38 cm³ cm³ SA=75 cm² cm²

32. V=216 in³ in³ SA=264 in² in²

33. V=280 cm³ cm³ SA=262 cm² cm²

34. V=318.09 in³ in³ SA=269 in² in²

35. V=105 ft³ ft³ SA=149.0 ft² ft²

36. V=168 in³ in³ SA=204.8 in² in²

37. V=230.91 in³ in³ SA=209 in² in²

38. V=168 in³ in³ SA=211.6 in² in²

39. V=105 in³ in³ SA=158.6 in² in²

40. V=175 ft³ ft³ SA=219.4 ft² ft²

41. V=75.40 ft³ ft³ SA=101 ft² ft²

42. V=128 in³ in³ SA=199.2 in² in²

43. V=120 in³ in³ SA=172.4 in² in²

44. V=90 cm³ cm³ SA=133.5 cm² cm²

45. V=157.08 in³ in³ SA=165 in² in²

46. V=180 ft³ ft³ SA=192 ft² ft²

47. V=252 in³ in³ SA=273.8 in² in²

48. V=98 ft³ ft³ SA=161.7 ft² ft²

49. V=12 ft³ ft³ SA=32 ft² ft²

50. V=101 in³ in³ SA=141 in² in²

51. V=60 in³ in³ SA=112.4 in² in²

52. V=192.42 cm³ cm³ SA=187 cm² cm²

53. V=324 in³ in³ SA=333.0 in² in²

54. V=180 cm³ cm³ SA=192 cm² cm²

55. V=90 in³ in³ SA=135.6 in² in²

56. V=100 in³ in³ SA=130 in² in²

57. V=224 in³ in³ SA=232 in² in²

58. V=126 cm³ cm³ SA=168.6 cm² cm²

59. V=441 in³ in³ SA=350 in² in²

60. V=450 ft³ ft³ SA=370 ft² ft²

Page 165: Pythagorean Theorem

1. S=136.788	2. S=159.154	3. S=145.997	4. S=183.371
5. S=102.176	6. S=59.397	7. S=210.488	8. S=207.617
9. S=56.533	10. S=132.401	11. S=96.177	12. S=46.765
13. S=203.470	14. S=53.600	15. S=18.762	16. S=139.223
17. S=132.382	18. S=188.290	19. S=77.026	20. S=14.799
21. S=90.526	22. S=16.882	23. S=142.955	24. S=54.332
25. S=100.757	26. S=85.082	27. S=43.451	28. S=138.780

29. S=50.289   30. S=13.964   31. S=81.333   32. S=102.995

Page 165: Exponents

1. 6,859
2. 20,736
3. 1/36
4. 28,561
5. 1/324
6. 1/343
7. 1/16
8. 400
9. 130,321
10. 1,728
11. 256
12. 1/1000
13. 2,197
14. 1/64
15. 1/6859
16. 65,536
17. 1/8000
18. 81
19. 1/100
20. 49
21. 4,096
22. 289
23. 1
24. 104,976
25. 1/289
26. 8
27. 1/169
28. 1/3375
29. 1/81
30. 3,375
31. 125
32. 1/1331
33. 324
34. 1
35. 1/361
36. 1
37. 1/400
38. 196
39. 169
40. 1/4
41. 2,744
42. 1/27
43. 1,296
44. 1,331
45. 1/2744
46. 1/225
47. 216
48. 36
49. 1/729
50. 1/49
51. 1/64
52. 1/196
53. 625
54. 4,096
55. 64
56. 121
57. 1
58. 1/9
59. 81
60. 512

Page 178: Scientific Notations

1. 4.5×10^4
2. 6.4×10^3
3. 4.2×10^4
4. 7,100
5. 7.4×10^5
6. 380
7. 4,430,000
8. 190
9. 48,000
10. 950,000
11. 830
12. 8.5×10^1
13. 5.6×10^4
14. 1,930,000
15. 5.5×10^1
16. 4.55×10^5
17. 8.8×10^1
18. 950
19. 390,000
20. 9.1×10^5
21. 830,000
22. 2.8×10^2
23. 7,000
24. 6.163×10^6

25. 9.4×10^1 26. 2,450,000   27. 8.6×10^3 28. 6.4×10^5

29. 4.7×10^1 30. 95   31. 320,000   32. 9.3×10^2

33. 35   34. 3.2×10^6 35. 21   36. 770

37. 3.8×10^5 38. 1.6×10^1 39. 1,100   40. 4,600,000

41. 8,700   42. 390   43. 7.9×10^6 44. 350

45. 720   46. 2.18×10^5 47. 8,344,000   48. 4×10^3

49. 6.4×10^4 50. 86   51. 18   52. 6.6×10^3

53. 8.96×10^5 54. 310   55. 4,300,000   56. 6.154×10^6